Winter 2009

Griffith REVIEW

Participation Society

Editor – Julianne Schultz

Griffith REVIEW is published four times a year by Griffith University in conjunction with ABC Books.

ISSN 1448-2924

Griffith University
South Bank Campus, Griffith University
PO Box 3370
South Brisbane Qld 4101
Australia

ABC Books
GPO Box 9994
Sydney NSW 2001
Australia

Telephone: (07) 3735 3071
Facsimile: (07) 3735 3272
Email: griffithreview@griffith.edu.au
Website: www.griffithreview.com

Subscription
4 issues incl p&h: $79.80 within Australia including GST (Recommended Retail Price)

4 issues incl p&h: A$120.50 outside Australia

Institutional and bulk rates available on application.

Letters to the Editor should be sent to:

The Editor, Griffith REVIEW
PO Box 3370
South Brisbane
Qld 4101 Australia

Alternatively, email to griffithreview@griffith.edu.au

The Editor reserves the right to edit letters for publication.

Publisher:
Marilyn McMeniman

Editor:
Julianne Schultz

Design/Production Manager:
Paul Thwaites

Copy Editor:
Katherine Delaney

Proofreader:
Sue Jarvis

Marketing Manager:
Erica Sontheimer

Picture Editor:
Paul Thwaites

Publication Assistants:
Brendan Lindsay
Jeremy Gates

Administration:
Cheryl Horner

ABC Books:
Lesley O'Brien, Brigitta Doyle, Lindsay Somerville, Liz White, Jane Finemore

Typesetting:
Midland Typesetters

Printing:
Ligare Book Printers

Distribution:
HarperCollins

Acknowledgement:
A special thanks to Liveworm Studio, Queensland College of Art, Griffith University for their assistance in the original design process.

CAL | Cultural Fund

Griffith REVIEW receives project sponsorship from Copyright Agency Limited.

Australian Government

Australia Council for the Arts

This project has been assisted by the Australian Government through the Australia Council, its principal arts funding and advisory body.

Griffith UNIVERSITY

Sir Samuel Griffith was one of Australia's great early achievers. Twice the premier of Queensland, that state's chief justice and author of its criminal code, he was a great, confident provincial who saw no reason why, as a Queenslander, he could not take a major role in the public life of the emerging nation.

Sir Samuel was best known for his pivotal role in drafting agreements that led to Federation and as the new nation's first chief justice. He was also an important reformer and legislator, a practical and cautious man of words. Griffith died in 1920 and is now best remembered in his namesakes – an electorate, a society, a suburb and a university.

Ninety-six years after he first proposed establishing a university in Brisbane, Griffith University, the city's second, was created. His commitment to public debate and ideas, his delight in words and art and his attachment to active citizenship is recognised by the university that bears his name with the publication of *Griffith REVIEW.*

This quarterly fosters and informs public discussion. Each issue is devoted to a topical theme and includes essays, reportage, memoir, fiction, poetry, photography and art. The range is deliberately wide. The complexity of contemporary issues cannot adequately be illuminated by one form alone. The who, what, when, where, how and why of events are important, but the feel for what they mean may better be understood through a novelist's eye, the cacophony of current activities better comprehended with an expert's insight into competing theories or the rhetoric of public debate unpacked by detailed behind-the-scenes reportage. *Griffith REVIEW* captures the spirit of the times.

Like Sir Samuel Griffith, *Griffith REVIEW* is iconoclastic and non-partisan, with a sceptical eye and a pragmatically reforming heart and a commitment to public discussion. Personal, political and [un]predictable, it is Australia's best conversation. ■

Contents

INTRODUCTION

ESSAY

MEMOIR

REPORTAGE

FICTION

ONLINE
www.griffithreview.com

OUR COVER:

Artist: Julie Shiels

www.julieshiels.com.au

Courtesy of the artist

Griffith REVIEW gratefully acknowledges the support and generosity of founding patron Margaret Mittelheuser.

Introduction: **Openness, collaboration & participation**

Writer: **Julianne Schultz**

It was always a thrill to find an email from the prospective president of the free world jumping out from the overnight clutter in Thunderbird.

'It's in your hands, Julianne' was the subject line of a tight four-line email Barack Obama sent me at 3.52 am on October 30, 2008. 'The next six days are going to be the toughest we've seen,' he cautioned, before entreating 'this campaign is in your hands' and thanking me 'for everything you are doing'.

'No wonder he looks tired,' I joked to my family over breakfast, 'he was up all night sending emails…'

In the final weeks of the 2008 US election campaign the notion of the global village took on a new meaning. Not only were all eyes trained on the consensus-busting contest in the world's increasingly troubled super-power, but countless millions who could not vote knew they had a stake in the outcome and, remarkably, felt involved.

Before 2008 earned a place in history for the election of Barack Obama, it had been tagged the 'year of social networking'. That Obama used social networking to raise more money, involve more people and create a more intimate sense of engagement, was emblematic..

Between one US presidential election campaign and the next, the number of people using Facebook, to network with friends skyrocketed from one to a 120 million – and continues to grow.

The lessons of community organising married with the tools of the internet and the power of a compelling narrative, created a new campaign paradigm that will be dissected and analysed for years. The era of mass media politics ended more abruptly, and with less fanfare, than it had begun. Goliath was wounded, if not slain, by what Glenn Reynolds presciently called *An Army of Davids* (Nelson, 2006) – who expected to be addressed by name, have an opportunity to propose and discuss policy, answer back, give a few dollars and be thanked.

First though, the lessons needed to be quantified. The election was still dominating conversations when David Plouffe, Obama's campaign manager lobbed another email into millions of inboxes. Like the diligent students of best practice that they were, his team wanted to know their strongest supporters – what their strongest supporters thought.

It was a fairly simple four-page survey, picking at the usual questions – how people got involved, what motivated them, what training worked, how they connected with others, the big future issues.

But at the bottom of the third page was the killer question, the one that symbolised the new paradigm, and took your breath away. It simply asked, 'Are you interested in running for elected office yourself?'

Nearly six hundred thousand people responded, without doubt the biggest survey of politically active people ever conducted. Remarkably, in a country that had come to believe it was apathetic, that knew in its bones that real power belonged to the goliaths of big business, big media, big politics – more than fifty thousand people said that yes, they would stand for election.

There was something reassuringly old fashioned and optimistic about this response – the new virtual world staked its claim in the old representative world.

It is one thing to click 'yes' in an online survey, another to do something about it, to throw yourself into the much more troublesome and demanding world of organising, lobbying, courting rejection and failure, because you think you can make a difference, that there is another way that things could be done. It takes imagination and optimistic confidence to conjure innovative ways of thinking and responding.

The era of mass politics depended on, and cultivated, passivity. Taking action was the exception. Policy was a matter for experts and vested interests. Layer on layer of official and informal monitoring organisations may have accreted in one country after another, but still ordinary folk expected to only play their part by getting on with their lives as conscientious consumers who voted now and then.

The promise and reward was increasing material well-being for most.

The new era of participatory politics recognises that money is not enough, it values a conversation where people answer back and seek social value. The screen-based world is just the beginning, energy is now directed at getting people from online surveys to local functions where they can build new networks, get to know others who are asking the same questions and thinking about ways of doing things with social as well as material benefits. Mark Zuckerberg, Facebook's co-founder and chief executive, declared his company's mission, 'is to make the world more open and transparent by giving people the power to share information.'

It is ironic that Big Brother's watchful screen, which George Orwell imprinted in our collective imagination as a system of control, should now promise collaboration, transparency and participation. It is doubly ironic that this paradigm shift has coincided with the world's most spectacular loss of personal wealth.

In the months that followed Obama's election it was clear that the old consensus was crumbling faster than anyone expected.

It is one thing to talk about participatory politics in a campaign, quite another to turn it into action within the cumbersome checks and balances of complex societies. In Australia it did not take long for the liberating potential of the 2020 Summit to hit the brick wall of interdepartmental committees, policy hierarchies, vested interests and budgetary restraint. Its potential, which could have been the first significant international experiment in talkback politics for an engaged citizenry, languished under the demanding routines of business as usual.

It remains to be seen whether Obama's presidency will change the rulebook of 'democratic system management' either. Managing an empowered and engaged citizenry is profoundly different – even when the technology works.

Facebook, which likes to describe itself as the world's sixth biggest country, confronted this challenge when it sought to change its terms of use. The suggestion that it might own the information posted by members caused a spectacular backlash and provoked an extraordinary experiment – the creation of a corporate bill of rights and responsibilities, and the promise that members could vote on contentious policy changes.

Openness, participation and collaboration are the new tools ready to be road-tested in business and government – at a moment when the evil twins of economic and environmental catastrophe conspire to produce the world's greatest crisis for decades.

On his second day as president, Obama issued a Memorandum on Transparency. It signalled his approach. 'My administration is committed to creating an unprecedented level of openness ... We will work together to ensure the public trust and establish a system of transparency, public participation and collaboration. Openness will strengthen our democracy and promote efficiency and effectiveness. Government should be transparent ... Government should be participatory ... Government should be collaborative ... '

The British government had already begun to experiment with this approach. Its Information Commissioner oversees a regime that puts the expectation of open access to government information at its core – a far cry from the old British model ready to defend official secrecy to the death. The Australian government has drafted legislation aimed at a similar transformation, and the Right to Know coalition of media companies is keen to flex its muscle.

Implementing such an agenda both demands and will produce profound culture change – information that was once the protected tool of insiders and vested interests becomes 'a national asset' available to all.

In this environment, those that enable citizens and consumers to be actively involved in finding and implementing solutions – involving public, private and not-for-profit sectors – are most likely to flourish. The success of the Obama campaign in collecting small donations from countless individuals has inspired other 'causes' to grow their own support online – the logic of the collaborative networked society is transformative.

Now as much as ever, where America goes, we follow. The principles of openness, collaboration and participation have not yet been grasped with gusto in official quarters in Australia, but on the ground they are already changing lives and the way things are done.

The combination of the global financial crisis, the enabling power of technology and the potential of social enterprises (in a closely intertwined world where the winners and losers are more visible) may force thinking about a new consensus. Australia will not be immune from this and it may be to our great benefit, unleashing productive and imaginative capacity that has lain dormant for years of good times to create a new settlement. If we dare.

In one of his victory addresses President Obama described his country's best export as the 'idea' of America – its democratic principles, its openness, its entrepreneurial spirit. This idea had become tarnished over recent decades, but the election outcome was akin to pouring a giant tin of Brasso over the grime and finding something still shiny underneath.

Almost a week after Obama's speech at Grant Park in Chicago, David Carr noted in *The New York Times*: 'The founders of America wanted a government that reflected its citizens, but would be at remove from the baser impulses of the mob. The mob, flush with victory, is at hand, but instead of pitchforks and lanterns, they have broadband and YouTube. Like every other presidency, the Obama administration will have its battles with the media, but that may seem like patty-cake if it runs afoul of the self-publishing, self-organising democracy it helped create … That's the thing about pipes today: they run both ways.'

Andrew Rasiej, the founder of Personal Democracy Forum, told Carr: 'Any politician who fails to recognise that we are in a post-party era with a new political ecology in which connecting like minds and forming a movement is so much easier will not be around long. Yes, we have met Big Brother, the one who is always watching. And Big Brother is us.'

That is the profound challenge and opportunity of a participation society. ■

Essay:
A quiet revolution

Author:
Cheryl Kernot

Image: Venturing into unexplored territory / From MATCH WINNERS – a guide to commercial collaborations between social enterprise and private sector business / www.can-online.org.uk

A quiet revolution

Once in a rare while the fundamental architecture of a significant part of society shifts. Over the last two and one-half decades the organisation of the social half of society, led by social entrepreneurs, has done so.

—Bill Drayton, Ashoka, 2002

Life has a way of leading you places. I have surfed on the wave of this transformational shift, this quiet revolution, which puts social value at its core, as my disillusion with the old ways of public policy formation has grown. Party political representative democracy, and its public sector, are unable to adequately respond to many areas of unmet social need. The new model which Bill Drayton describes, rewards initiative, specifically addressing the micro-detail of how society works (and fails) and engages with people wherever they are, whatever their circumstances. In the serendipity of life, this revolutionary approach also fits with the values that led me to seek elected office in the first place; to have a say in debate and policy choices; to harness the best in social innovation to create a fairer, more socially inclusive and economically just society for as many Australians as possible.

Social entrepreneurship is already having an impact on millions of lives, reshaping social, economic and political relations and making the impossible doable. Its impact is clear in politics, in business and in a rethinking of the old tenets of the welfare state. In the current economic situation the lessons from the early stages of this revolution are more important than ever. At the heart of this fundamental social change is a systemic challenge to the meaning of 'value' creation: who decides what matters, who measures that and how? And how is that reflected in national and global economies? It has created new tools to measure value that go well beyond a simple profit and loss account, and ways of making this possible.

I am indebted to my many British friends and colleagues, particularly those at the Skoll Centre for Social Entrepreneurship at Oxford University for the intellectual nourishment I draw on in this essay. Living and working in Britain for nearly six years, I was exposed in an immediate way to dynamic national discussions, a highly developed level of ethical consumerism and to the pressing social problems of Africa. This made me think again about many of the things I had taken for granted. It also led me to my 'adopted' Ugandan daughter, Olivia, who grew up on the streets and in a church refuge in Kampala, and her project to provide hope and opportunity for the next generation of street children in the same refuge.

But the first catalyst for my public policy interest in a profoundly new way of driving social change was a visit to Australia in 1999 by Andrew Mawson, a United Reformed Church minister who transformed an almost defunct parish in Bromley-by-Bow. Fifteen years earlier Mawson had arrived in the area of run-down housing estates deep in the East End of London, and found a place bisected by motorways, windblown, given over to generational cycles of poverty and unemployment. Over the years 'an army of well-meaning and socially conscious voluntary sector campaigners who had come to the area to do good' had made it their project, but the community lacked a heart. A sense of hopelessness pervaded.

Even by 2001 the census revealed that Bromley-by-Bow ward was one of the most deprived areas of Britain – almost half the people between sixteen and seventy-four had no qualifications; unemployment was three times the national level, a sixth of the unemployed had never worked and a third were classified as long-term unemployed. In the grim 1980s when Mawson arrived it had the highest level of poverty in Britain and he soon realised that countless government schemes over the decades had made no difference. When Mawson arrived in Bromley-by-Bow, his first assignment as a newly ordained pastor, he found a congregation that had dwindled to twelve septuagenarians. Within a ten-minute walk from the disused church people spoke more than fifty languages. He realised that if it was to survive his new church needed to adopt a very different approach.

Over the next couple of years Mawson persuaded his congregation to make the essentially unused assets of rundown church buildings available to the local community to create a multi-racial and multi-faith centre. Mawson's mission took him into the buildings that towered over the church. He knocked on the doors of the suspicious residents of the huge housing estates and talked to them about what they wanted. Along the way he found a few local artists who he persuaded to get involved and teach others their skills in return for rent-free workshops. Santiago, a Chilean political refugee saw an opportunity to use his carving and building skills to restore his spirit, and in the process created a centre for the community. A young woman wanted to teach art and pottery, another wanted to set up a ballet school. Local bureaucrats insisted that the poor would not send children to learn to dance, let alone pay for the classes, but within a year the school of arts was filled with local, fee-paying children.

As the community activities increased it was clear that a kindergarten was desperately needed. Mawson reorganised the schedule of weekday events, so that the unused space could become a childminding centre. More than a decade after he had begun the task of engaging and empowering this community Mawson again came face to face with the red tape that frustrates so many small businesses with seemingly insurmountable obstacles thus preventing the establishment of innovative and much needed start-ups. But Mawson was not the usual small-business operator with a dream. He did not accept the regulations that made it impossible to set up a childminding centre. Instead he lobbied hard and traded on his growing influence to persuade then Prime Minister Tony Blair to second a Treasury bureaucrat to work on site for twelve months. He told Blair that if civil servants could see the area up close rather than from a desk in far away Whitehall they would be more likely to help find solutions. As a result many of the problems were solved creatively, but still the pace of change was frustratingly slow.

Once the centre was established the socially excluded Bangladeshi mothers met for the first time, as they waited for their children. Over time these women graduated from sharing morning tea to running a community catering company. For most of them it was their first experience of employment in Britain, and their catering business gathered momentum. Other unemployed residents reclaimed and replanted community gardens and gained horticultural and landscaping qualifications along the way.

Mawson's mission had been galvanised in the mid-1990s by the failure of the National Health Service to adequately deal with the terminal cancer of Jean Vallis, an active worker in the community care program and a single mother who was also caring for her elderly parents. She died because she fell through the gaps in the system. When an inquiry was held into her death Mawson was furious as he listened to the face-saving justifications of failed services, of the doctor who failed to inform the cancer specialist of her deterioration because the specialist's fax number had changed. The support Vallis received in her final days came from the community, not the state-run services.

Mawson's rage at the way the system had failed Vallis and her family fostered a new model of health care in a centre which would be built and owned by the people it served. At the Centre, the doctors would prescribe 'more than just drugs', with activities and opportunities allowing local people to take control of their lives and their immediate environment. His team set about creating Britain's first Healthy Living Centre. Mawson recalls in his book *The Social Entrepreneur* (Atlantic Books, 2009) that the National Health Service blocked the endeavour at every step, worried this approach would allow other groups to try to take control of their own health care and this would be 'inequitable'. Eventually a directive from the Conservative Minister for Health released the money to build the Centre and staff it for three years. It had taken six years to secure a new purpose-built building owned locally and with tenants generating rental income.

Mawson's instinct and perseverance prevailed. When the Blair government allocated millions of pounds to replicate the model across the UK, many of the centres failed – the central lessons of local ownership and initiative and tangible measures of achievement were ignored.

Mawson's leadership qualities and pioneering methods modelled aspects of successful social entrepreneurialism: drive, passion, the ability to locate unused buildings and use them creatively as a community asset, and to build partnerships to generate income and in-kind support. Partners that some would consider risky and controversial helped the Centre achieve great things.

Contrary to the best instincts of many, our economic system has been dominated by a system which measures value creation in only one dimension – financial impact, profit and loss. In the last few years, there has been considerable effort, particularly in Britain and increasingly in Europe, to develop reliable systems and language to measure social impact more broadly. The social impact of the Bromley-by-Bow Healthy Living Centre and its central role in its local community can be tallied: about two thousand people use the Centre regularly; a quarter of local households take part in regular activities – as users or volunteers – and at least a third have had some form of direct contact with it over the past year; the Centre employs 115 staff and a regular volunteer presence of fifty; two-thirds of the staff live in Bromley-by-Bow and 86 per cent live within a six kilometre radius. The impact is both tangible and intangible as a community has remade itself, health outcomes and social connectivity have been improved and despair has been replaced with hope.

Bromley-by-Bow has inspired others to innovatively develop local resources to improve lives and the Community Action Network which Mawson co-founded now has 850 other British social enterprises, but there are many others as well. A pioneering Scottish mental health social enterprise, imaginatively named Rolls on Wheels, trains and employs people with enduring mental health problems to make lunches for day hospitals in a disadvantaged area of Edinburgh. Its profits are reinvested in employment and community development. The New Economics Foundation calculates that for every $250 spent by the local health authority on the contract, an additional $240 is generated for the local economy from the service. With total sales of $440,000 a year, this is a significant reinvestment. And the impact of providing socially inclusive contact, informal medical supervision and employment is just as valuable.

Ten years ago, Labor MPs Mark Latham, Lindsay Tanner and I had dinner with Andrew Mawson in Canberra. We listened as he described his fifteen-year journey to forge a new way, through trial and error and an unshakeable faith in the capacity of ordinary citizens and communities, to drive social innovation and community-centred responses to social need.

He described working outside government if necessary, working in funding partnerships with local people, businesses and councils, backing people not systems. It was hard not be affected by his enthusiasm for people-centred solutions and for his early successes. This was a significant move from the old grant-dependent community development model.

We are surrounded by the orthodoxy of risk aversion, but social entrepreneurs challenge orthodoxies, take risks and persevere. Mawson learned to embrace the risk and opportunity of each stage of new challenges. In the same way, 2006 Nobel Prize Winner Muhammad Yunus took a risk when he started the Grameen Bank giving micro-loans to the poorest Bangladeshi villagers – primarily women who traditional bankers said would never repay the loans. Mawson challenged the assumption that charities and corporations had few common meeting points, and the cultural assumptions of some charitable organisations which considered themselves 'pure' and 'noble', 'untainted' by profit-seeking activities. He approached big corporate sponsors and helped to pioneer the increased presence of corporate social investment and partnerships with local communities.

Initially, many in the third sector – charities, co-operatives, non-government, voluntary, community and employee-owned organisations – treated this with extreme suspicion. At first the suggestion that they should try to behave more like business was almost heresy, despite the role of the Australian third sector in Job Network. But the logic of this approach – helped by the high profile examples of Bromley-by-Bow, Grameen Bank and companies like The Body Shop, and Victoria Hale's not-for-profit pharmaceutical company One-World Health – prevailed. Over the following decade, especially in the UK and USA, the third sector became increasingly comfortable with the benefits that could come from generating income rather than always being dependent on handouts. The pioneering partnerships that emerged had the effect of blurring traditional boundaries which saw charities operating as not-for-profits on the opposite end of the spectrum from corporations operating with a profit motivation. Examining the question about the place of profit in this sector revealed a more central question about the role and source of profit. The logic of profits with a purpose, totally reinvested in the core purpose of social ventures, made increasing sense to the third sector and began to have an impact on traditional businesses as well.

Today that blurring has seen the emergence of a new spectrum of enterprises ranging from traditional non-profit organisations, non-profits with income generating activities, social enterprises and businesses and socially responsible businesses to corporations practising social responsibility within a traditional for-profit framework. Kim Alter, the founder of Virtue Ventures and a Skoll Fellow, describes not-for-profits and social enterprises as being focused on creating social value, using commercial methods to support their social mission. The for-profits with a social responsibility agenda focus on creating economic value, pursuing a sustainability strategy of 'doing well by doing good'.

The vast majority of third-sector organisations are engaged in creating public, social or environmental value, rather than private value. Yet in Australia we still use the limiting and negative description of 'not-for-profit' to describe distinctive third sector organisations that may be generating profits from income earning enterprises, and even relying on that for sustainability. Like the term 'philanthropy', 'not-for-profit' is one of those shorthand terms that inhibits understanding.

In early 2000, I visited Bromley-by-Bow to observe for myself. Noel Pearson has also visited and, like me, found an organic self-sufficiency belying the bleakness of the monolithic concrete housing estates; the community-based and led Healthy Living Centre was a lively community hub. Noel Pearson and the Cape York Institute and Partnerships have been at the forefront of developing this new model in Australia. Its links with Westpac, Boston Consulting and the National Australia Bank among others, have been central to the new approach of innovation and sustainability that has evolved in the disadvantaged communities of Far North Queensland. When Mawson visited Cape York last year the two leaders reflected on the way even a well-meaning public sector, with no institutional memory or strong local connections, can almost guarantee failure.

Pearson has much in common with Cherokee leader and social entrepreneur Rebecca Adamson, who in 1980 set up the First Nations Development Institute. It has a three-pronged strategy of educating grassroots practitioners, advocating systemic change, and capitalising Indian communities. The First Nations Development Institute 'works to restore Native control and culturally compatible stewardship of the assets they own – land, human potential, cultural heritage and natural resources – and to build new assets to ensure the long-term vitality of Native communities'. The Institute believes that when armed with appropriate resources, Native peoples hold the capacity and ingenuity to ensure the sustainable economic, spiritual, and cultural well-being of their communities. Others have referred to this as a paradigm shift – from passivity to entrepreneurialism.

In the days before successful corporate and third-sector partnerships, there was a pervasive business culture assumption that most charities were unbusinesslike and wasteful with their resources and practices. There were frequent calls to measure the efficiency of those who received grants and donations and this became a well-developed area of public reporting. As a result, successful third-sector organisations have worked hard to ensure that they have learnt the lessons of business efficiency. The First Nations Development Institute, for instance, manages to spend less than a tenth of its budget on its administration and a similar proportion on fundraising expenses so that well over three-quarters of its income reaches its programs. The daily deluge of revelations of excessive spending on executive salaries, conferences and travel put the old criticism of third-sector inefficiency into a context that makes the inference offensive. The lesson of the new model is that learning needs to occur at both ends of the spectrum; right and wrong are not the sole preserve of either sector.

One fantastic example of a corporate and social business partnership, based on mutual respect and an equality of voice, is the British partnership between HSBC and Green Works, a social business that removes surplus or unwanted office furniture, and trains and employs marginalised people to refurbish it before selling the furniture at reduced prices to third-sector organisations. The business challenge for Green Works was to match the market for recycled office furniture with the supply. My students at the School for Social Entrepreneurs loved listening to Green Works founder Colin Crooks honestly describe how the collaboration with HSBC came about. Eighteen months before HSBC was due to move to new headquarters at Canary Wharf in East London, Crooks sent a 'cold-call' letter. He knew that the relocation would leave the bank with surplus furniture. As it turned out the bank had been planning to send three thousand tonnes of furniture to the dump for land fill – seven thousand desks and workstations, equal to 178 double-decker buses. The letter arrived at the right time, and HSBC staff embraced the offer. Green Works could provide a simple, one-stop, environmentally responsible solution. The major impediment at the time was that Green Works was essentially one man with a van making collections before and after office hours: it did not have the capital, manpower, logistics or warehousing to handle such a big project. But it was a huge opportunity which Crooks was keen to seize. The bank had to be convinced that Green Works could deliver.

In a leap of faith, HSBC agreed to pay a proportion of the fees for removing the furniture in advance. This gave Green Works the financial clout it needed to make the project happen. Today Green Works is an award-winning social business with an annual turnover of almost $4 million, three London warehouses, forty-one employees, and five franchise operations with indirect employment generation, and the model of the possibilities of more embedded corporate third-sector partnerships. Green Works has become a trailblazer in showing how social enterprises can build equal business partnerships with big corporations, assisting them to meet corporate social responsibility goals in socially innovative, embedded ways. This is many levels up from the one-off donations, employee collections, sponsorship, volunteering and other common forms of corporate social responsibility. This is long-term, sustainable and transformative. 'What Green Works was able to deliver for HSBC was efficient furniture clearance at the right cost – but the key is in the added value it brought as a social enterprise: the social purpose of the best use of the furniture for the benefit of others; the embedded nature of the business relationships,' Crooks said.

In 2001 I was Shadow Minister for Employment and also keen to add an innovative dimension to the Labor Party's employment policy. I included funded, pilot programs to support identifiable social entrepreneurs with community-based employment and regeneration solutions in six of the most disadvantaged electorates in the party's platform. These initiatives would address particular local problems and empower communities. It is a matter of personal regret that these initiatives have fallen off the policy agenda as they are timelier than ever as we enter a period of high unemployment. After the collapse of Mark Latham's leadership, no one in the Labor Party has championed this model. It now falls naturally into the remit of the Social Inclusion Board established by Deputy Prime Minister Julia Gillard, but social businesses have not yet become a part of this agenda. This is partly because there has been no leadership for cultural change. There is a lingering public perception that much of the Australian third sector remains wedded to an old mode of charity and doing good.

After I lost the seat of Dickson in the Tampa-fuelled environment of the 2001 federal election, I moved to Britain to work on these pioneering policy ideas that had attracted me since that dinner with Andrew Mawson several years earlier. As Director of Learning at the London-based School for Social Entrepreneurs, founded by Michael Young in 1997, I was immersed in the innovative ideas that were driving this emerging field and able to observe the strengths and weaknesses from up close.

The term 'social entrepreneur' does not trip off the tongue lightly. Its associated entity, the 'social enterprise', is not commonly understood here either. In Australia we usually associate entrepreneurs with business – and then often with a tarnished sneer. This is unfortunate, because applying the best of the entrepreneurial spirit to enterprises and activities of direct benefit to communities has tremendous potential to unleash innovation, solve problems and improve the quality of life for many thousands of people here and abroad. It starts with an understanding of the role and character traits of a traditional entrepreneur like Sir Richard Branson – highly motivated, original thinkers and pragmatists who want to do things and are not constrained by the limits of old ways of thinking. The next step is to add a social/environmental aspiration to the business's core purpose, as distinct from the economic purpose of maximising shareholder wealth. This combination produces a marriage of entrepreneurial drive and social mission which leads to the creation of social businesses or ventures.

In a speech to the Skoll World Forum in 2006, Jeff Skoll, co-founder of eBay and through his eponymous foundation, the Skoll Centre for Social Entrepreneurship at Oxford University, said that social entrepreneurs are rebelling against one of the worst ideas that has ever gripped mankind – that the problems that surround us are so big that ordinary men and women can't make a difference. From his experience Skoll argues that social entrepreneurs see these problems as a call to action rather than a cause for despair: 'Some charities give people food. Some teach farmers to grow food. Social entrepreneurs have to teach the farmer to grow food, how to make money, turn it back over to the farm and hire ten more people. They're not satisfied until they have transformed the entire food industry.'

This encapsulates the difference between the nascent social enterprise space and the traditional third sector in Australia. There is still a narrow, welfare-oriented focus on creating employment as a tool of social inclusion. The contrasting model of large scale systemic change with a market orientation is happening around the globe, but is neither significantly embraced nor enabled here. This new model fosters the creation of employment, with jobs designed to address social and community problems, and owned by those directly involved. These jobs are qualitatively different from those produced as a result of private sector expansion or government stimulus.

Social market failure is not confined to one sector of the economy, or any one country. It can be seen in government inefficiencies in public service delivery, the rise of corporate power, and the retreat of the state in the face of free-market ideology. Australian social market failures include the lack of affordable housing and rental accommodation for those on low incomes, access to fair finance, affordable child care, real employment opportunities for Indigenous Australians, the proliferation of oil-based plastics in landfill and barriers to the use of renewable power. As a nation which prides itself on its technologically inspired innovative public policy genius, where is our Muhammad Yunus, Victoria Hale or Jeff Skoll, the socially innovative genius who has the capacity to inspire and transform?

One candidate might be Andrew Maher from Infoxchange Australia. For twenty years, Maher has been driving his socially innovative solutions to the unmet social need of 'digital inclusion'. He believes all Australians have a right to access and use information and communications technologies to participate in a socially inclusive society. In 1991 he began his Green PC social enterprise which trained unemployed and marginalised young people to refurbish recycled computers for resale at low prices. Since then Infoxchange has grown and diversified its business model and now employs sixty-five people in a range of related businesses and has forged partnerships with the government, corporate and third sectors. Its 'Parent Connect' wired a hundred households of families from Glen Orden Primary School in Melbourne's west, while Green PC supplied affordable computer and training packages to families with a child in the 'Learning for Life' program, in partnership with The Smith Family. Similarly, WorkVentures Connect IT offers quality, affordable, refurbished computer packs to people on Centrelink benefits, to schools, and to not-for-profit organisations. Infoxchange partners with corporations, including Westpac, which donate superseded computers which are then refurbished and loaded with donated software from Microsoft. Late last year Maher launched Infoxchange's largest digital inclusion project – Wired Community @ Collingwood. This is designed to provide computers, internet access and training to a thousand households in the Collingwood Public Housing Estate. Although Maher's enterprise has grown dramatically since he first had the idea to combine his computer skills with his concern for social justice, the question in terms of impact is one of replication and scalability.

Internationally, Infoxchange's sister organisation Info Timor earned a nomination for the prestigious Stockholm Challenge Award, which promotes the use of information and communication technologies to counteract social and economic disadvantage. The twelve Infoxchange-trained staff work at providing information technology services to schools, police, community centres and non-government organisations in East Timor. Recently, at a ceremony in Baucau, fifteen local village chiefs were presented with computers and a certificate recognising three months of computer training by Info Timor. These computers will be used to improve the governance of the District of Baucau.

Another contender for Australia's social inclusion genius might be mining magnate Andrew Forrest, Chief Executive of Fortescue Metals Group. In August 2008, Forrest launched an Australian Employment Covenant with the goal of signing up hundreds of companies to employ fifty thousand Indigenous people within the next two years to respond to an obvious unmet social need. Indigenous unemployment is more than twice the national rate. The Council for Reconciliation, of which I was a member, pioneered the development of partnerships between Indigenous leaders and mining companies in the 1990s under the chairmanship of Normandy Mining's Robert Champion de Crespigny. Two decades on this is still an unresolved problem. The question for 2009 and beyond is whether Andrew Forrest's plans can achieve the large-scale systemic change necessary, or whether his starting point is an incremental extension of corporate social responsibility which, in social entrepreneurial terms, is less market-oriented – in other words, whether this initiative is about companies creating extra jobs at the margin, or creating enterprises which produce sustainable, long-term employment.

Prior to the recent slump, which has hit the mining industry with particular ferocity, Forrest had obtained seven thousand commitments. If this number can be maintained, it is sufficient to have a quantifiable social impact and produce systemic change, as the covenant offers private sector jobs not simply work-for-the-dole obligations. It differs from other private sector commitments as the employer must commit to provide employment after training and assign a mentor for further on-the-job training. This is a big step forward, but depends on the largesse of companies and Forrest's personal authority. If Forrest's project were operating under Jeff Skoll's social enterprise model, these newly skilled Aboriginal employees would in turn train others, generate income from that training and use this income to buy training tools and machinery. This could ultimately transform Indigenous training and employment and produce an active Indigenous-led employment-ready trained pool of workers.

I was the Director of the Health Accelerator program at the Skoll Centre for two and half years until 2008. The Centre saw social entrepreneurship as the product of individuals, organisations, and networks that challenge conventional structures by addressing failures and identifying new opportunities in the institutional arrangements that cause the inadequate provision or unequal distribution of social and environmental goods. Social entrepreneurship can be defined as any action that displays three key characteristics: 'sociality', innovation, and market orientation. Sociality entails a context, process and outputs that might reasonably be considered to be of public benefit. Innovation is the creation of new ideas and models that address social or environmental issues. Socially entrepreneurial innovation can be manifested in new products and services. Institutional innovation uses existing goods and services in new, more socially productive, ways; incremental innovation reframes terms of reference to redefine social problems and suggest new solutions, and disruptive innovation is a performance-driven, competitive outlook that drives greater accountability and co-operation across sectors. Social enterprises specifically address conventional competitive markets, but social entrepreneurship broadens the conception of a 'market' beyond the neoliberal definition to suggest that markets establish exchange value that is inevitably socially embedded. Thus, market orientation also includes ideas of reciprocity and the common good. Social entrepreneurship can be the product of for-profit and not-for-profit organisations, as well as of many hybrids in between. It is also found in the public sector.

Professor Greg Dees from Stanford University was one of the first academics to publish on the subject in his 1998 report, *The Meaning of Social Entrepreneurship.*

Dees used the working understanding that social entrepreneurs play the role of change agents in the social sector. They do this by adopting a mission to create and sustain social value, not just private value; recognising and relentlessly pursuing new opportunities to serve that mission; engaging in a process of continuous innovation, adaptation and learning; acting boldly without being limited by resources currently in hand; and exhibiting a heightened sense of accountability to the constituencies served and for the outcomes created.

By these definitions, the British sociologist and politician Michael Young was a serial social entrepreneur. As the director of research for the British Labour Party in 1945, he wrote the party's manifesto and set the frame for the post-war welfare state. Young was a critical and original thinker and activist who went on to found the Consumers' Association in 1956 and then the Institute of Community Studies, the College of Health and the University of the Third Age. As these organisations turned up evidence of unfulfilled needs or unsatisfactory service he responded with yet more: the Open University; the International Extension College to spread distance learning to Africa and Asia; the Open College of the Arts to extend distance learning into the creative arts; Commuter Study Clubs so regular commuters could learn from each other; Language Line, a telephone interpretation service for doctors, police and the non-English-speaking people they dealt with; the Family Covenant Association to provide welcoming ceremonies for children; the National Funerals College to improve the conduct of funerals; Healthline to provide telephone information on health matters; the School for Social Entrepreneurs to train community innovators, where I later worked, and even a community garage in Milton Keynes offering professional support for people who wanted to service their own cars.

The Young Foundation operates from Young's original premises, a Victorian terrace in Bethnal Green, London. Now a centre for social innovation, the terrace is an expanding hub and home for numerous organisations, including the School for Social Entrepreneurs (SSE), engaged in social innovation from brand new start-ups to existing service providers and campaigns. Building on the Young tradition, the school undertakes research to identify and understand unmet social needs and then develops practical initiatives and institutions to address them – in fields as diverse as health and education, housing and cities.

Paul Hodgkin, a Sheffield general practitioner and one of my students, was a man imbued with the Young tradition. Prior to SSE he had begun a social enterprise training young disabled people as coffee bean roasters, and had also identified the need for the health system to be more responsive to the wisdom and insights of patients. He wanted to make the contemporary feedback of patients available to the National Health Service to assist them in developing and improving services and to give doctors, nurses and managers a feel for what patients were saying about the service they managed. The collated feedback could be used as part of the evidence that every British hospital had to submit each year to show the Healthcare Commission that the hospital used patient views to improve services.

From his long experience as a doctor, Hodgkin knew that the old ways of doing this – inviting a patient to sit on a working party or carrying out a survey – did not work very well. He devised a Web 2.0 feedback tool, Patient Opinion, as a way for thousands of patients to both share their own experience and gain support from others. He had start-up assistance from the Department of Health and the ongoing business model relied on selling data back to hospitals and a range of health authorities. Hodgkin calls this social innovation 'the democratisation of voice, allowing that public structured conversation about micro-aspects of health service delivery which hasn't happened up to now in the UK's NHS. And to which many hospitals respond'. Opinions are published online. They can also be sent directly to the health authorities with responsibility for administering the hospital and sometimes to individual managers in hospitals via a live feed. Opportunities also exist within the site for positive feedback to individual staff: nurses, doctors, cleaners. It is a model worth replicating in Australia. It is the 'real-time' aspect that makes it particularly effective, according to Hodgkin. Patients frequently make practical suggestions that the hospital can act on quickly, and because the site enables the hospital to announce online any changes, the patient gets speedy feedback. One of Hodgkin's considerations for the future of the model and plans for a national roll-out is that, while the Department of Health has been supportive, there is a risk that if the site is extremely successful, ministers might be tempted to establish a centralised, and therefore no longer independent, version.

It can be argued that socially entrepreneurial individuals have always existed. In the 1890s Australia was known as the 'social laboratory of the world' and the social innovations of Friendly Societies and Mechanics Institutes running libraries as social ventures generated significant and enduring social capital. Housing associations and cooperatives are also examples of early social enterprises. Robert Putnam, in his famous book, *Bowling Alone: The collapse and revival of American community* (Simon & Schuster, 2000), described social capital as the networks that are an integral part of social groupings and an indicator of the strength of social and community relationships.

Now the scale and confluence of powerful twentieth century drivers have led to the emergence of social entrepreneurship on a global level. This is quite different, as is the consequent response of the financial sector and some governments to the resulting social innovations. Social businesses and enterprises are the response of a critical mass of people throughout the world who have concluded that there can be a different way of doing business. They pursue new ways to harness capital market models, incorporating traditional business tools and strategies to add a social and environmental bottom line to the traditional profit and loss statement. Rather than being driven to maximise profits for shareholders, social businesses reinvest their surpluses in the pursuit of the business's core social and environmental purpose. This is not a passing trend. It didn't take a world economic crisis to create social entrepreneurs – the passion to design solutions for the unmet need inherent in social market failures was already driving them. The current economic crisis, however, offers a global opportunity to forge a new way forward; one which I have described as moving beyond the dichotomies of free or regulated, private or public. This demands a more creative and fairer form of capitalism that includes social and environmental value and impact when assessing prosperity and freedom.

Pamela Hartigan, director of the Skoll Centre, sees the current financial crisis as a global opportunity for economic transformation. Hartigan was the founding director of the Schwab Foundation for Social Entrepreneurship, the sister of the World Economic Forum, and co-author of *The Power of Unreasonable People: How entrepreneurs create markets that change the world* (Harvard, 2008). She sees an opportunity for a phoenix economy to rise from the ashes of the old, driven by accelerating entrepreneurial approaches and disruptive innovations, including new technologies, new business models, and new laws and regulations geared towards creating new market systems. To me, that is a checklist of twenty-first century solutions.

In the twentieth century, a sevenfold increase in per capita wealth in developed market economies drove the emergence of a widespread middle-class and an increased productive life expectancy. Drivers of social change included increased literacy and education, affordable information technology and a communications revolution, and at the political level the collapse of faith in hierarchies such as traditional politics, the social impact of deregulated markets and the failure of centralised public sectors created the space, and the demand, for social innovation.

While the Western world has enjoyed the fruits of this increased affluence, the global financial crisis and climate change is demonstrating its limits, even for those in the richest countries. Already this is most acute in the developing world, where the poorest half of the world's inhabitants accounts for 5 per cent of global income. The combination of increasing crises, market failures and resource depletion can be seen in the depleted resources that leave three billion people 'water stressed', the tens of millions predicted to be affected by HIV-AIDS by 2010 and the tens of millions likely to lose their jobs this year alone.

One response, which started to have an impact well before the global financial crisis, is the Grameen Bank founded by Bangladeshi economist and social entrepreneur Mohammad Yunus, who pioneered the use of micro-credit. Yunus challenged the fundamental banking orthodoxy of the necessity of collateral to secure loans. He reasoned that this perpetuated poverty and that 'these millions of small people with their millions of small pursuits can add up to create the biggest development wonder'. Yunus loaned $27 from his own pocket to forty-two women from the village of Jobra in 1976. They used the money to buy sewing machines and make clothes for sale. They used the income to pay back the loan and buy food, pay for their children's education and buy materials to continue their income-generating sewing. In a short time, the women had repaid the loan. The Grameen Bank, which defines itself as 'banking for the poor', sustains itself by charging a small interest on its micro-loans and recycling the capital to help other women. Its low default rates are the envy of traditional banks and its successful model has been replicated throughout the world. As of January 2009, it has nearly eight million borrowers, 97 per cent of whom are women. With 2,541 branches, the Grameen Bank provides services in 83,744 villages, covering all the villages in Bangladesh, it has disbursed over $11 billion since it started, and plans to disburse $1.5 billion this year.

The scale of its replication has been phenomenal: more than 106 million of the world's poorest families received a microloan in 2007, surpassing a goal set ten years ago. The loans have been used to start or expand a range of tiny businesses such as husking rice, selling tortillas, and delivering mobile phone services to remote villages. What is remarkable is that loans to more than a hundred million very poor families now touch the lives of more than half a billion family members around the world: half of the world's poorest people. The growth has been an extraordinary – 1,300 per cent, well beyond the dreams of the most growth-obsessed transnational corporation. This movement points to a systemic change that is responding to a huge unmet need which has now moved into secondary markets. Yet in Australia, the horizons of the mainstream political parties are still focused on degrees of Keynesian or neoliberal responses to free or regulated markets and the old duality of private and public; there is little focus on reciprocity or the common good.

The limits of this old model are evident in the sterility of the political debate, and the economic crisis itself. But there are other ways of operating and these provide useful models to consider at a time of profound shock. Take the example of Victoria Hale, an American pharmaceutical scientist who became increasingly frustrated by the market forces dominating her industry. 'In 2000, I was chatting with a cab driver about my work. When I told him I was a pharmaceutical scientist he burst into laughter and said,

"You guys have all the money." It wasn't the response I normally received when I spoke about my career, but I realised he was right. The pharmaceutical industry did have all the money and did make all the decisions about which drugs to develop – and we made those decisions based on the bottom line, the profit margin. The pharmaceutical industry is a business, and that is how a good business must operate. But what would happen if we took profit out of the equation?'

Driven by the purpose of creating financial profits for their shareholders, big drug companies which held patents for drugs to cure many infectious diseases chose to manufacture and market only those for which the well-off could pay for. To challenge this 'stable, but unjust equilibrium', Hale created the Institute for OneWorld Health, the first 'non-profit' pharmaceutical company whose mission is to ensure that drugs targeting infectious diseases in the developing world are accessible to those who need them, regardless of their ability to pay. Her business model involves her team of scientists identifying promising new drugs for neglected diseases and 'mentoring' them through clinical trials and regulatory approval. OneWorld Health contracts the manufacturing and distribution to companies and organisations in the developing world, creating in the process jobs and new economic pathways. In 2006 she began clinical trials in India and won approval to manufacture an off-patent antibiotic to treat a parasite which causes *visceral leishmaniasis*, the second deadliest disease after malaria in the country. The Indian government now distributes the drug free.

OneWorld Health received early and ongoing support from the Bill and Melinda Gates Foundation and has pioneered a collaborative space for pharmaceutical companies and universities to share and or donate intellectual property, professional expertise and, thanks to its tax-deductible status, financial donations. Involvement with OneWorld Health relies on the value of reputation enhancement: being seen to 'do good'. Whether Victoria Hale will manage to create a long-term sustainable model is uncertain, as OneWorld currently relies on collaborative goodwill, foundation and government funding.

Philosopher Peter Singer is at the other end of the spectrum. Singer recognises the reality of the existing corporate model but wants to find ways to use this to solve apparently intractable problems. He recently told corporate responsibility practitioners in Sydney that a better use of incentives might influence the behaviour of big pharmaceutical companies in their relationships with the developing world. He proposed the establishment of a Health Impact Fund whereby pharmaceutical companies are permitted to sell their drugs at high prices for the life of the patent, but then become part of a register for cheap generic copying. Through such a fund, rich nations would reward companies financially and enhance their reputation as they help reduce the global burden of disease.

Belu is another young, successful social business in Britain. It has taken commercial advantage of the current Western preference for bottled water, but unlike the oil-based bottles produced by the big beverage corporations, Belu's bottles are made of compostable cornstarch, the water is locally sourced and the product is not exported; it is available at a competitive price on the shelves of supermarket chains. While it produces bottled water, the business's core social purpose is to use its profits to invest in clean water products in the developing world. The bottles carry the distinctive marketing appeal – the purchase of one bottle in a British supermarket keeps one person in the developing world in clean water for a month. Since it began in 2000, with financial assistance from pioneering social entrepreneurs Anita and Gordon Roddick, who founded The Body Shop, Belu has generated net profits of over $2 million which, through a partnership with WaterAid, it has reinvested in hand pumps and wells for twenty thousand water-stressed people in India and Africa. Belu is primarily a business which needs to survive commercially in order to meet its core social purpose. That is very different from a re-crafted version of grant-dependant aid or charity.

Café Direct, another social business, is Britain's largest Fair Trade hot drinks company, turning over more than $35 million every year. Its tea, coffee and hot chocolate are on the shelves of every major supermarket. It buys coffee and tea from more than thirty-three producer organisations in eleven countries, ensuring that more than two hundred and fifty thousand growers receive a decent income from this trade by guaranteeing a fair price for their crops.

Fair Trade is one example of ethical consumerism, a world-changing social innovation of the last century. The sale of Fair Trade-marked food in Britain grew sevenfold in the five years from 1999, so that by 2004 the ethical consumption market was worth $57.3 billion and two-thirds of the population reported choosing a particular product or service on the basis of the company's reputation for social and environmental responsibility.

Yet in Australia shoppers have to rummage around, often on the bottom shelf of the big supermarkets, to find Fair Trade products. We tend to revisit the whole ethical consumption debate only at Christmas when we consider alternatives to the mass consumerism that swamps us. I don't believe that Australians are less interested or less 'ethical'. There is a failure of leadership to connect us to both our immediate region and the wider developing world. It would be easy for the corporate sector and Australian governments to lead Fair Trade coffee, tea and hot chocolate procurement practices, and to purchase from smaller social businesses as well. There is no reason to leave it all up to Oxfam.

Globally, the impact of leading social entrepreneurs is becoming clear as they drive systemic change transparency, accountability, certification and challenge methods of accounting for value creation beyond the one dimension of financial value. Social entrepreneurs are now fully integrated into the World Economic Forum program. Alongside the blurring and hybridising of the traditional boundaries between the private, public and third sectors, there has also been a dramatic change in the definitional boundaries of the financial sector and the emergence of a hybrid resource called social investment. This comprises the resources required to empower social and environmental change: financial capital – money; social capital – networks; and human capital – expertise and skills.

These are mobilised annually at the World Forum hosted by Jeff Skoll at Oxford to encourage the growth of the global network of social entrepreneurs. The theme of the 2006 Forum was an analysis of how philanthropy, social investment and mainstream capital could better lever social returns. Al Gore, in his presentation, made the prophetic observation that 'the investment market is functionally insane and we are operating the planet as a business in liquidation'.

In addition to his success with the film *An Inconvenient Truth,* Gore and his partner David Blood, the former chief executive of Goldman Sachs Asset Management, set up Generation Investment Management to challenge the prevailing orthodoxy that the only relevant tool for measuring 'value' is modernisation and the short-term mania in markets and the resulting irrational system for allocating capital. Investors have increasingly recognised the connection between the allocation of finance and its social and environmental impacts. This has resulted in a burgeoning field of players who have left conventional institutions to start new social investment organisations.

One such person is Australian Kylie Charlton, who recently teamed up with Eric Savage, an alumnus from Harvard's Kennedy School of Government, to launch Unitus Capital, one of the first financial advisory firms designed to meet the investment needs of social entrepreneurs. Unitus Capital is registered in India and operating initially in South-East Asia. It grew out of the capital markets group of Unitus Inc, a non-profit organisation that works to alleviate global poverty by increasing access to micro-finance. Unitus Capital has over $8 million in backing from private investors, and aims to become a boutique investment bank for social entrepreneurs working to improve the lives of those at the bottom of the economic pyramid. Charlton is managing director of the new organisation and is determined to transform the investment environment to better serve social entrepreneurs by working with them to ensure they have access to the growth capital they need. To me,

Charlton represents the values and mobility of her generation. She worked in investment banking in Australia and America and moved to the USA to work with Unitus leading its capital markets strategy before becoming part of the founding team for Unitus Capital. Her MBA studies at Oxford's Saïd Business School in 2004 were motivated by a desire to use her skills differently: 'I can stay an investment banker for the rest of my life, or apply my finance skills to initiatives aimed at improving the lives of the half of the world's population that lives on less than US$2 per day.'

As part of her MBA, Charlton did a strategic consulting project at the Cape York Institute of Policy and Leadership and this, combined with the Saïd Business School's elective course in social entrepreneurship, exposed her to the potential of applying capital markets to solve some of the world's most challenging social problems. There are lots of socially entrepreneurial 'Kylies' out there, changing our world, creating significant social value by challenging the old ways of thinking and doing.

Others have urged and inspired foundations to employ tools of venture capital to invest in the organisational rather than the programmatic needs of social-purpose organisations, and this has led to venture philanthropy. Conventional venture capital is high risk equity and loans capital directed towards new or young businesses with prospects of rapid growth and high rates of return. The aim of this type of investment is to accelerate growth. It is usually accompanied by the venture capitalist taking a hands-on role in the management of the venture being funded. The same principles apply in venture philanthropy to produce a new style of engaged philanthropy. Supporters argue that it brings the entrepreneurial spirit and fiscal discipline of the for-profit arena to innovative philanthropic investment portfolios of high potential, non-profit organisations. What is different though, is that it does not always seek a financial return on the capital invested. In North America, the vast bulk of venture philanthropy is based on non-returnable grants, with a greater emphasis on social rather than financial innovation.

In Australia, just as the venture capital industry has been slow to develop, so too has social venture capital. There are few social venture capital funds established specifically for the purposes of providing equity or debt financing for social enterprises or other disadvantaged small business groups. Foresters Community Finance is active in pioneering investment options for social enterprises and community assets and Social Ventures Australia has pioneered linking innovative social enterprise proposals with business mentoring to work the proposals into viable business and investment opportunities. Those judged capable of success have been provided with seed funding and close mentoring from skilled business professionals.

But, generally speaking, the access to capital for innovative community or individual social projects and ideas has been undeveloped. In Britain, Community Development Finance Institutions are a significant and registered presence in the field, raising finance and investing it in local community-owned or small business enterprises and providing business training and support to accompany the investment. This finance is usually grants and loans. Foresters recently assisted Logan Women's Health Centre in Queensland to design a financial plan and buy their building which was in danger of being sold by the developer owner. In an interesting twist, the developer bought into the new investment model.

A study by Mark Lyons and Kathryn Parker in 2003 examined parliamentary and other reports over the previous twenty years and found that, while there were several proposed policies that would have encouraged the emergence of community finance in Australia, these were ignored. The evidence of this lost opportunity is now obvious as there has not been identifiable investment in areas of unmet social need at the local level.

There are other examples of innovations designed to accelerate the flow of capital to social entrepreneurs with replicable, innovative start-ups including the experiment of Brazil's Social Stock Exchange, launched by the Sao Paulo Stock Exchange in 2003. It uses a brokerage model to bring together investors who wish to support those with a social mission and the organisations needing the capital. The investors purchase 'social shares' in initiatives recommended by the Social Stock Exchange Board. It's an innovative start but, as Muhammad Yunus wryly observed in his Nobel Lecture in December 2006, this new movement will require supportive infrastructure including new ratings agencies and *The Social Wall Street Journal*.

One such element of the supportive infrastructure needed is the development in Europe of Social Return on Investment (SROI), an impact measurement tool used to ascribe financial worth to the social value an organisation creates through its activities, outputs and outcomes. SROI is one of a range of tools that help third-sector organisations prove their impact. This is important in the new marketplaces in which third-sector organisations are operating: governments need to establish 'value for taxpayers' money' from contracting out services; funders want proof of the value and impact of their investments; and third-sector organisations themselves are keen to prove their added value to assist their chances of gaining funding and achieving success in these new markets.

SROI is a framework to help understand the value of social change from the perspective of those affected. It tells a compelling story of change, with a mix of narrative, qualitative and financial measures. It provides a financial proxy value of change, which can be understood alongside traditional financial costs.

It is transparent and consistent and aims to create a more tangible currency in social value that everyone can understand. For both governments and organisations, it can also help focus attention on particular activities and how well they are working to achieve social change.

One example of pilot work demonstrating how this can work can be seen in the British example of Fab Pad, a project which supports young homeless people to sustain new tenancies. Project leaders, Impact Arts believes that by engaging young people in making their new environment a home there will be less chance of them becoming homeless. The SROI evaluation carried out on Fab Pad revealed that for every pound invested by the government in support, £8.38 of social return was derived in reduced health care costs, reduced welfare benefits expenditure and reduced costs of repeat homelessness. The British Office of the Third Sector is currently working with UK Treasury to explore how SROI can be integrated into the Green Book methodology: in other words, into the way Treasury calculates 'value creation'. Are you with us, Mr Swan and Dr Henry?

There's nothing quite like a global system's failure to create the space for change. Geoff Mulgan, director of the Young Foundation which has a focus on the creation of a network of international Social Innovation Exchanges has been quick to draw attention to what he calls 'the mainstreaming of social innovation'. US President Barack Obama has created a new Office of Social Innovation as a venture capital fund to finance not-for-profit groups active in health, education and the environment. European Union President José Manuel Barroso is also leading a new push to link innovation strategy to social goals. Denmark has been integrating innovation into the work of its main government departments, from tax and social affairs to industry. Italy has set up a bank for social enterprise. Spain is setting up a 'Social Silicon Valley'. Korea's Hope Institute has been at the forefront of using the web to link citizen ideas to government. Foundations in North America have been experimenting with new forms of social investment, as well as using online collaboration to speed up problem solving. Contemporary examples include community wind farms, Linux software and other open source methods such as Wikipedia and Ohmynews, an online newspaper website originating in South Korea which employs over thirty thousand citizen reporters. These initiatives demonstrate exciting and inevitable capacity to drive changes in the way we currently operate our democracies.

So what, if anything, are we doing in Australia? There is an active hub of social enterprises in and around Brisbane fostered in part by the active support of the Brisbane City Council and some Queensland state departments in their use of social tenders for procurements contracts for social enterprises for such work as mowing parks and regular catering for large gatherings. The Howard Government established Business Community Partnerships. And the Centre for Social Impact was established in 2008 with funds provided by the Howard Government. It is a collaboration between the business schools of NSW, Melbourne and Swinburne universities with the stated ambition of 'helping to build an Australia centre renowned for its professionalism in delivering community benefit and its capacity to generate social innovation.' In February 2009 the South Australian government confirmed funding of its Australian Centre for Social Innovation in Adelaide. The School for Social Entrepreneurs Australia, supported by the Vincent Fairfax Foundation, and based in Sydney's inner west has also recruited its first students.

The Victorian Labor Government, the most progressive of the states in this field, has recently established Social Traders, a collaboration between it and a private philanthropic family trust. Social Traders will incubate social enterprises which help provide job training and work opportunities and will be run by a consortium of cross-sector organisations with extensive experience in community and social enterprise development. The Brotherhood of St Laurence has been actively developing community enterprises for some years.

But these endeavours are a very limited response to a trend which is gaining enormous momentum internationally. There is clearly a need to invest in technological innovation, but there is also a need to invest in social creativity. Australia needs the leadership to provoke and enable us to move beyond Hills Hoists, wine cask bladders, Victa lawnmowers and Speedos to the 'Social Silicon Valleys' – the places and institutions that will mobilise resources and energies to tackle social problems in ways that are comparable to the investments in technology made in the first Silicon Valley and its equivalents around the world.Since its election the Rudd Government has given policy priority to consultation with the third sector on a National Compact ('to develop effective relationships between Government and the sector to build social inclusion'), an inquiry into disclosure regimes for charities and not-for-profit organisations and a reference to the Productivity Commission 'to construct a new tool to measure the contribution of third-sector organisations to our economy as the starting point for maximising the sector's contribution to social inclusion, employment and economic growth.'

This is a disappointingly technocratic response. By all means let's continue to collect evidence to inform policy choices, but isn't a twenty-first century Australian government capable of multi-tasking, and forging ahead with what we already know from international best practice?

I find it enormously disappointing that, with an 'investment bank' of over $51 billion, the Rudd government with its 'Long Term Nation Building

Investments' (buildings, computers, physical infrastructure) has failed to grasp the enormous potential of this generational opportunity to invest meaningfully in transformative social infrastructure. How about a $500 million Social Investment Fund with matched funding from social investors? Perhaps that matched funding could come from a marshalling of the existing collective corporate social responsibility dollars into a consortia fund for the purpose of huge systemic impact?

Or a variation on a creative British idea: a Social Investment Bank with the capital to come from forgotten savings that are held by banks – so-called unclaimed assets. This bank could supplement funding for the work that third-sector organisations will be required to do in the next few years with those marginalised by the effects of the financial sector's instability.

Or investment in specific social innovation projects: again in the UK, the government has launched a collaboratively funded 'Next Practice Programme' which will support and showcase the best in third-sector innovation. Fourteen projects working across the issues of independent living and excluded young people will receive support packages that can include expert consultancy and a share of a $550,000 National Endowment for Science, Technology and the Arts and Innovation Exchange Fund.

It is important that Australia not be missing in action from this global revolution. What is clear is that governments need to enable a supportive policy and fiscal environment as a catalyst for change and as an investor in solutions that work. From its election in 1997, the British government under Tony Blair, and continuing under Gordon Brown, has enthusiastically embraced the opportunity for social enterprises to contribute to Labour's policy goals of a fairer, more just society by meeting unmet social needs, addressing environmental challenges, encouraging ethical markets and raising the bar for corporate responsibility. Gordon Brown when he was Chancellor of the Exchequer said: 'Today, corporate social responsibility goes far beyond the old philanthropy of the past – donating money to good causes at the end of the financial year – and is instead a year round responsibility that companies accept for the environment around them, for the best working practices, for their engagement in their local communities and for their recognition that brand names depend not only on quality, price and uniqueness but on how, cumulatively, they interact with companies' workforce, community and environment. Now we need to move towards a challenging measure of corporate responsibility, where we judge results not just by the input but by its outcomes: the difference we make to the world in which we live, and the contribution we make to poverty reduction.' Is our vision as comprehensive as this?

Within its first term, the Blair Government created a dedicated Office of the Third Sector within the Cabinet Office. This led to a specific Social Enterprise Action Plan in 2006 to actively foster across all departments a culture of building an evidence base, disseminating knowledge, enabling access to appropriate finance and making it possible for social businesses both to grow and participate in government procurement options.

Such an enabling policy environment has been a factor crucial to the success of the third sector's involvement in social solutions in Britain where there are now around 55,000 social enterprises, with indications that the numbers are rising. The total turnover of social enterprises is estimated at $60 billion, or 1.3 per cent of the total turnover of all businesses with employees; they contribute $18 billion to British gross domestic product; and a further $40 million is slated for investment in the next three years. A new, more appropriate legal structure that hybridised the best aspects of charities and companies – the first new legal form of company for a century – was created in 2005 and more than a thousand community interest companies (CIC) were created over the next two years. They are limited companies, with a 'community interest test' and 'asset lock', which ensure that they are established for community purposes and the assets and profits are dedicated to these purposes. Registration of a company as a CIC has to be approved by the regulator who also has a continuing monitoring and enforcement role.

I am an unapologetic, but not uncritical admirer of British intellectual leadership in social investment and innovation. Given our cultural and governance similarities, there are many simple but effective ideas which could assist Australia to catch up on social investment. Tax relief is one such area: it can support lending to enterprises in disadvantaged communities excluded from mainstream sources of finance, or be given to individuals and corporations investing in accredited Community Development Finance Institutions, which provide finance to qualifying profit-distributing enterprises, social enterprises and community projects. We could follow the British example of the national government investing directly in local community organisations, to enable them to run under-used local authority assets. The aim is to lead a sectoral cultural change so that governments and corporations move from seeing themselves as 'top-down providers' to 'social investment partners' with mutual aims, facilitating consultations with leaders in the sector but not expecting that sector leadership to neatly devolve to one person or one peak organisation. We have a great tradition in Australia of reducing complexity to one spokesperson: Tim Costello as the spokesperson on anything to do with 'social justice', one prominent unionist, one representative woman, one prominent business peak body, one 'welfare' spokesperson. Let's resist this and embrace the complexity and richness of diversity.

I want to contribute to a new reality of the third sector in Australia having a meaningful and equal voice in national conversations, alongside the public and the private sectors. I want to be one of the starting points for more meaningful interaction between the sectors and the legitimisation of opportunities for third-sector organisations to have the capacity to enter into equal business partnerships with the corporate sector and governments.

Today I read that the British are re-embracing their allotment system where communal gardens are grown as a local community-based response to the current financial crisis and rising unemployment and that cooperatives are experiencing a resurgence of investment. For me, learning about the third-sector and facilitating its growth has been a journey from the limits of being an Australian parliamentary representative, to a celebration of the global challenging to the 'accepted wisdoms' now finding new truths in social values-led systemic transformation. I draw inspiration from Victoria Hale, who has taken on a global mission, and from my 'adopted' daughter Olivia for her generosity in returning to Kampala to inspire another generation of Ugandan street children to find a way out of poverty through economic self-sufficiency. That nourishes me spiritually as well. ■

References and a vodcast of Noel Pearson in conversation with Andrew Mawson at www.griffithreview.com

Cheryl Kernot is the director of teaching and learning at the Centre for Social Impact, a collaboration of the business schools of the universities of New South Wales, Melbourne and Swinburne.

Get involved with Griffith REVIEW!

Griffith REVIEW presents popular events in capital cities and regions across Australia each quarter.

The Griffith REVIEW eNewsletter and website post details about upcoming events with links to podcasts from recent events.

Join us in person for Australia's Best Conversation!

Griffith REVIEW also welcomes 'Letters to the Editor', via post or email.

Selected letters will be posted on the Griffith REVIEW website. Please note that letters may be edited for clarity or length.

www.griffithreview.com

Essay:
Real communities

Author:
Hugh Mackay

Image: A volunteer in wet weather clothing collects donations on the steps of the Sydney Opera House at dawn on February 15, 2009 during a fundraising event for victims of the Victorian bushfires. / Photographer: Greg Wood/ AFP/Getty Images

Real communities

The former prime minister once dreamed of Australia as a nation of shareholders, enriched by their participation in the adventure of capitalism. Properly conceived, that is certainly one form of social engagement. If it looks a little less appealing to the punters today than it did back then, that might be because the full value of that kind of participation has not been widely or well enough understood.

Investing in our economic future is a worthwhile thing to do, and is most rewarding in the long term if, like philanthropy, it is undertaken as a form of social engagement. That's how the finest capitalists, from Adam Smith onwards, have approached it. Such investment is a symbol of the investor's faith in the future and in the integrity and potency of the enterprises they choose to support via their shareholding. Committed investment helps build communities and hold them together.

If, by contrast, the stock market is conceived of as a vast casino where buyers and sellers behave as if they are nothing more than gamblers, the system is bound to break down because the motivations are warped. Exploitation, motivated by greed, is a very different thing from investment. It is also a very different thing from social engagement.

Investment is the key to the creation of stronger communities and, ultimately, to a stronger nation.

But this is not only about dollars. We could dream a much larger dream about investment since, one way or another, we all make a social and emotional investment in the kind of society we are becoming. We could, for instance, choose to dream of a society where each of us understands that we are all part of one vast, vibrating web of interconnectedness. We could invest in the idea that all our actions – the way we save and spend our money, the way we occupy our time, the way we respond to the needs of strangers, all the ways we live – have consequences for the health and well-being of the whole. At its utopian best, this would be a dream about a nation – or even a neighbourhood – where our natural individualism is submerged beneath a concern for the common good; where, as a guiding story, competition gives way to a more egalitarian spirit of co-operation; where the shared values of citizens are shaped by a powerful sense of belonging to each other.

Belonging? Community? Shared values? These, surely, have become the weasel words of contemporary social analysis. Overblown and overplayed, they have been robbed of much of their meaning. They have come to sound more like mantras than social goals.

Indeed, the word 'village' is de rigueur if you're writing a real estate advertisement or creating a promotional brochure for a new high-rise development: the vertical village is with us. It's even become fashionable to speak of 'the Australian community', as if Australians were a close-knit little group, sharing in the life of some village where everyone knows everyone, everyone trusts everyone, and from which we draw a powerful and sustaining sense of identity and emotional security.

Yet we cling hopefully, and sometimes desperately, to words like community and village, precisely because we know, deep in our guts, that any successful, civilised society would aspire to that utopian prospect. Perhaps we also sense that the fondly imagined community is under threat, and we suspect the consequences of that might be serious. In fact, the consequences could hardly be more serious: our moral sense is, after all, a social sense.

It is only by learning how to live in a community that we gradually acquire our sense of right and wrong, as well as more subtle values like tolerance, compassion and respect for others. The fact that we don't even know our neighbours' names may have become a cliché of urban life and a favourite piece of anecdotal evidence for those who worry about the state of modern society. If you're concerned about the stability and cohesiveness of communities, there are more compelling pieces of evidence than that.

Take the upheavals in our patterns of marriage and divorce. A mere thirty years ago, the institution of marriage was still regarded by most Australians as a symbol of our stable society: 90 per cent of Australians were married by the age of thirty, and only about 8 or 9 per cent of marriages ever ended in divorce. Today, fewer than half of us are married by the age of thirty and over a third of contemporary marriages are expected to end in divorce.

While there's a strong argument in favour of easy divorce, and much to be said in praise of higher standards for marriage, a high-divorce society does have to contend with the fact that many friendship circles, neighbourhoods and communities are destabilised by marriage breakdown and family dislocation. Almost a quarter of families with dependent children are one-parent families and many of those solo parents are too busy, too stressed and too tired to participate in the life of any community.

About one million dependant children are currently living with only one of their natural parents, and about half of them regularly migrate from the home of the custodial parent to the home of the other parent for an access visit. This mass migration of children is a challenge to communities: not only is there inevitable disruption on a large scale, but there are additional needs for the care of children – and parents – distressed by all these comings and goings. The new Children's Contact Centres, designed to ease this pain, are a positive sign of our community's capacity to address the changing social order.

In the suburbs of the past, children typically acted as a social lubricant. But in spite of the present, probably temporary, lift in the birthrate, we have reached the point where, relative to total population, we are currently producing the smallest generation of children Australia has ever seen. That social lubricant is in short supply, especially in the middle and upper-middle socio-economic strata.

Not only is their birthrate falling faster than in lower socio-economic strata (where, among other factors, the $5,000 baby bonus is a major incentive), but parents are also becoming more protective of their children, less inclined to allow them to go outside and play and more likely to confine them to private cars on the way to and from school. A sharp decline in the number of stay-at-home mothers has further altered the dynamics of neighbourhood life, producing a generation of over-worked women and converting most of our suburbs into true dormitories with little daytime social interaction.

Increasingly, we need to make an appointment to chat with our neighbours. The mobility of the population also disrupts neighbourhoods: on average, Australians move house once every five or six years. That helps to explain why, according to research published by Edith Cowan University, only a third of us say we trust our neighbours.

Even the burgeoning numbers of wealthy Australians – and the widening gap between them and the rest – erode our sense of ourselves as members of a relatively homogeneous, middle-class society. It is now beginning to look as if our egalitarian dream might be evaporating, as a spirit of entitlement takes root among more affluent Australians.

Information technology plays its part, too, by blurring the traditional distinction between data transfer and communication, by tempting us to spend more time with machines than with each other, and by seducing us with the idea that online connections are just like the other kind. Indeed, for the rising generation of young Australians, words like 'community', 'connected' and even 'identity' have acquired new meanings in cyberspace.

Older people might think the idea of the global village was a hoax perpetrated by vested interests, but the young know better. If you doubt it, take a look at MySpace or Facebook, or any of the online networks and mobile phone links that facilitate constant contact between the members of the new cyber-tribes. They don't just feel as if these are real communities; they also have a range of online identities to go with them. The Symantec Identity Survey, conducted by Woolcott Research in 2007, found that heavy users of the internet typically had more than ten 'virtual identities' and that well over a third of users of internet social networks, virtual worlds or gaming sites believe their online identities are closer to their 'true self' than their physical or 'real-world' identities.

Back in that real world, our shrinking households are an intriguing sign of how radically and rapidly Australian communities are changing in ways that threaten social inclusion. (The fact that we are building ever larger houses to accommodate ever smaller households is also intriguing, but that's another story.) More than a quarter of Australian households now contain just one person and the ABS estimates that proportion will have risen to over one-third by the year 2026. One-person and two-person households already account for more than half of all households.

This is a complex picture, of course: we shouldn't automatically assume that aloneness equals loneliness. Many people cheerfully choose to live alone – often for brief episodes – but, at least in the short term, it looks as if the shrinking household heightens the risk of social exclusion and disengagement.

Longer term, I'm inclined to regard the shrinking household as an encouraging signpost to a more connected and more engaged community. We are, after all, herd animals and when the domestic herd shrinks below the normal herd size of seven or eight, we need to look elsewhere for herds to connect with. We may begin by grazing with the herd (it's no accident that the café revolution has coincided precisely with the upheaval in household composition), and then move on to a book club, a choir, a clean-up roster.

When we fear that the social fabric is fraying, it's tempting to assume the best solution is to impose a kind of regulated morality on society by creating more rules to compensate for the lack of social engagement. Calls for everything from anti-vilification laws to more regulation of corporate boards, tougher sentencing of criminals, tighter censorship of the media, all the way down to dog-walking laws … these are signs of our vulnerability to the idea that if we can't trust each other to act with restraint, compassion and moral sensitivity, we must legislate to create the kind of society we want.

As a response to social insecurity and anxiety, this is understandable – but unwise. Ever tougher rules and regulations won't make us a fairer, more compassionate society. In fact, it is more likely to do the opposite since excessive regulation tends to stifle, rather than quicken, the conscience. If we continue down the path of increasing regulation, we may well order our society in ways currently thought to be desirable, but at what cost?

The real challenge for anyone interested in rebuilding the sense of community is not to regulate more, nor to preach about ethics in the hope that people will start to act more considerately or compassionately in obedience to some written or unwritten charter of social responsibility. If we believe in the benefits that flow from being part of the life of a functioning community, the challenge is simply to find more ways of bringing people back together again.

For a start, we need to create more urban and suburban spaces conducive to the kind of spontaneous social interaction that facilitates friendly neighbourhoods – places where people can eat together, walk together, sit and talk together, or play together.

We need less emphasis on private space and more on public space, bearing in mind that two-income households have less time to maintain a traditional house and garden. We need to explore the concept of co-housing, where small living units are clustered around communal dining and recreation areas. We need to place more emphasis on shared transport, and less on the isolating cocoon of the private car. A great example is the 'walking bus' concept for kids, organising them into supervised groups for the walk to school. We need to accelerate the trend towards establishing commercial centres on the perimeters of our large cities, so more of us can work where we live and, in turn, have more time and energy to become engaged with our local communities. We need to encourage greater participation in community activities – everything from clean-up campaigns and bushcare groups to team sports, drama classes and poetry clubs – which reassure people that 'the village' exists and that they can belong to it.

In fact, the more you look at the ills of contemporary society – alienation, fragmentation, isolation, depression – the more compelling the need for communal participation in the arts seems. Surely, encouraging co-operative, collaborative creativity must be one of the better ways to foster a sense of community, promote mental health and well-being, and reduce the pressures of a competitive, materialistic society. Learning to paint or write (in a class that creates its own sense of belonging), putting on plays and musicals, organising festivals, making movies, taking up photography, puppetry or tapestry, singing in choirs, dancing, playing in bands ... these are all effective pathways to mental health for people whose daily lives are mostly spent in non-creative pursuits.

I recall my own experience of singing in a choir and resisting, every week, the demand to attend rehearsals: 'I'm too busy for this – I'll have to skip it this week' ... until the conductor's baton was raised, we began to sing and the therapeutic effects kicked in as reliably as any drug. We talk endlessly about the need for 'balance', by which we usually mean the balance between work, family and leisure. But there's another quite magical possibility: balancing the stresses, disappointments and tedium of life with the therapeutic release of tension through some form of regular creative outlet that restores your sense of perspective and your sense of worth, while connecting you to others.

Many people recall with intense pleasure their participation in school plays, orchestras, choirs and art classes. It wasn't just the music or the art or the performance: it was often the strong sense of group cohesion – of being a team player – that lingered most vividly in the memory. Sometimes they look back wistfully and wonder where all that pleasure (and all that talent) went. Why did it stop when they left school? And why couldn't it be recaptured?

Perhaps it's time to dust off all those Schools of Arts across the country and put them to the use for which they were originally intended.

Most of us find the richest source of life's meaning in our personal relationships. Being herd animals, we are born to communicate, to join, to gather, to connect and to share. When we deny those natural impulses, we diminish both ourselves and the communities to which we properly belong. The online revolution notwithstanding, I believe the most significant communities – significant, that is, in building a civilised, participative society – are still our local neighbourhoods. Grand visions of society have their place, but it's in the neighbourhood that we join the dots, a fact brought home to us with stark clarity whenever a crisis, like a flood or a bushfire, draws us together.

Getting along with friends and other like-minded people is easy: belonging to school or church communities, or even to gardening clubs or art classes, can be deeply satisfying and should be encouraged. But if we're not careful, such micro-communities can become tribal enclaves that add to the problem of social divisiveness. The real test of the civilising power (indeed, the moral power) of community is how we get along with people we haven't chosen to be with, don't especially like, and who don't necessarily share our interests.

Those unplanned, accidental encounters still happen in streets all over Australia, where people manage to get along with neighbours they never chose to live beside. But the pressures of our society are working against the miracle happening. We are tending to confine our contacts to the tried and trusted, at the cost of connections with our neighbours. That's unhealthy. There's no point in complaining about the loss of a sense of community if you haven't knocked on your neighbour's door and introduced yourself.

If you're serious about wanting to restore the health of your neighbourhood, join a choir or a book club, by all means. But don't forget to invite the neighbours in for a drink, as well. Find a few neighbours prepared to take it in turns to mow the lawn of the elderly person on the corner, or do the shopping for a harassed carer or single mother. Leave the car in the garage and walk around the block occasionally, greeting the people you meet.

That's participation; that's engagement; that's investment. ■

Hugh Mackay, social researcher and novelist, is the author of twelve books. His latest novel is *Ways of Escape* (Hachette). His essay, 'His eye is on the sparrow' was published in *Griffith REVIEW The Lure of Fundamentalism*.

Essay:
Consumer democracy

Author:
Mark Hopkinson

Image: Coney Island conceptual rendering / Courtesy of Coney Island Development Corporation / www.thecidc.org

Consumer democracy

The idea that it is the primary function of elected governments to raise the disposable income of their citizens is the great unwritten understanding of modern Western democracy. 'The social contract of Cold War liberalism' one commentator noted is, 'a state-sponsored guarantee of private consumption.' Tom Wolfe described the thirty-year boom that followed World War II as 'one of those facts that are so big and so obvious (like the Big Dipper at the showground) [that] no one ever comments on them anymore'.

The political propositions that came with that postwar boom now also seem as unremarkable as the Big Dipper. By the time that he wrote *The Affluent Society* in 1958, John Kenneth Galbraith presented his confident conclusions that the problem of production had been solved and that the class struggle was therefore obsolete. It was, however, a very new idea that the delivery of private material prosperity was the legitimate and credible purpose of government. This idea had two important components. The first was a new confidence in the productive potential of an economy managed by modern methods. The second was the emergence of the consumer as the pivot of the economic system, catching up with the individual's primacy in the political system since the creation of mass electoral franchises around the turn of the twentieth century. However, these two components created a feedback between consumer aspirations (including desire for welfare such as health and retirement income) and expectations about the capacity of the economy. Prosperity feeds expectations, but nobody knows how productive the economy will be.

The financial system has borne the burden of this contradiction. Financial innovation has allowed expectations of growth to be capitalised. The products that flow from this innovation are tied to the psychology of the consumer because of the rise of individuals as borrowers and savers. Now that the Big Dipper – to borrow Wolfe's metaphor – is on a sickening downward lurch, it takes a certain steadiness of nerve to consider, as it were, the engineering, but understanding how the ride was built may help to prepare us for the water dip.

A Frenchman, Ernest Renan, expressed the romantic idea of late nineteenth century nationalism in 1882 when he described the nation-state as a 'daily plebiscite' in which legitimacy was achieved by responding to the aspirations of the citizens. Max Weber, also thinking about the modern state in relation to the individual at this time, was more struck by the power of the state, and especially of its professional bureaucracy, than by the nation-state's attempts to appeal to its citizens. The power of modern governments was clear for all to see when they mobilised for World War I, but by 1918 the state was more obvious to its citizens in coercing them for war and taxes than in meeting their needs. As the German state collapsed around him in 1917–18, Weber concluded that a powerful bureaucracy was inescapable: 'socialism too has to reckon with this – the modern economy cannot be managed any other way'. Economic modernisation had led to 'the rule of things over men'. Although he thought that 'the anarchy of production' could conceivably be replaced with the meeting of needs, Weber could see neither where the leaders for such a change would come from, nor what their motives might be.

Meeting the needs of men became the crucial question in interwar Europe, and government failure to do this left the loyalties of the people open to other claimants. Europe at this time was a story of failed states as the new nation-states that had emerged in 1919 from the collapse of the Russian, Austrian and German empires struggled to establish democratic legitimacy. Of twenty-six continental states that existed in 1938, twenty had gone in one way or another by 1940.

The liberal economic system also faced a crisis of legitimacy during the 1930s. The great vulnerability of liberal capitalism, about which it had been harried by socialist parties since the mid-nineteenth century, was its attendant characteristics of waste and injustice. The Great Depression suggested that the system had failed this test. It has suited enthusiasts for activist government economic action like Galbraith to characterise the governments of the early 1930s as being locked into a nineteenth century conventional wisdom of small government and balanced budgets. World trade fell by two-thirds between 1929 and 1933; trade between France and Germany fell by four-fifths between 1929 and 1936. Faced with contraction on this scale, governments lacked a model that would release their inherent power to restore the economy. Britain's 'Treasury view' in 1929 was typical: 'We have no alternative now but to face up to the disagreeable reactionary necessity of cutting costs (including wages) in industry and cutting expenditure in public affairs.'

Behind this timid and constrained official response, however, and in contrast to the sweeping solutions being adopted in the totalitarian states of Germany and Italy, progressive thinkers were working on the rescue of the system.

The most historically prominent response was, of course, the case built by John Maynard Keynes for government spending and borrowing to counteract self-sustaining falls in private demand. Keynes joined a long British liberal tradition that sought to remedy the system's waste and injustice within the classical market freedoms. Keynes' work on these problems had begun as part of the New Liberalism movement before World War I. The British Liberal Party was destroyed by that war, so it is not clear what momentum the New Liberalism would have acquired, but its practical achievements, such as the unemployment provisions of 1911, were embedded in a broader critique of the economic cycle, developed by J.A. Hobson.

Hobson suggested that society could fail to develop its full economic potential due to under-consumption by the rich and inadequate spending power in the hands of the poor. It was an extension of this observation that Keynes developed in the 1930s into the rehabilitation of the liberal trading system.

Keynes became the polarising figure in postwar debates about the role of government in the market and the economy – champion to the active government lobby such as Galbraith, and demon to the free-market side. The attention given to Keynes has, unfortunately, served to obscure the work done by many others in the 1930s to develop the management tools for a better system.

Even during the Great Depression, these people could see the potential outlines of a productive economy based on a positive political conception of the citizen as consumer and a role for the state in promoting economic growth and social welfare. The Economic and Financial Organisation (EFO) of the League of Nations in Geneva provides one example of this work. The League had largely given up trying to develop a multilateral solution to the economic crisis after 1933 and focused instead on its technical work in areas such as public health – concentrating on the individual, not the state.

The EFO was led after 1931 by a Briton named Alexander Loveday who had recognised the relationship between social and economic problems from his study of Indian famines at the beginning of his career. Under Loveday, EFO accordingly worked on problems of nutrition and agriculture, developing, for example, schemes of agricultural credit. Four economists associated with EFO in the 1930s have won or shared Nobel Memorial Prizes for Economics since the prize was initiated in 1969. Loveday's EFO was an international network – the Nobel winners were Dutch, Swedish and British. The *World Economic Survey* was created at EFO and produced between 1931 and 1936 by J.B. Condliffe, an Australian-born New Zealander.

Loveday's network had connections to the 'Cambridge circle' of economists who developed Keynes' insights. James Meade, who worked on the *World Economic Survey* from 1937 until 1940, had been in this group in Cambridge in 1930–31. Meade returned to Britain in 1940 – driving through France with his wife and three small children just ahead of the German blitzkrieg – to join the Ministry of Economic Warfare. Here – with Richard Stone (who was also to win a Nobel Prize) sitting at a card table in a corridor with a mechanical calculator – Meade produced the first double-entry national accounts system for any country. This was done to marshal Britain's resources for the war effort, but measuring and comparing national growth rates, using the system developed by Meade and Stone, became an important part of postwar politics.

Loveday worked with Frank McDougall, Australia's economic adviser in London, to convince the League to establish in 1937 what Loveday called 'the mature bloom' of EFO's work: the Food and Agriculture Organisation. Loveday and McDougall designed the FAO's brief, which was to study ways to raise standards of living, mitigate depressions, increase agricultural credit, and link monetary policies to economic and financial trends.

This ambitious remit reflects the relationships that the economists who worked in this area at the time could see between problems of different kinds. In 1931, Loveday made a BBC broadcast as part of a series of responses by economists – the preceding week's broadcast had been by Keynes – to the unemployment crisis. Loveday was confident that improved productivity, together with lower population growth, would enable the world to become 'substantially richer per head than it has ever been before' and he also understood that one effect of this rising income would be relatively more discretionary spending, so that economic success in the future would depend upon 'satisfying those [secondary] needs'. In 1931, Loveday recognised the shift in economic activity towards servicing discretionary spending, but – whether significantly or not – he did not use the word 'consumer' at this time. By 1943, when writing of what would be possible after the war, with the 'whole apparatus of production kept actively engaged in producing what is required to meet human needs', Loveday said that this process 'must begin with the consumer'.

Franklin Roosevelt's New Deal in the United States embraced the consumer from the start. In his last campaign speech before the 1932 election, Roosevelt said: 'I believe that we are at the threshold of a fundamental change in our popular economic thought; that in the future we are going to think less about the producer and more about the consumer.' The role of the consumer was recognised through the creation of the Consumer Advisory Board. Roosevelt again acknowledged the economic component of citizenship in a campaign speech in 1936: 'If the average citizen is guaranteed an equal opportunity in the polling place, he must have an equal opportunity in the market place.'

America was the right place for the new political economy of the consumer. It had long been a relatively high-wage economy, but the introduction of mass standardised production by Henry Ford in 1910 transformed American consumption. 'Fordism' meant a widespread access to new products, based on a cycle of large-scale production, rising wages, lower costs, efficient distribution and attractive promotion. By the end of the 1920s, Americans could confidently see a self-sustaining system of economic growth, with the common man (and especially woman) at its heart. 'Consumptionism,' according to Mrs Christine Frederick in *Selling Mrs Consumer* in 1929, was 'the greatest idea America has to give to the world; the idea that workmen and masses be looked upon not simply as workers and producers, but as *consumers* ... Pay them more, sell them more, prosper more is the equation.'

The new way of life that was emerging in America also excited modernists in Europe, notably in Weimar Germany. More than fifty books were published in Germany in the 1920s on American culture, technology, prosperity and mass consumption. Some intellectual influences flowed the other way, adding modern Europe's more private insights to Mrs Frederick's breezy positivism. George Katona left Hungary for Berlin in 1919 to study experimental psychology. Germany's hyper-inflation in the early 1920s prompted Katona to study the psychological dynamics of rapid price rises. He became interested in American marketing methods in the 1920s and emigrated there in 1933. He worked on Wall Street, but returned to academic life after the war, founding the first systematic survey of consumer expectations and their effect on the economy.

Katona recognised that consumer aspirations were expansive, and predicted that the 'sweet poisoning emanating from America' would spread around the world, even to the communist countries. Another émigré, Ernest Dichter, worked more directly with the forces of the sweet poisoning. Dichter had extended his psychoanalytic practice in Vienna in the 1930s into commercial market research using in-depth interviews, and he put these methods to work for advertising agencies when he fled to America in 1938. One of his first clients was Ivory Soap, for whom he revealed an erotic element in bathing – 'one of the few occasions when the puritanical American was allowed to caress himself or herself'. But Dichter's fame came when *Time* magazine ran a photo story that described him as 'the first to apply to advertising really scientific psychology ... that tapped hidden desires and urges' in connection with his research for Chrysler that revealed men's associations between their choice of cars and their feelings about wives and mistresses.

Individual Europeans might have been excited by these forces of modernism, but the European politics of individual consumption were troubled. Among conservatives, access to material goods by the working class challenged notions of elite status that dated as far back as the medieval sumptuary laws which had classified permissible display according to social rank. Leaders on the left might have wanted to cushion the impact of adversity, but the left also had traditions of asceticism that became uncomfortable when aspirations moved from needs to wants. These European anti-materialist urges – then as now – gained much of their strength precisely from positioning themselves as the custodian of a perceived European tradition of restraint in opposition to the American psychology of abundance.

The mass market was politically challenging. A report by the International Chamber of Commerce in 1931 concluded that the purpose of the modern distribution system was 'to satisfy consumer wants by the most direct means and at the lowest costs'. That sort of system threatened the small-scale producers and distributors of the 'bourgeois' European commercial model, while the modern factory production of consumer goods challenged the basic and heavy industry bias that had existed so far for the European economy. A powerful constituency therefore existed to oppose these new forces – to be found, for example, in British trades unions and among smaller producers and retailers in Continental Europe. Businesses like these had been badly affected by the economic crisis of the early 1930s as falling prices and sales exposed their high fixed costs and inefficiencies. The question therefore was whether the state would favour the consumer by allowing market forces to lower prices and introduce new products, or favour producers by protecting the old ways of business.

The Nazi state was for the most part resistant to new forms of consumption. It was interested in some aspects of modernism – symbols of modern technology such as planes, *autobahns* and ocean liners were an important part of Nazi iconography. The material well-being of the German people mattered to the Nazis, especially the well-being of the artisans and clerks who formed their support base. The violence shown towards Jewish department store owners in Germany was derived in part from this Nazi support for the smaller shopkeeper but real power for individual producers and consumers was antithetical to the Nazi state. The Nazis portrayed themselves as the rebuilders of an older, purer, more fixed world for the German *volk*, which it was useful to contrast with a corrupt modern world of individual freedom and materialism. German attitudes to consumption had been shaped by hunger as a result of the British blockade during World War I and by the subsequent turmoil. In the 1920s, the Social Democrats had been interested in America's high wages, but they too believed that Germany was too poor for such a model and they saw modern production as a way to meet basic needs rather than to satisfy the desire for consumer goods. Nazi economic autarky required that imports be restricted, and the Nazis exploited the willingness of the German people to accept restrictions on consumer desire.

In Britain, by contrast, the interwar Conservative Party built its middle-class constituency around a supportive attitude to material aspirations. The 1930s are popularly associated with unemployment, but in practice, outside the old industrial areas, there was some prosperity after 1931. The devaluation and the lower interest rates that followed when Britain was forced off the gold standard gave a boost to demand that set British social and economic development on a path resembling that of America, based on the same products and desires – the home and conveniences to go into it, and the personal freedom epitomised by the motor car. New industry, based around electrical appliances and the car, boomed. Four million new houses were built between the wars – adding to a stock of homes that had only numbered eight million in 1918. Nearly two-thirds of middle-class government employees owned their own homes in 1938 – a fifth with no outstanding mortgage debt. Twelve new magazines about home decoration were launched between the wars. Retailing changed. In 1920, there were two hundred chain furniture stores selling less than a twentieth of furnishings; by 1939, eight hundred chain stores accounted for a fifth of the market. The suburban materialism of this time of fragile economic security – 'the Baldwin and Chamberlain era, when we messed about in our back gardens, [and] ran about in our little cars', according to J.B. Priestley – became part of the charge sheet of the appeasement era's 'Guilty Men' when the appeasement policy failed in May 1940.

Progressive economists like Loveday and his circle could sense the productive potential of a modern economy during the interwar years, but it was World War II that established this in the public mind. The war required all governments to run their economies at maximum productive power, with little regard for sound finance. The scale of the Red Army attack on Germany from the east was impressive, but the clear winner of the war, to its allies and its enemies alike, was the American economy. The American soldiers who arrived in Britain were conspicuously better paid and better equipped than their allies. Furthermore, by the later stages of the war, as the British economy reached the limits of its capacity, America became the major supplier of arms for the British war effort, using a very small proportion of its industrial capacity. Total supplies to Britain and her allies under lend-lease represented only a little more than a tenth of American arms production. The United States supplied a fifth of Britain's wartime combat aircraft and almost two-thirds of its transport aircraft, yet all these planes were only one eighth of American aircraft production. The US was producing two and a half times as many weapons as Germany by 1943, and six times as many as Britain by 1944, yet war production never accounted for more than 43 per cent of American gross domestic product, while both Britain and Germany committed well over half of their economies to war production.

George Orwell called the war 'the greatest of all agents of change' in his 1941 essay of revolutionary patriotism, *The Lion and the Unicorn*, and a 1942 Fabian pamphlet rather gleefully predicted that the war would be 'a holocaust of existing institutions'. This was certainly the case in continental Europe and Japan, where the nation-states collapsed, taking with them all previous claims to legitimacy. In retrospect, the components of the political arrangements for the post-1945 world in the West seem clear. These arrangements (with suitable variations for individual political traditions, especially between the European, Japanese and Anglo-Saxon economies) consist of government action to minimise consumer insecurity through welfare support and to sustain demand, as well as to transfer payments to special interests (for example, agriculture) to maintain economic demand and political support. This government action maintains a high and reasonably stable level of demand that allows a private corporate sector to get the benefits of scale in the mass production of goods, largely determined by consumer preference.

The American consumer democracy fell into place quite readily because delivering private prosperity was not a radical step. The only new feature was the postwar confidence about the role of the government. Government spending – both federal and state – had been less than a sixth of the US economy in 1930. By 1952 it had risen to over a quarter – all within an economy that had more than doubled since 1930. In continental Europe and in Britain, however, quite apart from the scale of economic devastation that the war had caused, it was not yet clear that the people wanted a political system based on individual material aspirations. West Germans seemed at first to believe that socialisation offered the best prospect of achieving reconstruction. Six of the German states passed socialisation laws between 1946 and 1948 and approval was high, garnering almost three-quarters of the vote in a plebiscite in Hesse. Britain elected an interventionist government in a landslide in 1945, but the undertakings of Attlee's Labour government were those of an austere security: 'meeting the people's needs' rather than permitting an economy of 'mink coats'.

Within a few years, this seemed to change. Erhardt's neoliberal platform was endorsed in West Germany under Allied sponsorship in 1949 as the benefits of the Marshall Plan began to flow. European economic integration which began with the formation of the Steel and Coal Commission in 1951 created the basis for a continental mass market. In Britain, the political appetite for equality in austerity was exhausted by 1951. Churchill's Conservatives, with their slogan of 'Freedom and abundance – these must be our aims', remembered the constituency that they had built on individual material aspiration in the 1930s. Satirising the postwar ethos of fair shares as 'queuetopia', the Conservatives beat Attlee's Labour government (campaigning on the basis of a 'just society') in the 1951 election and remained in office until 1964.

The durable constituency that emerged for a political economy based on growth suggests that social ambivalence between restraint and fulfillment had finally been resolved in favour of fulfillment. The cultural forces driving this resolution had been accumulating since the 1920s. Heavy industry, with its cohesion around the workplace and the communities that were formed by work, promoted identity based on productive roles and the associated group loyalties. These tribal loyalties were challenged by the growth of lighter industry, the suburbs and the increased personal mobility provided by the motor car. Options for mass entertainment increased in variety and excitement. The number of radio licences in Britain increased fourfold, to over nine million, between 1927 and 1939. When television became available, the number of licences that included television soared from fourteen thousand in 1947 to over 750,000 by 1951. More than 1,635 million cinema tickets were sold in Britain at the medium's peak in 1946, equating to a weekly visit by every person over the age of fifteen. The new entertainment experiences of radio, cinema, and eventually television offered fertile ground for individual identification. Cinema had rich visual content and exotic locations, with stars whose imagined lives were reinforced by film magazines. Radio programs might have been broadcast to millions, and films seen in identical form around the world, but cinema was watched in the dark, and radio was heard in private at home. *The Radio Year Book* for 1925 recognised this element of excitement: 'the first thrilling moment when the set is to be operated ... such as we seldom feel in this unromantic age'. The advertising industry developed in conjunction with the emerging system of mass production and consumption: the US advertising trade association was founded in 1917 and its British counterpart followed in 1926. Analysts of the consumption experience follow Ernest Dieter into the private places of the mind by comparing the acquisitive urge to a romance, with its cycle of desire, fulfillment and disappointment. Advertisers quickly realised the power of the emotional appeal to the individual – the benefits to be had if they could 'mobilise the instincts'.

The disposition towards consumer aspiration on which postwar politics has been based developed in the dreams evoked by these exciting new media. By 1950, this cultural force had become decisive. European voters, like their American counterparts, were inclined to elect on the basis of promises of material prosperity. Political platforms had evolved that could offer that preference. Of course, this promise had to be credible, and by the early 1950s belief in the new growth economics, emulating the American example, had begun to take root. Confidence developed in the growth potential of a modern economy, and in the capacity of governments to facilitate this. By 1954, *The Economist* magazine declared that 'the miracle has happened: full employment without inflation'. In 1955, the British Chancellor offered the hitherto extraordinary prospect that 'the size of the economy could double within twenty-five years'.

The new political arrangement was accidental. Demand for individual prosperity coincided with belief that it could be delivered, but it is easy to see why the political economy of growth appealed to all postwar politicians. The prospect of a growing economy made it easier to resolve the old arguments between sectional interests.

The weakness of the accidental settlement is that there is an unstable relationship between collective individual expectations and the productive capacity of the economy. If those, like Alexander Loveday, who could see the potential of a modern economy to improve the lives of its citizens were to be surprised by anything that has happened in the eighty years after the crisis of the early 1930s – years in which their optimism has been largely vindicated – it would perhaps be the extent to which growth seems to create new perceived needs as readily as it meets existing ones.

The phrase that seemed to catch the public imagination when William Beveridge's proposal for a universal social safety net in postwar Britain was released in December 1942 was the aspiration to 'slay the five giants' of Want, Disease, Squalor, Ignorance and Idleness. The notion that these dragons can be slain rather than just change form is based on a world picture of relatively fixed and objective needs.

It is unlikely that Loveday – who recognised in 1931 that the modern economy should be organised around meeting consumer needs and who later joined the Mont Pelerin Society – believed in a planned society, yet he too seems to have believed that demands on the economy could be managed against its ability to meet them. Loveday wrote in 1943: 'We want [to ensure that] this whole apparatus of production is kept actively engaged in producing what is required to satisfy human needs. We want to begin with the consumer and make sure that the essential needs of all people are satisfied first.' However, if consumer aspirations are fuelled but not limited by the growth of the economy, while its politics are based around satisfying those aspirations, then down-payments on future growth are likely to be stretched and accelerated.

It is a parallel part of this political economy that financial choice and risk have been handed to the individual consumer – most significantly, for the management of retirement savings. This most important and difficult process, which is the heart and purpose of the financial system, is now another arena for product choice, subject to the same mysterious cycle of aspiration and disappointment as any other consumer product.

The nature of the present crisis is that these pressures to overestimate economic performance have fuelled improbably optimistic claims on future income. These pressures emerge for example in rising levels of personal debt, in permissive attitudes to asset values, in underfunded welfare commitments and in lean corporate equity cushions. The situation has developed as a credit crisis because the credit mechanism has failed in its job of estimating what claims should be created, and on whom. The end of the crisis will require some consensus about the level of sustainable future growth, and therefore about the capacity of the economy to meet these future claims. Sharing the burden of reduced expectations seems likely to mean an uncomfortable return to conflict between sectional – and, increasingly, generational – interests. The challenge for the present generation of policy practitioners is to redesign the political economy of the individual to insulate the financial system, which brings together expectations about the present and future, from the strains under which it has suffered from being part of the consumer economy. ■

References available at www.griffithreview.com

Mark Hopkinson is a former banker, now completing a Master of Studies in History at University College, Oxford..

Memoir:

Working on big issues

Author:

Alan Attwood

Image: The Big Issue building, dating back to the mid-nineteenth century, houses one of the most unusual editorial offices in the country. Vendors like Gordon P, the magazine's man in Moonee Ponds, are regular (and welcome) visitors. He has participated in writing workshops. At one of these he came up with the beautiful lines: 'I believe in God / And God believes in me …' Photographer: Alan Attwood

Working on big issues

For a couple of years in the mid-1990s, I worked out of an office overlooking Times Square. Sounds of the midtown-Manhattan traffic, many floors below, were screened out by huge windows, which, when it grew dark, offered spectacular views of the neon advertising signs and the lights of the fast-flowing canyons of traffic. Not infrequently, I abandoned all pretence of work. I'd just sit there at my desk, gazing out at the view, knowing that this couldn't and wouldn't last, and that I'd never again have such an extravagant office.

I was right.

Even before my term was up as New York correspondent for *The Sydney Morning Herald* and *The Age*, the bean-counters had grown restless and the downsizing began. The operation moved to a less scenic location a few blocks from Grand Central Station. At street level there was a pizza shop; depending on the wind and quirks of the building's air-conditioning, we'd often get a blast of capricciosa or pepperoni late in the day. Yet still it was not exactly a hardship posting – how could it be with the stone lions outside the New York Public Library or the squirrels of Central Park within easy walking distance?

Now it's not unusual for my working days to begin with a minute or two spent brushing mouse shit off my desk, though I sometimes have to delay this while I twiddle with the bare light bulb above to get it to stay on. I work in a bluestone building that dates from the mid-nineteenth century: it's a heritage building and lovely to look at (from outside), but it often seems that much of the building's wiring and plumbing is only slightly more recent than its foundations. I know all about the plumbing: a toilet, used by many people, is next to my office. The computer I sit at is elderly and regularly shuts down without warning. Oh yes – the building has no air-conditioning, which makes working conditions interesting in the extremes of summer and winter.

Nevertheless, I feel more at home as editor of *The Big Issue*, the fortnightly magazine sold on streets around Australia by marginalised people, than I did for much of my time working in the mainstream media.

Part of the reason for this lies in the flip response I developed for those who ask me what it's like to go from somewhere like *The Age* – where I was on staff for eighteen years, on and off – to *The Big Issue*. 'Well,' I reply, 'you meet a better class of people.'

That usually prompts a snigger, but there's also some truth in it. One problem I had working for Fairfax was an unsettling suspicion that my labour was helping to make some fairly ordinary types even wealthier or more prominent.

(The appalling Conrad Black was my putative boss for a bizarre period in the 1990s.) At *The Big Issue,* I mix daily with the people who sell the magazine: people who are or have been homeless; people battling substance-abuse problems; people with mental illness; people doing it tough for all kinds of reasons, including disability. They are people, across the country, who buy the magazine for $2.50 per copy from our offices or outlets like The Body Shop, then go out to try to sell them for $5.

But the magazine doesn't just represent money for the vendors. I realised that early in my time as editor, which began in November 2006, when I asked a Melbourne vendor how many magazines he hoped to sell that day. 'Eight,' he replied. I quickly did the maths: the cover-price was then $4; eight sales meant a profit of $16, enough for cigarettes and not much more. But those eight magazines gave this bloke a sense of purpose and, importantly, something to do with his time. Days drag when you're unemployed. Those eight magazines represented a goal, which is why few workers ever look more pleased with themselves than a vendor who has sold his last magazine for the day. And it *is* work. Try it sometime: stand in a public place trying to interest passers-by in something you're selling – especially when everyone's feeling squeezed and daily papers are given away for free.

There are all kinds of reasons why people end up selling *The Big Issue.* It's often described as the magazine sold by homeless people. That's simplistic. Only some sleep rough. I don't know where most of the vendors (the vast majority of whom are men) spend their nights, nor is it my business to pry. But I generally only have to chat to a vendor for a few minutes to get a sense of why they are selling the magazine rather than doing something else. Most would struggle to hold down a 'regular' job, which is why *The Big Issue* is so important: it offers employment to those who would otherwise be jobless. Some vendors are quite entrepreneurial: they have sales spiels and put on a show for prospective customers. Their income can reflect their salesmanship. Others do little more than stand or sit with the magazine on display. They are the ones I admire the most. And they are used to being ignored. People, especially in cities, are good at not seeing things. They stream past a vendor with that blinkered look that says 'I'm not sure what you're selling, but I don't want any.' The biggest frustration, both for vendors and all of us working on the magazine, is that the Australian edition has existed for close to thirteen years now and yet too many people still aren't sure what it *is.* I hear myself saying all the time: 'No, it's not a greenie magazine.' (Or a leftie magazine. Or a union magazine. Certainly not the Scientologists' magazine.) It's simply a lively, general-interest magazine that exists to help those who sell it – a task that's becoming harder rather than easier.

Late last year, when the words 'global financial crisis' crept into common use, someone said to me, 'Well, your blokes aren't going to be affected, are they?' When I asked what he meant, he continued: 'Well, the magazine sellers don't have mortgages; don't have super funds; don't have share portfolios going backwards. They're insulated from all this, aren't they?' No they're not. They've been hit, like everyone else. In 2007, we set records for magazine sales; last year, figures started to dip. End-of-year sales picked up again (the Christmas spirit is not dead), but this year will be tough. Our sales are influenced by everything from bad weather to public-transport problems and holidays, but it seems clear that many people who, twelve months ago, would hand over $5 for a magazine without a second thought are now hanging on to it. *Everyone*, in different ways, is feeling the pinch, including our vendors. It wouldn't surprise me if some of the same people who, not long ago, walked past vendors without a second glance will have to consider the magazine as an employment option one day. It's happening already: tough times can make the unimaginable worth considering.

I didn't become aware of *The Big Issue* myself until I returned to Australia from New York in September 1998. (The first edition had hit the Melbourne streets two years earlier.) From my first encounter, it struck me as a brilliantly simple and practical idea: a magazine that directly helped those who sold it. I started buying copies whenever I saw a vendor, though often I'd hand over the coins in the same way I might give money to a busker or beggar: it was essentially a feel-good purchase, and I might only skim the magazine later. When I did read it, however, I'd often be impressed by the content: this was a magazine with personality and presence. I learned a little more about it; visited the bluestone office (donated, rent-free, by the Wesley Mission) to write a newspaper article on a literacy program being run for vendors and friends. This was an outfit with a clear sense of purpose.

But it wasn't until some years later, in 2003, that I actually got involved – after I'd finally left my staff position at *The Age*. There were several reasons for this, and only in retrospect is it apparent that I was wrestling with the notion of work, and what I really wanted to do. At the time, the most obvious reason for walking away from a secure, well-paid job was a delayed case of foreign correspondent's syndrome: after being out of the country for several years, reporting on stories like a US presidential campaign, it can be hard to feel engaged by domestic politics and events. There was also a sense of covering the same events again and again, of measuring out my life with Melbourne Cups or Australian Opens. I wasn't even sure that I wanted to be a journalist any longer.

I was fascinated by the career arc of a feature-writer I'd admired as a teenager in the 1970s, when I first started to get interested in papers. With great style, this bloke rode the wave of the so-called 'new journalism', then walked away from it all and moved to the country to try life as a restaurateur. Later I read a story in which someone asked him why he'd done this. His answer? 'I didn't want to keep asking people questions.' That was how I felt in 2003. There was another factor, too: my second novel had just been published, sparking a (short-lived) burst of interest. I was attending literary festivals not as a reporter but, rather, a guest. I was done with journalism; I was going to be an author.

Well, not *just* an author. I wrote a letter to *The Big Issue,* saying I'd always admired the publication and its purpose, and could I help? In response, the editor called. She'd be pleased to have me contribute some pieces, she said, but did I appreciate that they paid crap? That was fine; I wasn't doing it for the money. A little later, when I was contributing fortnightly columns for the magazine, I visited the office to meet her. I arrived on time at the bluestone building, announced myself and waited. Then waited some more. This was odd. I became conscious of a muffled banging from somewhere above. A young woman came down from upstairs, with an expression that seemed like a mixture of amusement and embarrassment. Sorry, I was told, the editor was locked inside the toilet. Seems she'd popped in for a quick visit before coming down to see me, only to have the door handle fall off. All that banging had been her trying to attract attention so she could get out.

Six years on, that visit seems like the perfect introduction to life at *The Big Issue.* Now I'm the editor, I sit in a small room next to that toilet, and I regularly tell people that I'd love to have them contribute some pieces, but did they appreciate that we pay crap? Six years ago, I wouldn't have anticipated this. After all, wasn't I going to be an author? Yes I was, until I discovered, predictably, that it wasn't as easy as it looks.

Other things were going on, too: my father, who'd already been in a nursing home for several years, inexorably slipped further down the ghastly slippery-dip of dementia. When I'd visit him I'd leave in despair; when I *didn't* visit I'd feel guilty. In between visits (or non-visits) I'd struggle with the next book, which had become a problem-child. In the scheme of things, spending too much time on my own talking only to the dog was not very healthy. My father's death in mid-2005 marked an end-point for all kinds of things, not least those incessant visits.

When it was all over, my sister and I looked at each other and asked: what *did* people do with their weekends? Suddenly I had more time. One thing I did with it was get more involved with *The Big Issue* and its people. I started going in once a fortnight to assist with proofreading, went along to Wednesday-afternoon soccer sessions, where my role was to prove to the motley mob who attended that none of *them* was the worst player on the pitch. No, that was

Where have I seen your face before?

Photographer: Alan Attwood

The Big Issue is sold on streets around Australia by disadvantaged men and women. They are used to being ignored. But *The Big Issue*'s main office in Melbourne is a place they can feel at home. The entrance corridor is lined with pictures of vendors past and present; people whom vendor support workers like Virginia Moebus-Nelson come to know well. Since 2006 I have tried to capture the essence of the 'Ish' – both the place and its people.

Molly has sung with the Choir of Hard Knocks. Last year, she eloquently expressed her pride in her Aboriginal heritage in a show, *Homeless, Not Artless*, put together under *The Big Issue* umbrella, which demonstrated what people have to say when given an opportunity.

Adam, an entrepreneurial vendor known for his rhymes on the pitch, is also handy on the soccer pitch: he was captain of the Australian Street Soccer team for the Homeless World Cup in Denmark in 2007.

Selling the magazine is not really Aaron's thing; few young people want to do it. Like Adam, he made the 2007 Street Soccer national team and is one of the many who is often around the place: helping out; chatting; chilling; enjoying being somewhere he's not judged or questioned or asked to move on.

Leo, with his ever-present dog, Herbie, out front of the magnificent old bluestone Wesley church next to the office. A long-term vendor, Leo is something of a philosopher and was also a participant in the *Homeless, not Artless* project. Vendors, he has said, are people on the margins of society, seeking a way in.

Jim is one of the best-known vendors. Any visitor to Melbourne's Queen Victoria Market is likely to have seen or heard him. He is a diehard Geelong supporter in the AFL and an extraordinary performer. Once seen (in drag), his alter ego, Daisy-Mae (the voice of his past), is never forgotten.

Gordon, who gets around on a motorised scooter, was seldom seen without his dog, Spooky, sadly no longer with us. For the magazine's last Christmas issue he wrote of the day: 'I have been left at home, watching pre-taped videos and DVDs, for the past 15 out of 20 years. But that doesn't mean I don't believe in Christmas.'

Owen is the magazine's poet laureate. Seldom does a week pass without another poem (or two) arriving from Owen, handwritten in capital letters, for the 'Streetsheet' page. He is also an expert on music; with the 60s his strong suit.

First-time visitors to the office invariably stop, transfixed, in the corridor ... All those faces without names; all those people who've done it tough ... Many of the vendors pictured have aged considerably since their pictures first went up. They arrive, have a cup of tea or bad coffee, then head out again with their magazines into a world where their welcome is less warm.

me. Over time, I realised I was gravitating to the 'Ish' and its people; there was something there – commitment, idealism, a sense of fun – I'd often found missing in mainstream journalism.

I was doing some of that again, too. I'd reconciled myself to the idea that journalism was essentially my trade. Some people are plumbers. Others are nurses. My trade was journalism, and there were worse things to do. Having wondered, in 2003, if I'd done my final interview, I headed out again with a notebook and tape-recorder for a magazine feature. Despite some early misgivings, it wasn't so bad. I felt like a footballer who'd missed a season with a bung knee and then found he quite liked being out on the field again, chasing a kick. Meanwhile, I'd also started volunteering.

It was planned as a one-off excursion on a weekend morning, nothing more. I took my youngest son to the Collingwood children's farm, just a few kilometres from Melbourne's business centre. For many city kids it's their only chance to see sheep and cows and goats. Parents like it too: for a couple of hours they can pretend they're in the country. Our outing went okay, though Gus had seen quite enough animals after an hour or two. Before we left, though, and without much thought, I'd scribbled down some details under a notice headed *Volunteers Wanted*. Then I followed it up and went along for an introductory session. They made it clear they wanted a degree of commitment, not just blow-ins who wouldn't show up again after a session or two. I nominated Friday afternoons as my preferred time: seemed like a good way to end a working week after too much time sitting at a desk.

So I became a part-time farmer. I helped weed the veggie garden; I shovelled shit, working my way around paddocks with a wheelbarrow; I bottle-fed newborn lambs; I learned to milk a cow (badly). After I'd been there for a while I was accepted, trusted with keys and a bit more responsibility. I enjoyed myself, coming home filthy but pleasantly tired.

The fact that I was earning nothing for my labour didn't bother me. On the contrary, it was immensely liberating *not* to be putting a monetary value on my time. Occasionally, my different worlds overlapped. I was doing some freelance pieces for *The Age*; one afternoon, a section editor rang to discuss an assignment while I was in a paddock. He said his piece, paused, then asked: 'Can I hear sheep?' Yep, I replied. I couldn't tell if he'd put down the phone envying my outdoor life or just shake his head sadly and tell my former colleagues that, clearly, I'd lost it.

Then, one afternoon, my duties changed dramatically. I was checking in with the woman who normally gave me my weekly task when another staff member came by, obviously looking for someone. Seeing me there, waiting, she asked if I had any problem working with disabled people. Not at all, I replied, though I wasn't sure what I was letting myself in for. I had been vaguely aware of a group that came on Friday afternoons: people in wheelchairs, a couple of Down syndrome blokes, others with callipers or walking frames and one big, noisy fellow who charged around a lot. They were all there for supervised outings, but our paths had rarely crossed – until then, when my Fridays became Afternoons With Paul.

Paul was, of course, the big, noisy fellow who charged around a lot. My job was to be his minder: to work with him closely, ensure he didn't get into trouble (given half a chance he'd slip away, find a kitchen and scoff whole jars of sugar or instant coffee) and, most importantly, tire him out a bit. A few hours of physical labour in the afternoon would make him more docile in the evening. So we chopped trees together, dug out roots, attacked huge compost-heaps with shovels. And all the while Paul would ask about the timing of afternoon tea. Same as last week, I'd reply. 'Four bloody o'clock.' Then he'd ask me again. A grown man, heavier than me, he was like a big kid. And we became a team. I'd hear him calling out my name when the group arrived and made their way down the driveway, Paul pushing one of the wheelchairs none too gently in his eagerness to start work.

It wasn't the sort of thing I'd ever planned. But I was surprised how satisfying it was. I learned that the last thing these people wanted was sympathy. They'd much rather laugh than be patronised or pitied. I'd joke with one guy about his Elvis sunnies; abuse another about his choice of football scarf; grew complicit with Paul in some of his minor crimes. (I told him one day that the supervisors would *never* believe his insistence that he hadn't got at the staff Nescafé, because there was a bloody great coffee ring around his mouth. Then I helped him wipe it off.)

My time at the farm – especially time spent with Paul and his mates – turned out to be perfect preparation for working with *Big Issue* vendors, with their myriad problems. Ironically, I had to give up one to do the other. I left the farm on my last Friday afternoon with considerable pangs, some of which were eased later when I learned that Paul, whom I was sure would miss me, apparently adapted remarkably quickly to my absence. Within weeks he was singing out 'Julia!' just as eagerly as he'd ever called my name.

Now that Barack Obama has emphasised the importance of 'community service' – one of his last acts before becoming president was to help paint a homeless shelter – my own experience as a volunteer seems significant.

My contribution to the farm was minor: one afternoon a week only goes so far. But that time helped shape some of my thoughts about work. In retrospect, much of that period between leaving *The Age* in 2003 and starting as editor of *The Big Issue* late in 2006, with my father's death falling in between, was spent doing some hard thinking about what I really wanted to do. Working for nothing at the farm, or as a fortnightly proofreader for the magazine, made it easier to go backwards (in terms of salary) when I took on the editor's job. That wasn't hard; after all, if money was what mattered most, I would never have left *The Age*. Staying somewhere just for the pay has always struck me as a slow death. It dismays me that several of my former colleagues, who couldn't call themselves happy in their jobs, have accepted this as their fate.

Looking back on a career path distinguished by several detours and a dead-end or two, it is clear that I've always been ambivalent about the nature of full-time work. And I've never been as concerned about pay as I probably should have been. Earning buckets of money has never been a priority. In fact, it has always seemed to me that huge salaries come at a high cost. It's simple: if someone is paying you ridiculous sums of money, they have the right to believe that they have bought you.

The summer of 1977–78, before I started at *The Age*, was spent as a labourer/beach-bum in Mallacoota, near the Victoria–NSW border. I was helping a bloke who ran some holiday flats and did some abalone-diving. In return for odd jobs, supplemented by shifts at the local abalone processing plant, I had free board in a tiny caravan without wheels at the back of his property. For transport, I had a bicycle; for clothes, I needed nothing more than tee-shirt, shorts and thongs.

This was my life when a message was relayed via my employer: ring *The Age*. I made the call from a public phone in Mallacoota's main street. I was being offered a coveted cadetship – on the strength of cuttings I'd sent in from the uni paper. But I guessed that the personnel manager on the other end of the line could sense my ambivalence when I learned that suit and tie would be required. 'I suppose that means I have to wear shoes, too,' I said. He thought that was a fine joke, so I decided it was wise not to let on I hadn't worn shoes for months. Standing in that phone box, with my bike leaning against it, I understood that my life was about to change dramatically, most likely forever. I was going to enter the workforce.

I got used to it. Sort of. Then again, after two and a half years I took a year's leave of absence to travel overseas, the sort of thing I possibly should have done before starting a uni course in which I really had no interest. Less than five years after coming back from overseas – having, by then, learned a truth of corporate life, that to advance you often have to leave – I quit and went to work somewhere else.

Down the track a little way, after marriage and fatherhood, I went part time – first to look after a child, then for good when I realised I preferred working from home to working in an office. And that's how it's been for much of my time since. Let's just say that over thirty-one years I've only once stayed long enough to earn long-service leave.

It may also be significant that my first day *back* from that long-service leave was the day I quit for good. A bit of perspective can be a very dangerous thing. I returned to my old desk, looked around, and at once it was perfectly clear: I didn't want to be there any more. I recall another moment of epiphany. This was in the US, I'm guessing around 1997. I was in transit in one of the huge hub airports, possibly Chicago, rushing from Gate 17 to Gate 53B. Suddenly I stopped and looked around, and was horrified by what I saw. There were hundreds and hundreds of people looking just like me: hurrying, hassled, with an overnight-bag on one shoulder, laptop on the other, and worried looks on their faces. This was no way to live your life. And it probably explains why, after I returned to Australia and a well-meaning editor tried to enthuse me with the prospect of further travel, that I told him I didn't want to go *anywhere* for a while. You see so much more when you're sitting still.

One last moment of lucidity – this time from my early days at *The Age*. I was waiting at the lifts. A door opened; a small group of people came out and shuffled away silently. When I commented on their lack of animation and the greyness of them all, I was told that these were members of the '25-Year Club' – long-serving staff members who'd been upstairs enjoying one of the perks of club membership, an annual sherry with the managing director. They seemed such a dispirited bunch that I resolved never to stay in one place long enough to earn twenty-five-year drinks.

As things have panned out, I've never been in danger of that. And I suspect fewer and fewer people ever get there. Once it was commonplace for people to stay in one place for much of their working lives; for a journalist to start as a copy-boy or girl and then, many years later, make it to editor or the ranks of senior management. Now it's expected that people will chop and change jobs and the concept of corporate loyalty seems as quaint as telex machines. These days, staff are more likely to be offered redundancy than invited upstairs for sherry. I know, too, that if a job application hit my desk from someone who'd been in the one place even for ten or fifteen years I might admire their steadfastness, but I'd also be asking questions about their lack of initiative and imagination.

One thing was clear to me from my earliest days at *The Big Issue*: I was there because I wanted to be. Being an editor is like being a footy coach. You can be sacked any time. It's an occupational hazard. If it happens to me, I'll simply move along. Then again, I may well run out of gas before anyone comes into my tiny office with some bad news. The same things that make the job challenging – the magazine being understaffed and under-resourced – can also make it exhausting. But there's something very satisfying and rewarding in working with people who could probably be earning more money elsewhere and are there, at least in part, out of affinity to a cause. I've never heard less whingeing in a workplace, which is ironic considering that the people often have more reason than most to complain. Maybe this is because there are usually vendors around the place to remind us that, in the scheme of things, a lack of flywire on an open windows or a flaky PC is really pretty small beer.

Others in our building have more to do with vendors and their welfare than me. I chat with many of the vendors, but my main role, plain and simple, is to ensure that a new magazine is ready every fortnight. My job is to give them something to sell. That's their job. And most are proud to do it. These people who have battled all kinds of demons in their lives have work, and something to do with their days. That's no small thing.

They are not always appreciative of our efforts. One morning, popping out for a coffee, I said 'hi' to one of the more cantankerous vendors and was dumped on in response. Well, I thought, walking away, this sucks. But I also recall another occasion, when a conversation with a different *Big Issue* veteran ended with him saying, quite softly, 'Thanks for what you're doing for us.' Those few words were more satisfying than any sherry upstairs with the MD. And can make mouse shit seem like nothing much at all. ■

Alan Attwood is the author of novels *Breathing Underwater* (Mandarin, 1997) and *Burke's Soldier* (Penguin, 2003). He is also a member of the MAP (Many Australian Photographers) Group, committed to documentary photography. (www.mapgroup.org.au)

Essay:

Monitory democracy and media-saturated societies

Author:

John Keane

Image: Ben Heine / Barack Obama US President / Courtesy of the artist / www.benheine.com

Monitory democracy and media-saturated societies

There is a need for a fundamental revision of the way we think about democracy in our times. An epochal transformation has been taking place in the contours and dynamics of representative democracy. From roughly the mid-twentieth century representative democracy began to morph into a new historical form of 'post-representative' democracy. The fundamental implications of this change for democracy in the coming years need to be explored. The 'end of history' perspectives and maritime metaphors are too limited to grasp the epochal change – too bound to the surface of things, too preoccupied with continuities and aggregate data to notice that political tides have begun to run in entirely new directions.

My claim is that our world is now living through an historic sea change, one that is taking us away from the old world of representative democracy towards a form of democracy with entirely different contours and dynamics. In media-saturated societies which bristle with communicative abundance – questions about the causes and causers of this new historical form of democracy, its advantages and disadvantages, have fundamental implications for media and politics, and profound implications for how we think about and practise democracy and journalism in the coming decades.

It is hard to find an elegant name for the emergent form of democracy, let alone to describe and explain in a few words its workings and political implications. The strange-sounding term 'monitory democracy' is the most exact for describing the great transformation that is taking hold in regions like Europe and South Asia and in countries otherwise as different as the United States, Japan, Argentina, Australia and New Zealand.

My opening conjecture is that monitory democracy is a new historical type of democracy, a variety of 'post-Westminster' politics defined by the rapid growth of many different kinds of extra-parliamentary, power-scrutinising mechanisms. These monitory bodies take root within the 'domestic' fields of government and civil society, as well as in cross-border settings. In consequence, the whole architecture of self-government is changing. The central grip of elections, political parties and parliaments on the lives of citizens is weakening. Democracy is coming to mean more than elections, although nothing less. Within and outside states, independent monitors of power begin to have tangible effects. By putting politicians, parties and elected governments permanently on their toes, they complicate their lives, question their authority and force them to change their agendas – and sometimes as former West Australian Premier Brian Burke found, can smother them in disgrace.

Whether or not the trend towards this new kind of democracy is a sustainable, historically irreversible development remains to be seen; like its two previous historical antecedents, monitory democracy is not inevitable. It did not have to happen, but it has.

Certainly when judged by its institutional contours and inner dynamics, monitory democracy is the most complex form of democracy yet. Those with a taste for Latin would say that it is the *tertium quid*, the not fully formed successor of the earlier historical experiments with assembly-based and representative forms of democracy. One symptom of its novelty is the altered language through which millions of people now describe democracy. In the name of 'people', 'the public', 'public accountability', 'the people' or 'citizens' – the terms are normally used interchangeably in the age of monitory democracy – power-scrutinising institutions spring up all over the place. Elections, political parties and legislatures neither disappear, nor necessarily decline in importance, but they most definitely lose their pivotal position in politics.

Democracy is no longer simply a way of handling the power of elected governments by electoral and parliamentary and constitutional means, and no longer a matter confined to territorial states. Gone are the days when democracy could be described – and in the next breath attacked – as 'government by the unrestricted will of the majority' as Friedrich von Hayek once wrote. Whether in the field of local, national or supranational government, or in the power-ridden world of non-governmental organisations and networks, some of them stretching down into the roots of everyday life and outwards towards the four corners of the earth, people and organisations that exercise power are now routinely subject to public monitoring and public contestation by an assortment of extra-parliamentary bodies.

In the age of monitory democracy, the rules of representation, democratic accountability and public participation are applied to a much wider range of settings than ever before. Here is one striking clue for understanding why this is happening: the age of monitory democracy that began around 1945 has witnessed the birth of nearly a hundred new types of power-scrutinising institutions unknown to previous democrats.

Defenders of these inventions often speak of their importance in solving a basic problem facing contemporary democracies: how to promote the unfinished business of finding new ways of democratic living for little people in big and complex societies, in which substantial numbers of citizens believe that politicians are not easily trusted, and in which governments are often accused of abusing their power or being out of touch with citizens, or simply unwilling to deal with their concerns and problems.

By addressing such concerns, the new power-scrutinising inventions break the grip of the majority rule principle – the worship of numbers – associated with representative democracy. Freed as well from the measured caution and double speak of political parties, some inventions give a voice to the strongly felt concerns of minorities that feel left out of official politics. Some monitors, electoral commissions and consumer protection agencies for instance, use their claimed 'neutrality' to protect the rules of the democratic game from predators and enemies. Other monitors publicise long-term issues that are neglected, or dealt with badly, by the short-term mentality encouraged by election cycles. Still other monitory groups are remarkable for their evanescence; in a fast-changing world, they come on the scene, stir the pot, then move on like nomads, or dissolve into thin air.

By making room for opinions and ways of life that people feel strongly about, despite their neglect or suppression by parties, parliaments and governments, these inventions have the combined effect of raising the level and quality of public monitoring of power, often for the first time in many areas of life, including power relationships 'beneath' and 'beyond' the institutions of territorial states.

It is little wonder that the new power-monitoring inventions have changed the language of contemporary politics. They prompt much talk of 'empowerment', 'high energy democracy', 'stakeholders', 'participatory governance', 'communicative democracy' and 'deliberative democracy'; and they help spread, often for the first time, a culture of voting into many walks of life. Monitory democracy is the age of surveys, focus groups, deliberative polling, online petitions and audience and customer voting. Whether intended or not, the spreading culture of voting, backed by the new mechanisms for monitoring power, has the effect of interrupting and often silencing the soliloquies of parties, politicians and parliaments.

The new power-scrutinising innovations tend to enfranchise many more citizens' voices, sometimes by means of unelected representatives skilled at using what Americans sometimes call 'bully pulpits'. The number and range of monitory institutions have so greatly increased that they point to a world where the old rule of 'one person, one vote, one representative' – the central demand in the struggle for representative democracy – is replaced with the new principle of monitory democracy: 'one person, many interests, many voices, multiple votes, and multiple representatives'.

Caution must be exercised when trying to understand these new methods of restraining power; they are not cut from the same cloth and therefore need careful examination. The new monitory inventions are not exclusively 'American' or 'European' or 'Australian' or 'Western' products. Among their more remarkable features is the way that they have rapidly diffused around the globe. They mushroom in a wide variety of different settings – participatory budgeting is a Brazilian invention; truth and reconciliation commissions hail from Central America, while integrity commissions first sprang up with force in Australia – and there are even signs, for the first time in the history of democracy, of mounting awareness of the added value of the art of invention – as if the democratic ability to invent is itself a most valuable invention.

Monitory mechanisms are not just information-providing mechanisms. They operate in different ways, on different fronts. Some scrutinise power primarily at the level of citizen input to government or civil society bodies; other monitory mechanisms are preoccupied with monitoring and contesting what are called policy throughputs; still others concentrate on scrutinising policy outputs produced by governmental or non-governmental organisations. Quite a few of the inventions concentrate simultaneously on all three dimensions. Monitory mechanisms also come in different sizes and operate on various spatial scales, ranging from 'just round the corner' bodies with merely local footprints to global networks aimed at keeping tabs on those who exercise power over great distances.

Given such variations, it should not be surprising that a quick short list of the post-1945 inventions resembles – at first sight, to the untrained eye – a magpie's nest of randomly collected items. The list includes: citizen juries, bioregional assemblies, participatory budgeting, advisory boards, focus groups and 'talkaoke' (local/global talk shows broadcast live on the internet). There are think tanks, consensus conferences, teach-ins, public memorials, local community consultation schemes and open houses that offer information and advisory and advocacy services, archive and research facilities and opportunities for professional networking. Citizens' assemblies, democratic audits, brainstorming conferences, conflict of interest boards, public meeting trigger clauses, global associations of parliamentarians against corruption and constitutional safaris (famously used by the drafters of the new South African constitution to examine best practice elsewhere) are on the list. So too are the inventions of India's banyan democracy: railway courts, *Lok Adalats*, public interest litigation and *satyagraha* methods of civil resistance. Included as well are consumer testing agencies and consumer councils, online petitions and chat rooms, democracy clubs and democracy cafés, public vigils, peaceful sieges, protestivals (a South Korean speciality), summits and global watchdog organisations set up to bring greater public accountability to business and other civil society bodies.

The list of innovations extends to deliberative polls, boards of accountancy, independent religious courts, experts' councils (such as the 'Five Wise Men' of the Council of Economic Advisers in Germany), public 'scorecards' – yellow cards and white lists – public planning exercises, public consultations, social forums, weblogs, electronic civil disobedience and websites dedicated to monitoring the abuse of power (such as Bully OnLine, a British initiative that aims to tackle workplace bullying and related issues). And the list of new inventions includes self-selected opinion polls and unofficial ballots (text-messaged straw polls, for instance), international criminal courts, global social forums and the tendency of increasing numbers of non-governmental organisations to adopt written constitutions, with an elected component.

Let us pause, for evidently the list of inventions is disjointed, and potentially confusing. Clear-headed thinking is needed to spot the qualities that these inventions share in common. Monitory institutions play various roles. They are committed to providing publics with extra viewpoints and better information about the operations and performance of various governmental and non-governmental bodies. Because they appeal to publics, monitory institutions are not to be confused with top-down surveillance mechanisms that operate in secret, for the private purposes of organisations of government or civil society. Monitory mechanisms are geared as well to the definition, scrutiny and enforcement of public standards and ethical rules for preventing corruption, or the improper behaviour of those responsible for making decisions, not only in the field of elected government, but in a wide variety of settings. The new institutions of monitory democracy are further defined by their overall commitment to strengthening the diversity and influence of citizens' voices and choices in decisions that affect their lives – regardless of the outcome of elections.

What is distinctive about this new historical type of democracy is the way all fields of social and political life come to be scrutinised, not just by the standard machinery of representative democracy, but by a whole host of non-party, extra-parliamentary and often unelected bodies operating within and underneath and beyond the boundaries of territorial states. In the era of monitory democracy, it is as if the principles of representative democracy – public openness, citizens' equality, selecting representatives – are superimposed on representative democracy itself. This has many practical consequences, but one especially striking effect is to alter the patterns of interaction – political geography – of democratic institutions.

Once upon a time, in the brief heyday of representative democracy, the thing called democracy had a rather simple political geography. Within the confines of any given state, democracy meant (from the point of view of citizens) following an election campaign and on the great day of reckoning turning out to vote for a party or independent candidate. He – it was almost always a man – was someone local, a figure known to the community, a local shopkeeper or professional or someone in business or a trade unionist, for instance.

Then came democracy's great ceremonial, the pause of deliberation, the calm of momentary reflection, the catharsis of ticking and crossing, before the storm of result. 'Universal peace is declared', was the sarcastic way the nineteenth-century English woman novelist George Eliot (1819–80) put it, 'and the foxes have a sincere interest in prolonging the lives of the poultry.' Her American contemporary, Walt Whitman (1819–92), spoke more positively of the pivotal function of polling day as the great 'choosing day', the 'powerfulest scene', a 'swordless conflict' mightier than Niagara Falls or the Mississippi River or the geysers of Yosemite, a 'still small voice vibrating', a time for 'the peaceful choice of all', a passing moment of suspended animation when 'the heart pants, life glows'.

If blessed with enough votes, the local representative joined a privileged small circle of legislators, whose job was to stay in line with party policy, support or oppose a government that used its majority in the legislature, to pass laws and to monitor their implementation and administration, hopefully with results that pleased as many of the represented as possible. At the end of a limited stint as legislator, buck passing stopped. Foxes and poultry fell quiet. It was again time for the swordless conflict of the great choosing day. The representative either stepped down into retirement or faced the music of re-election.

This is obviously a simplified sketch of the role of elections, but it serves to highlight the different, more complex political geography of monitory democracy. Just as representative democracies preserved the spirit and form of ancient assemblies, so monitory democracies preserves legislatures, political parties and elections, which (to the contrary) are often bitterly fought and closely contested and sometimes (as the recent American presidential and senate election shows) exciting affairs. But such is the growing variety of interlaced, power-monitoring mechanisms that democrats from earlier times, if catapulted into the new world of monitory democracy, would find it hard to understand what is happening.

The new democracy demands a headshift, a break with conventional thinking in order to understand its political geography. For this purpose, let us imagine for a moment, as if from an aerial satellite, the contours of monitory democracy. We would spot that its power-scrutinising institutions are less centred on elections, parties and legislatures; no longer confined to the territorial state; and spatially arranged in ways much messier than textbooks on democracy typically suppose. The vertical 'depth' and horizontal 'reach' of monitory institutions is striking. If the number of levels within any hierarchy of institutions is a measure of its 'depth', and if the number of units located within each of these levels is called its 'span' or 'width', then monitory democracy is the deepest and widest system of democracy ever known. The political geography of mechanisms like audit commissions, citizens' assemblies, web-based think tanks, local assemblies, regional parliaments, summits and global watchdog organisations defies simple-minded descriptions. So too does the political geography of the wider constellation of power-checking and power-disputing mechanisms in which they are embedded – bodies like citizen assemblies and juries, audit and integrity commissions and many other watchdog organisations set up to bring greater public accountability to business and other civil society bodies.

Both the novelty and complexity of monitory democracy make it vulnerable to a handful of misconceptions, beginning with the claim that the struggle to bring greater public accountability to government and non-government organisations that wield power over others is in effect a struggle for 'grassroots democracy' or 'participatory democracy' or 'popular empowerment'.

Such metaphors rest on a misunderstanding of the trends. The age of monitory democracy is not heading backwards; it is not motivated by efforts to recapture the (imagined) spirit of assembly-based democracy – 'power to the people', as some supporters of groups like Students for a Democratic Society liked to say during the rebellions of the 1960s. Many contemporary champions of 'deep' or 'direct' democracy still speak as if they were Greeks, as if what really counts in matters of democracy is as Archon Fung and Erik Olin Wright put it, 'the commitment and capacities of ordinary people to make sensible decisions through reasoned deliberation and empowered because they attempt to tie action to discussion'.

The reality of monitory democracy is otherwise, in that all of the new power-scrutinising experiments in the name of 'the people' or citizens' empowerment rely inevitably on representation. These experiments often draw their ultimate legitimacy from 'the people', but they are not understandable as efforts to abolish the gap between representatives and the represented, as if citizens could live without others acting on their behalf, find their true selves and express themselves as equals within a unified political community no longer burdened by miscommunication, or by misgovernment.

Monitory democracy thrives on representation. Take the much-discussed example of the Citizens' Assembly on Electoral Reform in the Canadian province of British Columbia. Backed by the local legislature, the Citizens' Assembly worked for the best part of a year as an independent, non-partisan assembly of representatives charged with the task of casting a critical eye over the province's electoral system. The Assembly had 161 members; it included one woman and one man drawn randomly from each of the province's seventy-nine electoral districts, plus two indigenous citizen representatives, as well as one representative from the province's Legislative Assembly. The member representatives of the Citizens' Assembly were not elected, but drawn by lot. In contrast to the Greek trust in the deities as underwriters of decisions determined by lot, the Assembly members were chosen at random by a computer, from a pool that was supposed to reflect the age, gender and geographical make-up of British Columbian citizens. Granted its own budget, the Citizens' Assembly was designed to operate outside the system of political parties, and to keep its distance from the legislature, organised lobby groups and journalists. Its duty was to act as an unelected body of temporary representatives of all British Columbians.

Another misconception, to do with the changing status of elections, prevents many people from spotting the novelty of monitory democracy. It is vital to grasp that this new type of democracy does not dispense with questions of suffrage, or voting in national or local elections. It is not an age that has settled once and for all the issue of who is entitled to vote, and under which conditions (think of the emerging legal and political controversies about who owns the software of unreliable electronic voting machines). In fact, some people – for instance, felons – have their votes withdrawn; others, including diasporas, minority language speakers, the disabled and people with low literacy and number skills, are disadvantaged by secret ballot elections; still other constituencies, such as women, young people and the biosphere, are either poorly represented, or they are not represented at all.

Struggles to open up and improve the quality of electoral representation are by no means finished. And yet in the era of monitory democracy the franchise struggles that once tugged and tore whole societies apart have lost their centrality. As the culture of voting spreads, and as unelected representatives multiply in many different contexts, a brand new issue begins to surface. The old question that racked the age of representative democracy – who is entitled to vote and when – is compounded and complicated by a question for which there are still no easy answers: are people entitled to representation between and outside elections and, if so, through which representatives?

A symptom of the changing definition of democracy is the advent of election monitoring. During the 1980s, for the first time in the history of democracy, founding elections in new or strife-torn polities began to be monitored systematically by outside teams of observers. The practice was admittedly an older invention, first used in 1857 when Prussian, French, British, Russian, Turkish and Austrian representatives jointly supervised a plebiscite in Moldavia and Wallachia; but in the new circumstances, the methods of election monitoring assumed a much more powerful and publicly visible role, this time on a global scale.

The net effect of election monitoring is to heighten globally the sense that elections matter; that efforts should be redoubled to find and apply contextually sensitive quality standards; that election observers themselves need watching; and that 'fair and open' methods – the elimination of violence, intimidation, ballot-rigging and other forms of political tomfoolery – are expected of all countries, including the most powerful democracy, the United States, where observers from the Organisation for Security and Co-Operation in Europe played a role for the first time in the presidential elections of November 2004 and where, in the 2008 elections, the competing sides proved that the legal monitoring of elections is becoming as common a campaign tool as fundraising and advertising by assembling literally thousands of lawyers at state level to protect their supporters at the polls, help untangle ballot problems and run to court should litigation be necessary – Senator Barack Obama's campaign for instance sent five thousand lawyers to Florida alone.

Among the remarkable features of monitory democracy is the way power-scrutinising mechanisms gradually spread into areas of social life that previously were untouched by democratic hands. The extension of democracy downwards, into realms of power beneath and cutting across the institutions of territorial states, has the effect of arousing great interest in the old eighteenth-century European term 'civil society'; for the first time in the history of democracy, these two words are now routinely used by democrats in all four corners of the earth.

The intense public concern with civil society and with publicly scrutinising matters once thought to be non-political is unique to the age of monitory democracy. The era of representative democracy, as Alexis de Tocqueville spotted, certainly saw the rise of self-organised pressure groups and schemes for 'socialising' the power of government, for instance through workers' control of industry. Few of these schemes survived the upheavals of the first half of the twentieth century, which makes the contrast with monitory democracy all the more striking.

The trend towards public scrutiny is strongly evident in all kinds of policy areas, ranging from public concern about the maltreatment and legal rights of children and bodily habits related to exercise and diet, through to the development of habitat protection plans and non-carbon and non-nuclear sources of energy. Initiatives to guarantee that the future development of nanotechnology and genetically modified crops is governed publicly in the interests of the many, not the few – efforts to take democracy 'upstream' into the tributaries of scientific research and technical development are a further example of the same trend.

Experiments with fostering new forms of citizens' participation and elected representation have even penetrated markets, to lay hands on the sacred cow of private property. A notable example is the German system of codetermination known as *Mitbestimmung*; following the near-collapse of banking systems during 2007–08, many new proposals are now on the political table to extend monitoring mechanisms into the banking and investment sectors of global markets that previously operated with little or no regulatory restraint.

There is rising awareness as well of the possibility and desirability of exercising rights of criticism and casting a vote in large-scale global organisations. An example is the International Olympic Committee: once an exclusive private gentlemen's club, it became during the 1980s the focus of muckraking journalism. Scandals ensued. Public outcries followed. Under pressure, against considerable odds, the IOC began to apply monitory mechanisms to its own corrupted structures. Some things didn't change. By 2002, the IOC body of 115 co-opted members included only twelve women; in that year, not one woman was among the sixty-six new member nominations.

But some things did change. Visits by IOC members to candidate cities were banned. An IOC Ethics Commission and a World Anti-Doping Agency were formed. Reports of income and expenditure were published, for the first time. IOC meetings were thrown open to the media. A so-called Nominations Committee was set up for the purpose of more fairly deciding IOC membership, which was restricted to an eight-year term, renewable through election. Olympic athletes were granted the right to elect their own representatives directly to the IOC. The upper age limit of IOC members was reduced from eighty to seventy.

The rules of representative government were for the first time applied to its inner workings, at least on paper.

The vital role played by civil societies in the invention of power-monitoring mechanisms seems to confirm what might be called James Madison's 'Law of Free Government': no government can be considered free unless it is capable of governing a society that is itself capable of controlling the government. Madison's sketch of The Law in *The Federalist Papers,* number 51, has tempted some people to mistakenly conclude that governments are incapable of scrutinising their own power. The truth is otherwise. In the era of monitory democracy, experience shows that governments, unlike ducks and turkeys, sometimes vote to sacrifice themselves for the good of citizen guests at the dinner table.

Government 'watchdog' institutions are a case in point. Their stated purpose is public scrutiny of government by semi-independent government agencies. Scrutiny mechanisms supplement the power-monitoring role of elected government representatives and judges, even though this is not always their stated aim; very often they are introduced under the general authority of elected governments – for instance, through ministerial responsibility.

In practice, things often turn out differently. Especially when protected by legislation, well resourced and well managed, government scrutiny bodies tend to take on a life of their own. Building on the much older precedents of royal commissions, public inquiries and independent auditors checking the financial probity of government agencies – inventions that had their roots in the age of representative democracy – the new scrutiny mechanisms add checks and balances to the possible abuse of power by elected representatives. Often they are justified in terms of improving the efficiency and effectiveness of government, for instance through 'better informed' decision-making that has the added advantage of raising the level of public trust in political institutions among citizens considered 'stakeholders'.

The process contains a double paradox. Not only are government scrutiny mechanisms often established by governments who subsequently fail to control their workings – for instance, in cases of corruption and the enforcement of legal standards; the new mechanisms also have democratic, power-checking effects, even though they are normally staffed by un-elected officials who operate at several arms' length from the rhythm of periodic elections.

The independent 'integrity systems' that came to enjoy an important public profile in various states in Australia from the 1980s are good examples. Following repeated media exposure of fraud and corruption among politicians and police, in some cases with links to business and organised crime, monitory agencies were established to bring new eyes, ears and teeth to the public sector. The aim was to crack down on intentional wrongdoing or misconduct by elected representatives and appointed officials; fingers were pointed as well at the lax and self-serving complaints systems operated by the police, who are to democratic governments as sharp edges are to knives. Misgivings were also expressed about the reluctance of elected ministers to oversee publicly sensitive police operational matters. Two royal commissions in the state of South Australia during the 1970s led to the establishment in 1985 of the first Police Complaints Authority. Other states followed suit, culminating in Queensland's Criminal Justice Commission (later the Crime and Misconduct Commission). Established in 1990 as a combined anti-corruption and criminal detection body, it was charged with the job of exposing corruption within the public sector, undertaking crime research, gathering evidence of organised crime, and tracking and recovering criminal proceeds.

In the age of monitory democracy, a great wall of prejudice still surrounds the whole idea of 'cross-border' or 'international' democracy. The prejudice dates from the era of territorially bound representative democracy, and almost all leading scholars of democracy today defend its supposed truth. One interesting thing about monitory democracy is that it begins to confront that wall with a hammer. Its latticed patterns of power monitoring effectively fudge the distinction between 'domestic' and 'foreign', the 'local' and the 'global'. Like other types of institutions, including business and universities, democracy too is caught up in a process of 'glocalisation'.

Monitory mechanisms are dynamically interrelated, to the point where each functions simultaneously as both part and whole of the overall system. In the system of monitory democracy, to put things a bit abstractly, parts and wholes in an absolute sense do not exist. Its units are better described as sub-wholes – 'holons' is the term famously coined by the Hungarian polymath Arthur Koestler – that function simultaneously as self-regarding and self-asserting entities that push and pull each other in a multi-lateral system in which all entities play a part.

The example of summits, a remarkable invention of the second half of the twentieth century, helps bring this language down to earth. A strange fact is that summits began as exercises in big power politics, as informal ad hoc meetings of heads of state or leaders of government, or foreign ministers – the kind of meetings that first took place during the fragile Soviet/American/British alliance against Hitler. Some people have said that the word 'summit' was first used to describe the so-called 'percentages agreement' at the October 1944 meeting in Moscow, when Churchill and Stalin speculated about their ratios of influence in the post war world. The strange mathematical origin of the word (a corruption, perhaps in Stalin's virtually non-existent English, of 'sum it') was a one-off. It soon morphed into a mountaineers' term. Churchill himself long continued to advocate the tactic of high-level informal meetings in international relations. He spoke of 'summit diplomacy' and the benefits of a 'parley at the summit', which is the sense that prevailed in Geneva in 1955, when the climbing word 'summit' was used for the first time to describe a Cold War meeting of the political leaders of the United States, the Soviet Union, France and Britain.

From the end of World War II until the time of the famous Vienna Summit meeting between Kennedy and Khruschev in June 1961, there were well over a hundred such summits, each using broadly similar methods. The meetings were preoccupied with the dynamics of the Cold War, and so had both a global reach and a strong bipolarity about them. Whether used as tools of amity or enmity, these early summits were also marked by a strong measure of predictability. The rule was that no statesman was willing to risk the certainty of humiliation. Hence the great attention paid to dramaturgy. 'It ended, as it began, with two firm hands firmly clasped,' began the rather ritualised

Newsweek report of the Kennedy–Khruschev summit. Such media coverage usually put ceremonial trivia on a pedestal; at one point, during the summit preparations, the question of whether Jackie Kennedy should be given a silver tea service was reportedly decided by Khruschev with the blustering judgement that 'presents can be given even before a war'. The effect – like the old rituals of European monarchy – was to reinforce the sense among audiences that these were top-down affairs, instances of how the world was run by just a handful of men.

During the last decades of the twentieth century, the wholly surprising thing about summits was their dramatic transformation into sites where the power of elected representatives was publicly contested. Summits morphed into monitory mechanisms. The altered meaning and function of summits was evident at the series of high-level meetings between Reagan and Gorbachev, including the 1986 Reykjavik gathering, where without prior consultation with NATO and other bodies the abolition of ballistic missiles and strategic nuclear weapons – including all nuclear weapons – was proposed. From there on, summits began to be used by leaders to 'bounce' their bureaucracies into policy shifts. That had the knock-on effect of politicising government, making it clear to wider audiences, both inside and outside government, that different political options existed.

The growth of summitry cloaked in secrecy and pageantry backfired. Summits began to attract the attention of thousands of journalists eager to report stories and images of this exclusive and powerful club. Beginning with the Bonn G7 Summit in May 1985, which attracted thirty thousand demonstrators demanding greater global justice, its annual meetings provided an opportunity for civil society organisations and protesters to press their concerns related to matters ranging from international trade and terrorism to energy development and cross-border crime – in effect, by turning rulers into culpable representatives. Attempts to transform top-down governmental summits into new channels of bottom-up representation of the interests of civil society were not confined to the G7 and G8, though they have attracted some of the most spectacular attention – for instance, in July 2005 at the Live 8 'global awareness' concerts to encourage political leaders to 'Make Poverty History'.

It is sometimes said that the business of power scrutiny changes very little, that states and corporations are still the 'real' centres of power in deciding who gets what, when and how in this world. Evidence that this is not necessarily so is suggested by the fact that all of the big public issues that have erupted around the world since 1945, including civil rights for women and minorities, American military intervention in Vietnam and Iraq, nuclear weapons, poverty reduction and global warming, have been generated not by political parties, elections, legislatures and governments, but principally by power-monitoring networks that run 'parallel' to – and are often positioned against – the orthodox mechanisms of party-based representation.

The powerful civil rights movement that sprang up during the 1950s in the United States was among the pacesetters. Its inventive tactics – bus boycotts, improvement associations, co-ordinating committees, sit-ins, kneel-ins, 'jail-no-bail' pledges, freedom rides, citizenship schools, freedom singing, voter registration drives, mock elections – were proof positive that monitory bodies could have effects upon existing power relations by forcing many people to sense their contingency, often through bitter battles, sometimes resulting in surprising victories for those bent on humbling the powerful. The tactics produced two historic pieces of legislation. The Civil Rights Act, signed by President Lyndon Johnson on July 2, 1964, barred racial discrimination in public accommodations, education and employment. The Voting Rights Act he signed a year later on August 6, 1965, abolished literacy tests, poll taxes and other restrictions on voting, as well as authorised federal government intervention in states and individual voting districts that continued to use such tests to discriminate against African Americans.

The enactment of the double-barrelled legislation was monitory democracy in action. It proved that the powerless had the power to change things, and that change had to begin in the home, the workplace and in other public fields of everyday life, before spreading across the whole of the political and social landscape of the American democracy – eventually resulting in the election of the first black president of the United States.

Now that we have tackled some misconceptions about the contours and main dynamics of monitory democracy, let me pause finally to ask one short question: how can its unplanned birth be explained?

This is not an easy question to answer. The motives behind the hundred or so inventions described above are complicated; as in earlier phases of the history of democracy, generalisations are as difficult as they are perilous. But one thing is certain: the new type of democracy has had both its causes and causers. Monitory democracy is not a monogenic matter – a living thing hatched from a single cell. It is rather the result of many forces. As in the two earlier phases of democracy, changes usually happened only when cracks developed within ruling circles, so allowing the courage of citizens and the resolve of public-spirited leaders to do the rest.

A half-century of total war, dictatorship and totalitarianism that very nearly finished off democracy – in 1941 there were only eleven democracies left on the face of the earth – proved to be the initial catalyst. The widespread despair and troubled thinking about political evil triggered by the disaster undoubtedly helped inspire one of the most remarkable features of monitory democracy: the marriage of democracy and human rights, and the subsequent worldwide growth of organisations, networks and campaigns committed to the defence of human rights.

Personal ambition, monkey business, power games and the quest for more effective or cheaper government – and government eager to offload blame on to others for policy disappointments and failures – have all also played their part. So too have conservative instincts, radical demands, geopolitical considerations and market pressures. Opportunities for building 'social capital' – cultivating the connections and skills among people at the local and regional levels – and the lure of winning power or revenue growth from the provision of outsourced government services has strongly motivated some organisations, especially non-government organisations, to push for stronger monitory institutions.

Unintended consequences and plain good luck have also played their part in the early history of monitory democracy. Not unimportant as well has been a factor famously outlined by de Tocqueville: the contagious force of the belief among citizens and their representatives that the removal of particular grievances enables other grievances to be addressed, and resolved.

All these pressures have conspired to push actually existing democracies in the direction of monitory democracy. But one force is turning out to be the principal driver: the emergence of a new galaxy of communication media.

No account of monitory democracy would be credible without taking into account the way that power and conflict are shaped by new media institutions. Think of it like this: assembly-based democracy in ancient Greek times belonged to an era dominated by the spoken word, backed up by laws written on papyrus and stone, and by messages dispatched by foot, or by donkey and horse. Representative democracy sprang up in the era of print culture – the book, pamphlet and newspaper, and telegraphed and mailed messages – and fell into crisis during the advent of early mass communication media, especially radio and cinema and television in its infancy.

By contrast, monitory democracy is tied closely to the growth of multimedia-saturated societies – societies whose structures of power are continuously 'bitten' by monitory institutions operating within a new galaxy of media defined by the ethos of communicative abundance.

Compared with the era of representative democracy, when print culture and limited spectrum audio-visual media (including public service broadcasting) were much more closely aligned with political parties and governments, the age of monitory democracy witnesses constant public scrutiny and spats about power, to the point where it seems as if no organisation or leader within the fields of government or social life is immune from political trouble.

The change has been shaped by a variety of forces, including the decline of journalism proud of its commitment to fact-based 'objectivity' which was an ideal born of the age of representative democracy, and the rise of adversarial and 'gotcha' styles of commercial journalism driven by ratings, sales and hits. Technical factors, such as electronic memory, tighter channel spacing, new frequency allocation, direct satellite broadcasting, digital tuning and advanced compression techniques, have also been important. Chief among these technical factors is the advent of cable- and satellite-linked computerised communications, which from the end of the 1960s triggered both product and process innovations in virtually every field of an increasingly commercialised media.

This new galaxy of media has no historical precedent. Symbolised by one of its core components, the internet, it is a whole new world system of overlapping and interlinked media devices that, for the first time in human history, integrate texts, sounds and images and enable communication to take place through multiple user points, in chosen time, either real or delayed, within modularised and ultimately global networks that are affordable and accessible to many hundreds of millions of people scattered across the globe.

All institutions in the business of scrutinising power rely heavily on these media innovations; if the new galaxy of communicative abundance suddenly imploded, monitory democracy would not last long. Monitory democracy and computerised media networks behave as if they are conjoined twins. To say this is not to fall into the trap of supposing that computer-linked communications networks prefigure a brand new utopian world, a carnival of 'virtual communities' homesteading on the electronic frontier, a 'cyber-revolution' that yields equal access of all citizens to all media, anywhere and at any time.

Hype of this kind was strongly evident in the *Declaration of the Independence of Cyberspace* (1996), a document drawn up by the self-styled cyber-revolutionary John Perry Barlow, the former lyricist of famous rock band the Grateful Dead and subsequent campaign manager for infamous American vice-president, Dick Cheney. *The Declaration* proclaimed the end of the old world of representation within territorial states.

Making hype seem profound, it claimed that computer-linked networks were 'creating a world that all may enter without privilege or prejudice accorded by race, economic power, military force, or station of birth'. Barlow said that communicative abundance heralded nothing short of 'a new social space, global and anti-sovereign, within which anybody, anywhere can express to the rest of humanity whatever he or she believes without fear'. 'There is in these new media,' he concluded, 'a foreshadowing of the intellectual and economic liberty that might undo all the authoritarian powers on earth.'

Such utopian extravagance prompts a political health warning, not least because the new age of communicative abundance produces disappointment, instability and self-contradictions – for instance, in worrying patterns of closure or 'privatisation' of digital networks and in the widening power gaps between communication rich and poor,

A majority of the world's people are too poor to make a telephone call; only a tiny minority have access to the internet; thus they seem almost unneeded as communicators, or as consumers of media products. The divide between media rich and media poor citizens blights all monitory democracies; it contradicts their basic principle that all citizens are entitled equally to communicate their opinions, and periodically to give elected and unelected representatives a rough ride.

Yet, despite such contradictions and disappointments, there are new and important things happening inside the swirling galaxy of communicative abundance. Especially striking is the way the realms of 'private life' and 'privacy' and wheeling and dealing of power 'in private' have been put on the defensive. From the point of view of monitory democracy, that is no bad thing. Every nook and cranny of power – the quiet discriminations and injustices that happen behind closed doors and in the world of everyday life – become the potential target of 'publicity' and 'public exposure'. Routine matters such as birth and death, diet and sex, religious and ethnic customs are less and less based on unthinking habit, on unquestioned, taken-for-granted certainties about 'normal' ways of doing things. In the era of communicative abundance, no hidden topic is protected unconditionally from media coverage, and from possible politicisation; the more 'private' it is, the more 'publicity' it seems to get.

Nothing is sacrosanct – not even the efforts of those who try to protect or rebuild what they claim to be sacrosanct. Past generations would find the whole process astonishing in its global scale and democratic intensity. With the click of a camera, or the flick of a switch and the tap of a keyboard, the world of the private can suddenly be made public. Everything from the bedroom to the boardroom, the bureaucracy and the battlefield, seems to be up for media grabs. Thanks to stories told by journalists, themselves unelected representatives of publics, this is an age in which private text messages rebound publicly, to reveal marital unfaithfulness and force the resignation of a government minister as happened in Finland in 2008.

It is an era in which so-called reality TV can cut from an afternoon children's program to a man on a freeway setting his truck ablaze before turning his shotgun on the police, and then himself, live, courtesy of a news helicopter and a satellite uplink. These are times in which Sony hand-held cameras are used by off-air reporters, known as 'embeds', to file ongoing videos and blogs featuring election candidates live, unplugged and unscripted; and this is the age in which video footage proves that soldiers in war zones raped women, terrorised children and tortured innocent civilians.

In the age of communicative abundance, the private lives of politicians, unelected representatives and celebrities, their romances, parties, health, drug habits, quarrels and divorces, are the interest and fantasy objects of millions of people. And thanks to talk shows, blogs, user-generated social networking sites, wiki platforms, YouTube video exchanges and other media acts, there is an endless procession of 'ordinary people' talking publicly about their private fears, fantasies, hopes and expectations. Some of them are sometimes lucky enough to morph into media stars, thanks to simulated elections, in which audiences granted a 'vote' by media companies are urged to lodge their preference for the star of their choice, by acclamation, cell phone or the internet.

Helped along by red-blooded journalism that relies on styles of reporting concerned less with veracity than with 'breaking news' and blockbusting scoops, communicative abundance cuts like a knife into the power relations of government and civil society. It is easy (as many do) to complain about the methods of the new journalism. It hunts in packs, its eyes on bad news, egged on by the newsroom and bloggers saying that facts must never be allowed to get in the way of stories.

Professional and citizens' journalism loves titillation, draws upon unattributed sources, fills news holes – in the era of monitory democracy news never sleeps – spins sensations, and concentrates too much on personalities, rather than time-bound contexts. The new journalism is formulaic and gets bored too quickly; and it likes to bow down to corporate power and government press briefings, which helps explain why disinformation (about such matters as weapons of mass destruction and excessive leveraging of risks within financial markets) still whizzes around the world with frightening speed and power.

But these trends are only half the story. For in spite of all the accusations made against it, red-blooded journalism helps keep alive the old utopias of shedding light on power, of 'freedom of information', 'government in the sunshine' and greater 'transparency' in the making of decisions.

Given that unchecked power still weighs down hard on the heads of citizens, it is not surprising, thanks to the new journalism and the new monitory inventions, that public objections to wrongdoing and corruption are commonplace in the era of monitory democracy. Thanks to journalism and the new media of communicative abundance stuff happens. Shit happens. There seems to be no end of scandals, and there are even times when '-gate' scandals, like earthquakes, rumble beneath the feet of whole governments.

The profusion of '-gate' scandals reminds us of a perennial problem facing monitory democracy: there is no shortage of organised efforts by the powerful to manipulate people beneath them; and hence the political dirty business of dragging power from the shadows and flinging it into the blazing halogen of publicity remains fundamentally important.

Nobody should be kidded into thinking that the world of monitory democracy, with its many power-scrutinising institutions, is a level playing field – a paradise of equality of opportunity among all its citizens and their elected and unelected representatives. We still live in the age of the put-on. The combination of monitory democracy and communicative abundance nevertheless produces permanent flux, an unending restlessness driven by complex combinations of different interacting players and institutions, permanently pushing and pulling, heaving and straining, sometimes working together, at other times in opposition to one another.

Elected and unelected representatives routinely strive to define and to determine who gets what, when and how, but the represented, taking advantage of various power-scrutinising devices, keep tabs on their representatives – sometimes with surprising success. The dynamics of monitory democracy are thus not describable using the simple spatial metaphors inherited from the age of representative democracy. Talk of the 'sovereignty' of parliament, or of 'local' versus 'central' government, or of tussles between 'pressure groups', political parties and governments is just too simple. It is obsolete. In terms of political geometry, the system of monitory democracy is something other and different: a complex web of differently sized and more or less interdependent monitory bodies that have the effect, thanks to communicative abundance, of continuously stirring up questions about who gets what, when and how, as well as holding publicly responsible those who exercise power, wherever they are situated. Monitory democracies are richly conflicted. Politics does not wither away. Everything is never straightforwardly okay.

There is something utterly novel about the whole trend. From its origins in the ancient assemblies of Syria-Mesopotamia, democracy has always cut through habit and prejudice and hierarchies of power. It has stirred up the sense that people can shape and reshape their lives as equals, and not surprisingly it has often brought commotion into the world.

In the era of monitory democracy, the constant public scrutiny of power by hosts of differently sized monitory bodies with footprints large and small makes it the most energetic, most dynamic form of democracy ever. It even contains bodies, including Human Rights Watch, the Democratic Audit network and the Global Accountability Project, that specialise in providing public assessments of the quality of existing power-scrutinising mechanisms and the degree to which they fairly represent citizens' interests. Other bodies specialise in directing questions at governments on a wide range of matters, extending from their human rights records through to their energy production plans and the quality of the drinking water of their cities.

Private companies are grilled about their services and products, their investment plans, how they treat their employees, and the size of their impact upon the biosphere. Questions are raised about which SUVs are most likely to roll over, and which companies retail the worst fast food, and which are the biggest polluters. Various watchdogs and guide dogs and barking dogs are constantly on the job, pressing for greater public accountability of those who exercise power.

The powerful consequently come to feel the constant pinch of the powerless. In the era of monitory democracy, those who make decisions are subject constantly to the ideal of public chastening, tied down by a thousand Lilliputian strings of scrutiny.

When they do their job well, monitory mechanisms have many positive effects, ranging from greater openness and justice within markets and blowing the whistle on foolish government decisions to the general enrichment of public deliberation and the empowerment of citizens and their chosen representatives through meaningful schemes of participation. Power monitoring can be ineffective, or counterproductive, of course. Campaigns misfire or are poorly targeted; power wielders cleverly find loopholes and ways of rebutting or simply ignoring their opponents. And there are times when large numbers of citizens find the monitory strategies of organisations too timid, or confused, or simply irrelevant to their lives as consumers, workers, parents, community residents and young and elderly citizens.

Despite such weaknesses, the political dynamics and overall 'feel' of monitory democracies are very different from the era of representative democracy. Politics in the age of monitory democracy has a definite 'viral' quality about it. The power controversies stirred up by monitory mechanisms follow unexpected paths and reach surprising destinations. Groups using mobile phones, bulletin boards, news groups, wikkies and blogs sometimes manage, against considerable odds, to publicly embarrass politicians, parties and parliaments, or even whole governments.

Power-monitoring bodies like Human Rights Watch or Amnesty International regularly do the same, usually with help from networks of supporters. Think for a moment about any current public controversy that attracts widespread attention: news about its contours and commentaries and disputes about its significance are typically relayed by many power-monitoring organisations, large, medium and small. In the world of monitory democracy, that kind of latticed – viral, networked – pattern is typical, not exceptional. It has profound implications for the state-framed institutions of the old representative democracy, which find themselves more and more enmeshed in 'sticky' webs of power-scrutinising institutions that often hit their target, sometimes from long distances, often by means of boomerang effects.

In the age of monitory democracy, bossy power can no longer hide comfortably behind private masks; power relations everywhere are subjected to organised efforts by some, with the help of media, to tell others – publics of various sizes – about matters that previously had been hidden away, 'in private'. This denaturing of power is usually a messy business, and it often comes wrapped in hype, certainly. But the unmasking of power resonates strongly with the power-scrutinising spirit of monitory democracy.

The whole process is reinforced by the growing availability of cheap tools of communication (multi-purpose mobile phones, digital cameras, video recorders, the internet) to individuals and groups and organisations; and communicative abundance multiplies the genres of programming, information, and storytelling that are available to audiences and publics. News, chat shows, political oratory, bitter legal spats, comedy, infotainment, drama, music, advertising, blogs and much more clamour and jostle for public attention.

Some people complain about effects like 'information overload', but from the point of view of monitory democracy, on balance communicative abundance has positive consequences. In spite of all its hype and spin, the new media galaxy nudges and broadens people's horizons. It tutors their sense of pluralism and prods them into taking greater responsibility for how, when and why they communicate. I recall days from my early years in South Australia when children were compulsorily bathed and scrubbed behind the ears, sat down in their dressing gowns prior to going to bed, and required to listen to radio or television program with their families – those days of representative democracy and party or government-linked broadcasting and mass entertainment are over. So, too, are the days when millions of people, huddled together as masses in the shadows of totalitarian power, found the skilfully orchestrated radio and film performances of demagogues fascinating, and reassuring.

Message-saturated democracies encourage people's suspicions of unaccountable power. All the king's horses and all the king's men are unlikely to reverse the trend. Within the world of monitory democracies, people are coming to learn that they must keep an eye on power and its representatives, that they must make judgements and choose their own courses of action. Citizens are tempted to think for themselves; to see the same world in different ways, from different angles; and to sharpen their overall sense that prevailing power relationships are not 'natural', but contingent.

Communicative abundance and monitory institutions combine to promote something of a 'Gestalt switch' in the popular perception of power. The metaphysical idea of an objective, out-there-at-a-distance 'reality' is weakened; so too is the presumption that stubborn 'factual truth' is superior to power. The fabled distinction between what people can see with their eyes and what they are told about the emperor's new clothes breaks down. 'Reality', including the 'reality' of the powerful, comes to be understood as always 'produced reality', a matter of interpretation – and the power to force particular interpretations of the world down others' throats.

There is admittedly nothing automatic or magical about any of this. In the era of monitory democracy, communication is constantly the subject of dissembling, negotiation, compromise and power conflicts – in a phrase,, a matter of politics. Communicative abundance for that reason does not somehow automatically ensure the triumph of either the spirit or institutions of monitory democracy. Message-saturated societies can and do have effects that are harmful for democracy. In some quarters, for instance, media saturation triggers citizens' inattention to events. While they are expected as good citizens to keep their eyes on public affairs, to take an interest in the world beyond their immediate household and neighbourhood, more than a few find it ever harder to pay attention to the media's vast outpourings.

Profusion breeds confusion. There are times, for instance when voters are so pelted with a hail of election advertisements on prime-time television that they react frostily. Disaffected, they get up from their sofas, leave their living rooms, change channels, or mute, concluding with a heavy sigh that the less you know the better off you are. The coming age of internet protocol television is likely to deepen such disaffection and if that happens then something more worrying could happen: the spread of a culture of unthinking indifference.

Monitory democracy certainly feeds upon communicative abundance, but one of its more perverse effects is to encourage individuals to escape the great complexity of the world by sticking their heads, like ostriches, into the sands of wilful ignorance, or to float cynically upon the swirling tides and waves and eddies of fashion – to change their minds, to speak and act flippantly, to embrace or even celebrate opposites, to bid farewell to veracity, to slip into the arms of what some carefully call 'bullshit'.

Foolish illusions, cynicism and disaffection are among the biggest temptations facing citizens and their elected and unelected representatives in existing democracies. Whether or not the new forms of monitory democracy will survive their deadly effects is for the future to tell us. ■

References available at www.griffithreview.com

John Keane is Professor of Media and Politics at the University of Westminster, London. His new book, *The Life and Death of Democracy* will be published by Simon and Schuster this year. It expands this analysis and also considers the counter-trends and dysfunctions of monitory democracy. This essay is based on a contribution to the workshop 'Media, Power and Democracy – Old Dilemmas, New Issues', held at the University of Sydney, November 2008.

Reportage:

How cyber-activism changed the world

Reporter:

Anne Coombs

Image: GetUp! billboard cycled around Parliament House, Canberra in April 2008 to pressure for strong action on Climate Change / Courtesy of GetUp! / www.getup.org.au

How cyber-activism changed the world

I can't thank you enough for providing the tools I've always wanted for social change. With MoveOn, I feel like I have a voice in the world and an organisation fighting for the same things that are important to me. As a working professional and mother, I don't have time to look up whom to contact on what issues. You make it possible for me to fight against the infuriating things that I see either destroying or about to destroy our country.

Three years before the twin towers were destroyed, three months before Bill Clinton was impeached, two Silicon Valley entrepreneurs sent an email to a hundred of their friends, born out of their frustration at the way American political life had been hijacked by drawn-out attempts to remove Clinton. The email was a call to Congress to: 'Censure President Clinton and Move On to pressing issues facing the nation.' Within days, thousands had signed the online petition. By the time Congress impeached Clinton in December 1998, the organisation spawned by that email had half a million members. Ten years later, more than five million people have signed up to MoveOn.org.

The America of a decade ago now looks like another country. The kind of people power mobilised by MoveOn is just one of the reasons. MoveOn was one of the first of what was then a new phenomenon – ordinary people becoming activists and using the internet to do it. Barack Obama's success in his race for the White House was in large part due to the phenomenal social mobilisation that took place around him. Through his years working as a community organiser in Chicago, he had direct experience of the difference that grassroots action could make. In the internet age this has translated not into thousands of people mobilising behind an issue or an individual, but hundreds of thousands. Millions even. Obama was the right candidate at the right time, because in the past decade cyber-activism has taken centre stage. At the time of his presidential win, Obama's own email list of supporters stood at more than ten million, and has grown since.

MoveOn spawned GetUp! in Australia and, last year, the international Avaaz.org. These, together with thousands of specific-issue online networks, have transformed the way that individuals interact with the issues of the day and exert influence – perhaps even to the extent of changing the political process. Early last year one American online commentator wrote, 'Is there something about this moment in history, and the medium dominating it, that suggests that progressive organizing can genuinely take power? I think so … The tools are there. The internet, unlike the direct action organising of the 1960s and the mass medium of the time, allows for civic engagement to be a sustainable part of one's life, as well as for clear communication among small and large progressive groups and individuals … We're part of the silent majority this time, only we're no longer silent.'

While MoveOn did not succeed in its first ambition – getting a Democrat elected to the White House in 2004 – it had a victory in 2006 when Democrats gained control of Congress. By then the MoveOn model had been imported into Australia by David Madden and Jeremy Heimans, who had seen MoveOn first hand during the 2004 campaign.

GetUp! was launched here in August 2005, soon after the Howard government gained control of the Senate. At a time when the Senate looked like becoming a mere rubber stamp, GetUp! set out to prevent that by sooling the membership onto Coalition senators. The campaign was launched with a television ad and the slogan 'Now You Answer to Us'. The initial plan was to prevent the passage of ideologically driven conservative legislation by pressuring Coalition backbenchers, flooding their inboxes with email. Inevitably, this was derided by government ministers as 'spam'.

Yet it had an effect. For one, it emboldened MPs who may have had reservations about particular legislation. Three examples come to mind: the first was the RU486 campaign, the attempt by Health Minister Tony Abbott to assume the power to veto drugs, in this case, the abortion pill. A cross-party alliance of women MPs (from all parties), facilitated and publicised by GetUp! and backed up by tens of thousands of emails, stopped that legislation in its tracks. Similarly, Howard's attempt to have all asylum seekers processed offshore hit a brick wall when GetUp! mounted a campaign pointing out that that would mean putting children back in detention. One hundred thousand GetUp! members signed the petition and Howard withdrew the legislation when it became clear that Coalition MPs were prepared to cross the floor. Above Parliament House GetUp! had written in the sky, 'Just Vote No'.

The third campaign that showed GetUp!'s ability to build a coalition across the political parties was aimed at increasing funding to the ABC. The ABC has wide support in the community and GetUp! was able to exploit that. In May 2006 it gathered more than forty thousand signatures in four days. The outcome? The best funding result for the ABC in twenty years.

It would be a mistake to think that these wins were solely due to GetUp!s's interventions, but what GetUp! does very cleverly is choose campaigns that are both dear to the hearts of progressives and winnable. It forms partnerships with groups who have been working on the issue for years, so have the knowledge and credentials, but who don't have the number of supporters that GetUp! can provide. It goes for campaigns that, for the most part, are already in the media or on which it can mount a good media campaign. Stunts and photo opportunities are very much a part of that. Not only has that ensured wide media exposure for the issue (which hopefully prompts some reaction from politicians), it has also given GetUp! itself wide exposure, which leads to more members.

The former executive director of GetUp!, Brett Solomon (who last year moved to Avaaz.org in the USA), considers GetUp!'s most important campaign was that around David Hicks. 'Hicks was fundamental to the end of Howard. Hicks was everyone's son. A whole lot of different constituencies came together around that campaign. There was the rusted-on left, the predictable left, the radical fringe. But there was also Hanson voters, pissed off because here was another example of an Aussie bloke being abandoned by the government. Then there was the legal fraternity. Plus the Major Mori fans. David and Terry were Adelaide people, and they gathered support from South Australians in [Alexander] Downer's own corner of the country.'

Brett Solomon remembers a tabloid banner headline: 'Howard feels the heat over Hicks'. It was one of several 'got ya!' moments. There were a number of key moments over the years that galvanised the different elements of the resistance: in 2000, the failure of the government to apologise to Indigenous people; going to war in Iraq; the treatment of asylum seekers; the failure to sign the Kyoto protocol. Each one of these created more disaffected people ready to be mobilised by an organisation like GetUp!.

As with MoveOn, the thing that has driven people to get involved with GetUp! is frustration with the political process. At a time when the membership of political parties is tiny, where arcane preselection processes are far removed from most people, there has been a general sense of alienation from political life. GetUp! has made it possible for people to have a voice and feel they are making a contribution. The sense of apathy and alienation from the political process, which seemed endemic just a handful of years ago, has largely disappeared. Hundreds of thousands of people now feel empowered; they've seen that they can make a difference. The model has been around for several years but it was Barack Obama's use of it that made it visible to a mass audience. Everyone can now see the value of people power.

GetUp! offers sustained political activity in an easy format. The ease of online activism has been the key to its success. The campaigns of course must be ones that people care about; and the politicians encouraged to take a particular line of action must believe it is worth their while. But none of this would work if it weren't easy to participate. You come into your office in the morning and a GetUp! email is in your inbox. In less than five minutes you are briefed on a pressing political or social issue, are told what needs to be done and who needs to be pressured to do it, have written a brief email in your own words (but with notes provided), sent it, donated $20 to the campaign coffers, and forwarded the material to a dozen of your nearest and dearest.

Initially most of GetUp!'s funding came from a handful of wealthy and progressive individuals, plus some union money. But with 330,000 members most of its funds now come direct from the membership. One of the things that the Obama campaign showed so effectively was the way a grassroots support base can change political funding. When millions of people give small amounts of money it frees a politician from the clutches of powerful vested interests and their lobbyists. So too with an organisation like GetUp!.

One of the differences between activists of the 1960s and 1970s and those now is age. It is no longer a youth thing – most of the new wave of online activists are over forty. Until recently only a quarter of GetUp! supporters were under thirty-four – this has now crept up to a third. Despite GetUp!'s youthful image, and the youth of its staff (the current executive director is twenty-three), this is activism for the old and crotchety, or at least cranky – the empty-nesters, the professionals and the self-employed.

One of the intentions of GetUp!'s founders was to unite the liberal middle-class and working-class unionists. Fighting Howard's industrial relations laws was held up as an important campaign, and certainly one that resonated with the broader community. Yet it is climate change rather than industrial relations which seems to have really activated the GetUp! membership. More GetUp! members belong to a professional association than to a union. And a quarter of them belong to an environmental organisation, compared with only 7 per cent of the general community.

Decisions about which issues GetUp! takes on are taken by a small core of staffers. According to one of the founders, David Madden, this structure works when the membership is in sympathy. He calls it a form of 'radical transparency' – if the membership is not with them, then it becomes obvious very quickly. The most significant feedback for GetUp! is that from people who say they have never been involved in politics before. Madden says, 'It's empowering for people and can lead to greater participation.'

Signing up to an email campaign is one thing, but true political involvement means getting together with other people. This aspect got underway in 2006 with hundreds of GetUp! get-togethers in people's homes around the country. Madden says this offline work was always part of the plan, 'because people like face-to-face'. Local mobilisations were important in the lead-up to the 2007 federal elections – particularly in John Howard's Bennelong electorate, where GetUp! concentrated major resources and GetUp! members volunteered from far and wide. Since then, climate change has been the principal rallying point for the offline work. A survey in 2008 put climate change as the principal issue as far as most members were concerned.

GetUp! invested such extraordinary effort and passion into defeating the Coalition government that there was always a danger that the organisation would fall into irrelevance once this goal was achieved. That hasn't happened. It's as if, once woken, the citizenry don't want to go back to sleep. GetUp!'s membership has continued to grow, albeit at a slower rate. But the organisation will need to evolve if it is to continue to be effective. This is the challenge for the new executive director, Simon Sheikh, who took over last year. Drawing in the under twenty-fives is one of his major tasks. And it is going to involve looking at the means by which GetUp! communicates with its members. If email was the tool of the first phase of internet activism, SMS, Facebook and Twitter will be the tools of the second. According to David Madden, GetUp! uses old strategies but new technology. It's a recipe that Simon Sheikh wants to push further.

Just how far can online political activism go? Has it the potential to fundamentally change the way democracy operates? Using online activism as a mechanism that brings people together, either physically or virtually, does enable people to participate more fully in the democratic process. Holding simultaneous meetings in private homes, then collating the results, staging real or virtual town hall meetings … these activities generate a lot of energy. David Madden says that while the 2020 Summit in Canberra last year was an interesting event, it was also very old-fashioned. It would have been possible to engage more people and generate more universal interest if it had been accompanied by hundreds, or thousands, of house parties in homes across Australia. What would have been the result if tens of thousands of Australians had participated? Possible chaos, given how unwieldy it was to get even a thousand delegates to come up with coherent goals. But certainly it would have generated a wider sense of participation in the intellectual process of setting an agenda for the country.

It seems hard to believe that the internet revolution won't be accompanied by new ways of conducting this business called democracy. It would be feasible in the not-too-distant future for every citizen to vote on every piece of legislation. But that would hardly be an improvement – most people wouldn't bother and those who did might well do so with a lot of passion and too little knowledge.

California has a form of direct democracy that allows people, by direct ballot, to rescind laws or propose new laws or even remove elected officials, all bypassing the legislature and the Governor. This kind of direct democracy, whereby citizens can have a say on a whole range of matters – including, potentially, removing (or creating) laws at odds with the views of the elected representatives – is interesting but problematic. While it came about in the early twentieth century in response to corruption within the government, it has been found to be riddled with unintended consequences. In 2002, a coalition of right-wing organisations put forward a referendum that proposed that only marriage between a man and a woman be deemed legally valid in California. Proposition 22, as it became known, received majority support and became law, thus undermining decades of work by gay activists. But it was opposed by 40 per cent, thus highlighting one of the problems with direct democracy. Proposition 22 was overturned by the Supreme Court in May 2008. But it has become law again as a result of another referendum held in conjunction with the November elections, making it part of the Californian Constitution.

Direct democracy might be problematic but direct *communication* between citizens and elected politicians has never been so possible. And this can be effective too, particularly if politicians start to see these communications not as an onerous burden but an enormous resource. Governments now have a huge and highly educated citizenry to tap into.

GetUp!'s new executive director has ambitious plans as to where GetUp! might go from here. Sheikh sees the campaign-based actions as just the first step and expects in the next few years to see a major change in the relationship between the people and their government, brought about through the power of grassroots action. The next step for GetUp! will involve far more member-to-member communication and providing members with the tools to act on issues they care about. It will take web politics to a new level, and one that, according to Sheikh, has not yet been tried anywhere in the world. The point is not to have ten or twenty thousand GetUp! groups around the country, but to resource progressive groups that are self-organising and have a shared vision as to where they want to see the country go.

In diversifying the ways in which members can act, Sheikh is moving away from the usual debate about the effectiveness of online campaigns versus on-the-street action. He wants to see GetUp! members involved in both. The key to grassroots action, to involving and keeping new members, is not about online versus offline but about method of contact. Contacting people, particularly young people, via SMS and social networks like MySpace and Facebook will be the new growth areas. The potential to mobilise those who have not traditionally been interested in politics was demonstrated late last year when GetUp! ran a strong campaign against internet censorship. That campaign brought in tens of thousands of new members, many of them the kind of IT geeks not usually associated with progressive politics. Most have stayed on board and a significant number joined a subsequent action in support of a *Human Rights Act.*

For GetUp!, the next phase is about building democracy. For Simon Sheikh, growing the grassroots, involving people in a shared vision while giving them the tools to be proactive citizens, is a sure-fire way to build a progressive national agenda. And the key is getting local politicians listening to local people. He says he'll know they have succeeded when MPs start crossing the floor, because that will show politicians are listening to their constituents and not just the party bosses.

For this to happen will require more than just an expanding membership base and clever technology. The kind of inane comments endemic on many sites, including those with a progressive agenda, will drive away as many people as they attract. The quality of the engagement is at least as important as the quantity of it. Getting people communicating with one another may be a good thing but that doesn't mean it will amount to much. So any social mobilisation is going to require rigorous leadership, no matter how democratic its goals. It may be that intelligent political engagement will always be a minority sport ... Then again, a big minority is still an awful lot of people. ■

Anne Coombs is a GetUp! member and a regular contributor to Griffith REVIEW. Her essay on Rural Australians for Refugees 'Mobilising rural Australia' appeared *Griffith REVIEW 3: Webs of Power.*

Memoir:
Assemble at home
Author:
Kate Cole-Adams

One afternoon in late July 2003 I turned up at a café in Brunswick Street Fitzroy to have coffee with a man. I carried, for reasons still partly obscure to me, a small orange case – a child's reinforced cardboard 1950s school bag – and arrived several minutes late.

The man I was to meet had told me over the phone that he would be carrying a 'crumpler', which I did not at that point realise was a brand of satchel, and I, flustered, had told him I would carry this bag, which I was now half regretting. As I neared the café, trying to look composed, I saw a man sitting in the window seat. When I looked towards him, he raised a stripy bag into the air, and I, in response, raised my orange case.

About six weeks earlier, I had had a revelation of sorts. In the wake of a painful separation and a long period of soul searching over what – or, to be more honest, who – might actually make me happy, I had a sudden intimation that I already knew the answer. 'You know,' I said to no one in particular, 'I just want to find someone – *lovely*.' I couldn't have told you then exactly the ingredients of this 'lovely' but I could feel it, I could taste it in my mouth. 'And if I can't find anyone lovely,' I continued (tasting it again, the small word like a smooth stone at the back of my tongue), 'I'd rather not be with anyone at all.'

It was probably this second stanza that was the critical departure – the final acceptance that being single was better than being incompatibly partnered. But it was the word 'lovely' that stayed with me – and that I teased into its constituent parts as I sat at my computer one afternoon soon after, composing a personal profile and listing the qualities I was seeking in a mate, to put on the internet.

Not so long ago internet dating was considered a port of last resort. Something if not shameful, at least embarrassing; an admission that in the real world of spontaneous friendships and slow burn courtships, you had been found wanting. But to me it offered a sense of freedom.

British research on internet dating has shown that women in cyberspace tend to be more flirtatious and sexually explicit than in the flesh, while men online find themselves more than usually emotional and soulful. If anything I fell closer to the second camp. I wanted to allude at the outset to the parts of myself I habitually underplayed in relationships.

The trick though was in the writing – the tone light, yet precise; hinting at depths, but never earnest; implying but not quite announcing skills, attributes, vulnerabilities. 'Good head. Good heart,' I wrote in the two-line bill board designed to entice prospective suitors. 'Great friends. Terrible sense of direction. Erratic cook. Thoughtful, creative, funny(ish). Work in progress.' I felt that in the pauses and clauses of the written language I could communicate rhythms and dispositions that had little to do with the standard lists of likes and dislikes, music preferences and body shape. There was a code.

Entering an internet dating site is a bit like the first five minutes at an Ikea store – everything is possible and seemingly affordable. It is to teeter on the edge of a boundless, perilous sort of pleasure. An abundance that congeals, almost as soon as you reach for it, into something small and insistent, the colours too bright, everything packed too close around you, pressing on your eyes.

The site is set up so that each person appears under an alias. Each entrant has room for about twenty-five words and a postage stamp-sized photo to entice someone to click on their profile. Once you have joined and put your profile online, you can, if you see anyone who interests you, send them a cyber 'kiss', signalling your interest. On the first night I sat at the computer for nearly four hours, until the rims of my eyes were red and hot.

For me, though, looking on the internet was a symbol not of desperation, but of taking control of my life. My relationship history had been marked in part by a sort of passivity – a sense of waiting to be chosen; or of not being prepared to take the risk of rejection. Now, I decided to ask for what I really wanted.

To do that I had to decide what that was. Armed with that one small word, *lovely*, I made a list of all the qualities I was looking for in a mate. I was clear from the start that it was a mate I was seeking. Not just a friend or a short-term relationship. Not just sex. It can be oddly sobering asking for what you want. Not what you think you should want, or would like as extras – not all the daydreams or wish lists or fantasies – just the things you will not do without. I sat for a while with my eyes closed.

I wrote: 'Would like to spend time with a man who is smart, sweet, funny, sexy, serious – at least some of the time.' Not an exhaustive list, but, I felt, an essential one. (Later, and for longer than was seemly or even funny, I chided myself in public for not having stipulated a few more criteria: 'employed', for instance, or 'owns a car', or even 'drives a car'. It was almost galling to have got everything I had asked for.)

Having set the bar, I decided to give no one the benefit of the doubt. I discounted immediately anyone who said he was looking for a lovely/nice/foxy/etc *lady*. I dismissed anyone who aspired to romantic evenings, or sunsets. I ignored anyone who said he had 'no baggage', who was clearly lying or deluded. Then I discarded anyone whose sole attraction was that they seemed nice. I wanted more than nice. I wanted more even than decent and good and worthy. I kept tasting at the back of my tongue that smooth stone. It was a relief. I made no excuses for anyone, and it narrowed the field a lot.

By the end of the first evening I had noted down nine or ten aliases, two or three of which I had already started to feel attached to. Fourth on my list was an entry that had made me laugh. 'art loving music loving coffee loving Melbourne loving daughter loving single dad looking for more friends and well a girlfriend too ... '

His profile said he was a forty-five-year-old vegetarian. 'I love to cook dinners for people, and love people who haven't had an irony bypass and whose sense of humour extends to themselves / I find people who Don't Drink faintly alarming ... ' Funny, I thought, and smart. But then I thought: perhaps a bit too funny, a bit too smart. Plus, he had listed various obscure films in his favourites section, including one in French, and (while I like French) I wondered if he might also be a bit of a wanker. A friend wondered if he might also be a bit of an alcoholic.

The next day though, along with a message from a man who wanted to tie me up, was a kiss from the vegetarian. I took this as a sign. I messaged him back and a delicate email exploration began. In the meantime, however, I too had sent out a few kisses and received a few others unsolicited.

My life was suddenly busy. In the solitude of my small study, I spent evening after evening trawling through a sea of men. Apart from the maybe-too-smart-by-half vegetarian, I exchanged emails with three or four other cybermen. And in the midst of these exchanges a strange thing happened. I started seeing myself as if from a distance. It was not a great distance: perhaps only a centimetre or two, but it was enough to be able to observe with some surprise my own mating rituals. It was like watching my brain dancing with itself.

The first thing that happened was that almost immediately I started to believe that these marks on the computer screen were real people, and that I was having real relationships with them. I started to attach feelings to them. Warm feelings, hopeful feelings, and then, if they didn't respond quickly to my 'kisses', wounded rejected feelings.

The feelings weren't intense, but they were undeniable – and instructive. I watched entire relationships come and go overnight like weather. It was funny and sometimes painful. For a start, I didn't like rejecting people. I felt mean sending back the little pro-forma slips the site thoughtfully provided. Thanks but no thanks. I found myself worrying about people's hurt feelings. I worried about my own. I found myself feeling responsible for other people's feelings. I wanted everyone to like me. But I sent the slips anyway. From emailing, the next step was talking on the phone. And then, when that proved oddly easy, meeting.

Inside the café, I made my way over to the corner table and the vegetarian bag-waver. He had a face that was neither handsome nor unhandsome, or perhaps both, although I noticed that one of his teeth was cracked and discoloured. Again we talked easily. We discussed our children and schools and head lice. He talked about the multimedia course he was doing. My heart sank a little when I realised he didn't have a job. Or even a car. 'Well I don't know about you,' he wrote the next day, 'but I thought that was jolly good fun … (he was English, it had turned out) so I hope you'll fancy catching up again … '

We met next at an inner Melbourne haunt with great food but no alcohol. It was a drizzling winter's evening and as I drove past the restaurant looking for a car park I caught sight of him making his way on foot down the road. With his hunched shoulders and overlarge coat he looked to me like a little hobo. I had an impulse to keep driving.

Inside we made polite conversation and exclaimed at the food. The restaurant was crowded but our dishes came quickly and within an hour we were standing to leave. In an attempt at salvage, one or other of us suggested we go and have a quick drink. We looked in vain for a small convivial bar and retired instead to the lounge of a large and ugly hotel, with Foxtel on the TV. Here, over beer and cigarettes, the vegetarian proceeded to give me a précis of his life so far. He told me that his mother had died when he was young and that his wife had died four years before, and about the circumstances of her death, and about the child he was now bringing up alone.

It was a big story and after it was out it sat uncomfortably there between us on the polished wooden bar. I said what I hoped were the right sorts of things and we smoked the last of the cigarettes and eventually pulled on our coats and left. It was still damp, and the vegetarian, now motherless, was about to head up the street to his bus stop. My car was in the other direction. We turned to each other in the street, and I made as if to shake hands, but he stepped forward and kissed me lightly goodbye on the lips. I knew the nice thing to do would be to offer to drive him home. But I couldn't bring myself to. It was all too much and not enough.

I raised my hand in a salute and turned and walked away, relieved. And then something unexpected happened. As I was walking I could hear my head talking (this wasn't unexpected; this was normal), confirming all the reasons why the vegetarian was not the man for me: the non-job, the stained tooth, the too-short trousers, the dead wife etc. etc.

So it took me a while to notice that something was happening in my body. There was a strange warmth, heat almost, emanating from behind my breast bone. I was flummoxed. I actually looked down at my chest, expecting to see, I don't know what – a small brazier perhaps. I couldn't or wouldn't understand what was happening, but I remember in my puzzlement the words that came to me, a throwback to the years I had spent reporting on local council meetings with their interminable agenda items, each needing to be voted upon or deferred.

'Received and noted,' I said to myself politely. A startled little voice. And then I got in my car and drove home.

I did not, it has to be said, wake up the next morning and realise I was in love with the vegetarian. My brain was still clutching onto its list. The next day he emailed me. After a longish preamble, mostly without full stops or capitals, he wrote: 'I am finding that I am quite refreshed about the world after I talk to you, and although this is almost disconcerting, because after all the last thing one expects is what one wants, it is a very pleasant kind of *bouleversement* (ah got there in the end!) I hope that makes a modicum of sense. x'

I was furious. I didn't know why but the tone of the letter – sweet and carefully careless and finally (obscurely but unmistakably) confessional – enraged me. How dare he be so – so – so what? I didn't know. So vulnerable perhaps. I felt – and I am not proud of it – as if I were being asked to care for a waif or stray.

It seems unfair for me not to record my own responses here, but I didn't keep copies of my outward mail. I know that I dashed off an ungracious rant about the fact that I had a deadline looming for a feature story I was struggling with – to do with psychosomatic illness and the ways in which some people express psychological conflicts through the body.

I saw no irony in this. Nor any connection with myself.

For a week I avoided contact. And then suddenly and spontaneously, the following Sunday afternoon, I rang and when he answered, said, 'I'm going to see a really crappy movie – nothing arty – do you want to come?'

'Yep!'

And so we met a couple of hours later at a cinema in town, both wearing our overlarge overcoats, and the film (the remake of *The Italian Job*) was suitably crappy, and afterwards we wandered down the street and found a small convivial bar, and over the next two hours had more fun talking and laughing than I could remember ever having had. Eventually we left, at which point he realised, or at least confessed, that he had missed the last bus, so I dropped him at his place, where we kissed chastely goodbye, and then I drove back to mine alone, feeling light and happy and free.

A week later I returned to his house for a dinner party, at which he turned out not to be a vegetarian after all (he served sorrel soup followed by chicken, and later argued that he had once gone a decade without meat and was thus, in effect, an honorary vegetarian). But I didn't mind. His friends were raucous and funny and laughed like drains. He stood at the stove in the kitchen and served course after course of wonderful food. He was smart and sweet and funny and sexy and, yes, serious – at least some of the time.

Reader, I stayed. ■

Kate Cole-Adams is a Melbourne writer and journalist. Her novel *Walking to the Moon* was released by Text last year. She is now working on a non-fiction exploration of anaesthesia and consciousness.

Memoir:

When elections need protection

Author:

Marian Arkin

Image: Bush attack / Source: www.f3tisha.deviantart.com

When elections need protection

The call came at the very end of my four-hour shift on election day 2008: 'Ma'am, I'm calling from Missouri, where I'm a poll worker, and my sister tells me – she's over at another polling place – there's a man there giving $100 bills to folks, mostly to black folks, to get off the voting line. I didn't know what to do, so I'm calling you there at 1-866-OURVOTE. Can't you do something? Can't you stop this thing? It's a long, long line – and people are sick of waiting, and they sure could use that money.'

I took a deep breath. This was what I had thought would happen when I signed up to work the hotline: dirty tricks, racial targeting, insufficient and crowded facilities in African-American and Hispanic neighborhoods. Many people, myself included, believe that the 2000 and 2004 US Presidential elections were stolen by the Republicans – there were so many incidences, especially in Democratic districts. But until the end of my shift, there was nothing extraordinary to report.

As I listened to the caller I looked at the list of frequently asked questions for Missouri. The statement, 'There are people at the polls trying to intimidate voters' seemed appropriate, as was the response: 'Alert a Commander immediately.'

'If you'll wait a second I'll get my supervisor,' I told my caller, and ran to the control area. In minutes I was surrounded by young lawyers, vying to help her. 'Tell her to call the cops,' one shouted. 'No,' said another, *we'll* call the cops.' I handed the phone to one of the supervisors so he could get the information from her directly, wished everyone luck, and went home to watch the election results.

Elections in the United States are quirky, to say the least. Everything about them works against the electorate's ability to choose those who represent them – the stakes are high and the Electoral College system antiquated. Logistically, if not practically, it would be possible to lose by ten or twenty million votes and still be elected president. The popular vote does not elect a president – Al Gore beat George Bush by half a million votes in 2000, but because the Supreme Court chose to let the Florida Legislature's certification of a Bush victory stand, and stop the recount, Bush became the forty-second president.

The problem goes back to the late eighteenth century and the compromise between the Federalists who wanted centralised government led by a president and governed by a constitution, and the anti-Federalists who wanted to protect the rights of states, and feared 'big' government and presidential power. The Federalists wanted the president to be chosen by Congress, while the anti-Federalists wanted elections based on popular vote. The compromise was the Electoral College, a system by which electors would be chosen by popular vote in each state and these electors would then vote for president. To this day, the United States technically remains a republic, not a democracy.

The number of electoral votes for each state is based on its population and the number of representatives it has in Congress. Every state has two senators, but the number of congressional representatives is based on population. California has the most with fifty-three representatives; Vermont, Delaware and Wyoming have only one each. It is difficult to say whether the system favours the larger states or the smaller states. Certainly the larger states have a more significant say in electing the president, but in the less populous states each vote is worth more. The winner of each state's election, whether by one vote or one million, gets all the electoral votes (except in Maine and Nebraska) and this can encourage voter fraud and intimidation because just a few hundred votes can determine the leader of a country of nearly three hundred million people.

While the US Constitution sets out the main outlines of the electoral system, each state has the right to regulate discrete provisions and the laws in each state are so different and complicated that a hefty book is required to explain them. Also, these regulations change, so it is difficult for people – even those who vote regularly – to keep up with them. While party poll workers are charged with knowing their state's elections laws, many do not and make mistakes, sometimes out of ignorance, sometimes out of partisanship.

Election Protection was formed after the 2000 election, which was decided when Florida's twenty-seven electoral votes were given to George Bush. The process was marred by punch ballots that weren't clearly punched, tens of thousands of ballots that disappeared, and also by the massive disenfranchisement of minority voters. Some people in largely African-American areas received telephone calls the day before the election telling them that the voting would take place over two days, the regular day for Republicans and the day after for Democrats. Others were purged from voting rolls when their names were maliciously put on a list of felons, making them ineligible to vote. (Once people are purged from lists of eligible voters, it is very difficult and time consuming to restore them.) Some poll workers shut down the polls despite long lines; others did not report broken voting machines, so people had to wait for hours and finally gave up and went home. Not only were candidates buying elections, but they – and their minions – were also stealing them.

Many civil rights organisations called for something to be done and one of the first responses to the election crisis was from the Lawyers' Committee for Civil Rights Under Law. Together with a number of other public-interest organisations, the committee coordinated a pilot program to protect American voters. This small program grew quickly to become a year-round effort and the largest pro bono project in America.

The election day hotline not only helps people comprehend the voting laws, but keeps careful records of calls, so that lawyers can investigate and resolve problems, address issues that need reform and suggest the legislation necessary to repair the system.

In 2004, after four years of the Bush presidency, determined to do something to help change the course of US foreign and domestic policy, I joined my daughter, then a paralegal, for Election Protection training at Cardozo Law School in Manhattan. The advertisement very clearly stated that only attorneys, law students or paralegals could participate, but I was certain they would make an exception for me as a college professor with a deep interest in politics. The session, run by law students, was fascinating. We were told all the ways that things can and have gone wrong and how to safeguard voters' rights. It was also made very clear how important our contribution would be.

As we were leaving, I confidently approached one of the trainers: 'I'm not working in law but I'm a college professor,' I told him. 'Is it okay for me to join the hotline?' 'Of course not,' he answered. 'We must be able to stand behind the integrity and legal training of our staff.' I thought his words were delivered with a sneer, but my daughter felt I was taking it way too personally. And so it was that on election day 2004, my daughter, a paralegal for a mere four months, went off to help save the election, while I watched John Kerry lose to George Bush. I despaired as Ohio become not only another victim of voting malfeasance but also the state that delivered Bush victory.

I don't know why I thought my participation would be any more acceptable to the Election Protection team in 2008; perhaps I hoped my sheer desperation might engage their sympathies. Like many Americans in the run-up to the 2008 polls, I was excited, inspired and hopeful. I had registered voters and made phone calls to prospective volunteers, but I needed to be active on the election day and so, on a cold night in October, I went to a midtown law firm and sat at a conference table with a group of young legal professionals, mostly all dressed in dark suits and sporting blackberries, to be trained for the hotline.

The workshop was more sophisticated than the one I had attended four years previously. While Powerpoint and video presentations informed us, the number 537 glared at us from the white board at the front of the room – the number of Florida votes by which George Bush had won the 2000 election – to make the point that every vote counted. Even the most serious corporate lawyer types looked energised. What we were doing was critical. Can you blame me then, for being guilty of the sin of omission? I did not tell them I was not a lawyer, or a paralegal, or even a law student, and no one asked.

There were several hotline sites in Manhattan, all at large law firms. Mine, in downtown Manhattan, was one of the most renowned, and fifty of us were responsible for answering questions from voters in Missouri and Texas. We were each given a pamphlet of FAQs for our states, and big black tee-shirts with Election Protection emblazoned in white across the front. I put mine on immediately, and was assigned to a phone. There were tables with breakfast, then a full lunch, and coffee all day long.

It was not until the calls started that I fully realised how impossibly dysfunctional the US electoral system is. While it makes sense to have different voting facilities in each state (schools, gyms, town halls), it does not make sense to open and close polling places at different times, or for each state to require different forms of identification. Maybe it made sense when America was a collection of states divided by distance and custom, but in a world of air travel and internet, and cell phones and blackberries, distances are not so great and customs not as different. And a system as complicated as this is dependent on human intervention – poll workers who know and interpret regulations and make sure ballots are recorded correctly, election officials who interpret the intention of ballots in the process of counting them and campaign workers who are meant to be honest and nonpartisan in allowing all qualified voters to vote.

My first caller was from Texas. She had moved a few years before but had not reregistered. Now she wanted to vote and hoped I could help her. I checked a website to see if she was still registered at her old address. She was, and I told her to go to her former polling place and vote. I found out later that I was wrong. She should have gone to her new polling place, reregistered and voted provisionally – tantamount to not voting at all. My supervisor wanted me to call her and revise the information, but I didn't. She so wanted to vote. I didn't want to take that away from her.

Statutes affecting people with disabilities have proliferated in recent years and my next mistake was about accessibility. The wife of a married couple in wheelchairs called because she had heard that the lines were very long and was afraid it would be too hard for them to wait. They did not know, and neither did I, that the election statute in Missouri demands that polling places be accessible, and if not, that an election judge must bring the ballot and/or equipment to the disabled voter to 'within two hundred feet of the polling place'. All I could suggest was that they would surely be allowed to go to the front of the line – something they were loathe to do. However, following instructions, I made a notation on their record, and several hours later, after my shift had ended, received a call from a Missouri attorney asking for details so he could follow up to make sure they were able to vote. Eventually they got help to get to the polls.

I had some calls from mothers. One, from Missouri, had (like many of my callers) moved to another county many years previously and hadn't bothered reregistering. It hadn't seemed important then, but now she was desperate to vote; she so wanted to be 'part of this wonderful election'. She was African-American and had promised her kids she would vote for Obama. But the Missouri statute clearly says that if she moved before the deadline to register, she could not vote. We stayed on the phone far longer than necessary, although there was nothing I could say to make her feel better. 'Next time,' I said. Another African-American mother was desperate for her son to vote. He was just eighteen, and she felt it would be a matter of great pride for his first vote to be for the first African-American president. He had registered by mail and was told he would be sent a voter's registration card, but it hadn't arrived. I was able to find his name on the Missouri registered voters' website, and his joyful mother told me she would walk him personally to the polls to vote for the first time.

In the end, it wasn't even close: Obama won by a landslide. The quirkiness of the Electoral College did not factor in; the none-too-subtle appeals to racism did not work; whatever 'dirty tricks' were tried, they failed to make any meaningful impact. The country was weary of soul after eight years of the Bush administration. By the end of my shift it became clear that the election of Barack Obama as the first African-American president of the United States was not just a reaction to Bush's presidency. Many of the people I spoke with were African-American, and for them it was a miracle they never thought they would see, one in which they wanted, needed to play a part.

John McCain won Missouri by a very narrow margin. It was the only one of the very close states he took. I don't know whether a bundle of well-placed $100 bills made any difference, or whether the culprits were ever caught. And, in a sense, this single case does not matter because we made this election fairer and will make the next one fairer still. Election Protection will be back in 2012 – presumably bigger, better organised and more efficient – and I'll be back too, if they will have me. After all, now I have the legal training. ■

References available at www.griffithreview.com and at http://www.866ourvote.org/tools/documents/files/0077.pdf

Marian Arkin is a Professor of English in the City University of New York. She is the author of several textbooks on writing and editor of *The Longman Anthology of World Literature by Women*.

Essay:

When the whistle is blown

Author:

A.J. Brown

Image: www.gettyimages.com.au

When the whistle is blown

It was early 1996, and getting late in the evening. Somewhere in a nondescript building in central Canberra, I was prowling a largely empty open-plan office, killing time while an Australian Federal Police investigator and I waited for yet another police officer to come off the late shift, somewhere across town, and make his way to us for a confidential interview.

My job, as a young lawyer in the Commonwealth Ombudsman's office, was simply to 'sit in' on the interviews as the police tried to resolve some complex allegations. A junior police whistleblower – let's call him Constable Tim – was claiming he had been harassed by colleagues after he told AFP Internal Security about serious misconduct in another part of the force. The misconduct was proven, and action taken. But since then, life for the constable had not gone smoothly.

Our office was involved because Tim himself had come to us that morning, concerned about the police investigation into the alleged harassment. After due consideration, someone decided we had better take a look at the AFP's internal inquiry. So there I was, that same night, observing silently while more young police were hauled in to tell internal investigators whether they knew of any bad treatment being dished out to the stressed constable. Of course, none did. Why would they? But the process of interviewing them was certainly helping alienate Tim from the rest of the organisation.

One of Tim's concerns was even stranger. The previous week, AFP staff had arranged what he thought was a meeting with an outside psychologist, to help manage the stress of the various investigations. But at the end of the session, his 'counsellor' revealed he was actually a psychiatrist, and that AFP staff had asked him for a report on whether Tim's feelings of persecution were simply paranoid delusions. The doctor's conclusion: no, he was perfectly sane and rational. As the Ombudsman later reported publicly, the doctor also found it 'extraordinary' that no one at the AFP had not told Tim the true purpose of the consultation.

When he came to us, Constable Tim was in obvious distress – with good reason. Was he, as one AFP employee later suggested to us, being 'bricked up as a nutter'? Surely not, I thought; such a thing could not happen in modern-day Australia. But later that night, as I moped hungry and tired in a building whose air-conditioning had gone off some hours before, I noticed a letter in the investigators' 'out' tray. It was to a consultant forensic psychiatrist in Sydney, asking for an opinion on Tim's state of mind. We later established that the letter was sent with tapes and transcripts of interviews. There was no plan for this doctor to actually meet Tim in person.

At the time, I simply turned to my AFP host, a burly but fatherly plain-clothes federal agent, and asked: 'I see you've written to Dr So-and-so; what's that about?'

'Oh, we're a bit worried about Tim. We think he needs some support to help manage this thing. This doctor's very good, we think he can help Tim with some stress management strategies and counselling.'

The interviews were finished, but instead of going home, I went back to my office and wrote up a detailed file-note of what the agent had said. As it turned out, it was a long way from the truth. As the Ombudsman reported, in the end 'no adequate explanation was given' for why the investigators felt it necessary to seek this second psychiatric opinion. Especially given the results of the first, and as there was no plan for Tim to ever meet the man supposedly enlisted to 'help' him.

The consultant was actually a 'profiler', a specialist in diagnosing the mental state of people he never met, usually criminal suspects and besieged hostage-takers. Another AFP investigator admitted they were really just seeking a professional opinion on the veracity of Tim's evidence about being harassed. Under the pressure of stress, perhaps he was making it all up – the mystery harassing phone calls in the middle of the night; the dog faeces in his locker; the fellow officers who refused to work with him on the basis they no longer trusted him. There was no effort to help Tim. Instead, as the Ombudsman reported, it appeared the AFP investigators were simply 'shopping around' for psychiatric opinions until they obtained one that excused them from completing an investigation on its merits.

The Ombudsman's office oversaw the rest of the investigation. The attempt to get further psychiatric opinions was terminated. There was, in fact, no reason to disbelieve Tim, and every reason to conclude that he had not been adequately supported and had indeed suffered harassment. It was fortunate he came to us when he did, and that, by luck more than design, we were able to intervene at a point where it was possible to save his career. Because it was one thing that a few fellow police had started turning against Constable Tim, aligning themselves with the officers who had been disciplined or sacked for misconduct – that kind of adverse workplace reaction can be anticipated and managed. The real damage started when the police managers responsible for his welfare, and for the good functioning of the force generally, failed to anticipate this behaviour. It got worse when they failed to stomp on it, instead throwing up their hands and letting the workplace be paralysed by conflict.

The damage got worst of all, however, when the internal investigators faced the task of recognising the evidence that the police managers had dropped the ball. Instead of facing up however, the investigators took the easy way out and were positioning to discredit the poor suffering whistleblower. Tagging Tim as 'paranoid' and 'delusional' would have meant the end of his career; he would have been a sad case of collateral damage. As a messenger he had been heard, and even congratulated for revealing real wrongdoing. But as in many organisations, this was still not sufficient to prevent him from becoming the messenger who almost got shot.

Constable Tim's lucky escape was also lucky for the Australian Federal Police, which learned a great deal from his case. As in many organisations, there was a battle going on. Welfare professionals and senior managers in the organisation, simultaneously trying to support him, were horrified at the actions of those who almost succeeded in ending his career. In the final wash-up, a number of heads rolled. But the case proved it did not have to be that way. The AFP went on to develop and introduce its own, unique strategy for monitoring and managing the welfare of officers who speak up about possible wrongdoing, and began preventing further such disasters.

A decade later, over $1 million in Australian Research Council and integrity agency funding has been spent researching how scores of federal, state and local government agencies manage these types of 'whistleblowing' incidents – what happens when insiders try to report things that are going wrong within their own organisation. In September 2008, the first report from the *Whistling While They Work* project was launched by the Special Minister of State, Senator John Faulkner.

While individual organisations are not named in the research, the AFP is among those studied. Effective management of public interest whistleblowing remains a complex problem, even for agencies which make an effort – whistleblowing is only one way of flushing out wrongdoing, and it only takes one major mistake to send the message that it is not safe for staff to speak up. But the evidence shows that not all whistleblowing has to end in trauma. Indeed by 2006, when the data was collected, the AFP had become one of the best agencies in the country at managing this difficult job.

The big problem for Australian governments is that recognition of the importance of public-interest whistleblowing – and of the need for systems to manage the welfare of public officials who speak up – is still left too much to chance. Everyone knows how important whistleblowing can be. Employees are usually best placed to accurately identify when things are going wrong, in any organisation. When there is fraud, corruption, mismanagement or failures in administration, it is widely recognised that it is a public servant's duty and responsibility to speak up.

On the other hand, whistleblowing is also fraught with risks and conflicts. It is easily confused with disgruntled employees simply having a grizzle – something few managers want to encourage. But we know from experience it is often much more than that.

The *Whistling While They Work* project team hoped to find many public agencies putting a concerted effort into responding constructively to employee concerns, and looking after the welfare of public servants who spoke up about wrongdoing. Our aim was to collect data about cases where wrongdoing was being identified and rectified, and whistleblowers were quietly getting on with their careers, without their case becoming a drama of mutual destruction played out on the front page.

Unfortunately we found that the agencies who were making the effort were more the exception than the rule. Of the 304 federal, state and local agencies that answered our first survey about systems for managing whistleblowing, close to half said they had no procedures for identifying whistleblowers who needed management support. By their own account, nearly three-quarters of agencies had no procedures for ensuring that when an employee reports wrongdoing, there was any assessment of the risk that they could suffer reprisals. Since risk management must start with risk assessment, it is not surprising that many agencies continue to struggle with the fallout and conflicts that reporting by insiders easily provokes.

The research also shows, however, how vital it is that agencies and governments grasp this challenge. The importance of whistleblowing is well-recognised in the media – but only a fraction of whistleblowing reaches the public domain. Only in New South Wales does legislation provide protection for whistleblowers who go to the media when other remedies have failed.

When we surveyed over 7,600 individual public servants in the agencies, we found that over a quarter had reported at least one incident of wrongdoing within their agency over the previous two years. A fifth of all respondents had reported outside their normal organisational role – as a potential act of whistleblowing. The types of wrongdoing tell us that over half of these were public-interest whistleblowers. This is a very substantial proportion of the public sector workforce. Extrapolated nationally, it would equate to at least 179,000 public officials blowing the whistle on a problem of potential public interest over a two-year period.

However ,very few of these employees are seeking fame or glory, or rushing to see the issue plastered across the nightly news. In 97 per cent of the cases, the whistleblower first reported the matter internally, within the organisation; and in 88 per cent of cases that was where the matter stayed. Only 3 per cent of initial reports, and 10 per cent of further reports, were to anyone outside the organisation – and then most were to regulatory or integrity agencies such as the Ombudsman, not to the media.

Most public servants who see problems, just want them fixed. They see reporting these problems as part of their obligation as diligent employees, or upset employees, or both – in any event, as a way of fully participating at work. Many find they are listened to, and carry on their careers as normal. A few are prepared to go to the media as a last resort, especially if they have been mistreated and begin to feel they have nothing left to lose. But most conscientious public servants will give up long before that point, even if the problems they perceive have not been rectified. They will simply quit before the matter takes too high a toll, or become silent victims of a process they would have preferred never to start.

How organisations manage this vast amount of 'unseen' whistleblowing is crucial for the wellbeing of every organisation, and the whole of society. We now know that some organisations are doing it relatively well. We also know that many are not.

On one hand, the averages across the totality of whistleblower experience are not as negative as feared. About two-thirds of all public-interest whistleblowers in the public sector are likely to have suffered at least some stress in the experience, with just under half experiencing high levels of stress. But less than a third of public interest whistleblowers in our survey felt they had actually been treated badly by co-workers or their organisation for speaking up.

However, even if not all whistleblowers are suffering, the outcomes for those who do can be bad – and in any organisation, it only takes a few cases of bad treatment to freeze the willingness of other employees to speak in a timely fashion. The research shows that most mistreatment falls at the 'hard' end of the problem – cases where the suspected wrongdoing is more serious, more systemic, or implicates more senior people. It may be widely recognised that employee reporting is the single most important avenue by which wrongdoing comes to light. But there is still policy disarray over how employee reporting should be managed, with organisations generally left to themselves, showing wildly differing levels of management understanding and commitment, and vastly differing results.

Nowhere is the range of experience broader than among Commonwealth government agencies – the only Australian jurisdiction still with no comprehensive public sector whistleblowing legislation. Our research surveyed employees in twenty-seven Commonwealth agencies, and in seventeen of them, the responses permitted a reliable estimate of the proportion of public interest whistleblowers who claimed bad treatment by their management. In three agencies, the proportion claiming mistreatment was rewardingly low – below 15 per cent. But in twelve of the seventeen Commonwealth agencies studied, the proportion of mistreated whistleblowers was above the national average, and in one case was more than double.

In each of the state governments studied, similar challenges apply, but the results provide no reassurance that the Commonwealth government is somehow naturally immune to these pressures. When the comprehensiveness of agencies' whistleblowing procedures was assessed, nationwide, the Commonwealth agencies also showed the greatest variation. Some federal agencies provided examples of the best approaches, but twenty-one out of fifty-six federal agencies assessed fell significantly below the national average. The research team's benchmarks were not massively onerous – for example, whether procedures made convincing statements about the 'benefits and importance' to the agency of having whistleblowing mechanisms. Across the entire study, fewer than 3 per cent of agencies supplied procedures that reasonably satisfied the requirements of the Australian Standard for Whistleblower Protection Programs (AS 8004-2003).

What can and should be done to ensure that governments are properly valuing and managing whistleblowing? Australia boasts a long history of high integrity in standards of public accountability, but we can be slow to notice when standards are slipping, and when the rest of the world might be starting to pass us by.

In the early 1990s, a range of Australian states began passing quite innovative 'public-interest disclosure' legislation, trying to address this issue at least in respect of the public sector. But much of this effort was flying blind, without a clear idea of the practical options for managing whistleblowing in the workplace.

Further, public sector reform in that decade was dominated by the ideal of 'letting the managers manage'. There was low recognition that when it comes to dealing with whistleblowing, no organisation is likely to escape the need for external support or an outside watching eye. Even for agencies that make a good effort, the need for independent oversight will arise at least occasionally – in fact, this is most needed just when the internal pressures to quietly shoot the messenger are likely to be strongest. Just ask Constable Tim, or the AFP.

The legislative responses have also been blind to other fundamentals. It was assumed that if it was a criminal offence to undertake a reprisal against a whistleblower, detrimental actions would be deterred. But the *Whistling While They Work* research reveals that specific, deliberate, harmful actions for which individuals can be held criminally liable are rarely the major problem. The more common problems are the kind suffered by Tim – a downward spiral of stress, harassment, underperformance and conflict, leading to management actions to extricate the organisation from a mismanaged situation. The most commonly neglected duty is the duty of organisations to provide employees who speak up with a safe and supportive work environment. It is this duty that needs to be supported and enforced much more systematically – not just the rare instance where anyone sets out to cause criminal harm.

Even when whistleblowers do persist and seek compensation for mistreatment, the avenues are inappropriate. How many whistleblowers, having been mistreated, are prepared to face all the costs and risks of a Supreme Court civil action? The statistics show the answer to be precious few. More public employees are inclined to fight for redress in an industrial tribunal, under general employment law, where the cases are more difficult to track because they are not recorded as such. But most who are currently coming off second-best are more inclined to cut their losses, and try to rebuild a career elsewhere without a further fight.

Yet others persist with their careers, having had their organisation act on their disclosure, without the indirect costs being adequately recognised or compensated. One whistleblower told us they remained 'proud to have had the courage' to report a substantial internal fraud, on which the organisation took action – but that at the same time, 'part of me doesn't want to know about it': 'This incident has done nothing for my career in this organisation as I have tended to just stay in low-key positions and away from the stress of finding fraud again.'

Another conspicuous silence in Australian legislation so far has been limited recognition of the legitimacy of the last resort – public whistleblowing – even in exceptional circumstances. Only in New South Wales does the *Protected Disclosure Act* 1994, in an inadequate way, recognise the principle that a public official might in some cases be justified in taking a disclosure to a journalist. In 2004, the Liberal and National Parties moved for Queensland legislation to be extended to include the same principle – but were unsuccessful. In all other cases, governments have seen the question as so hard that they prefer to pretend it does not exist.

The reality, of course, is that in a democracy we know that some public-interest disclosures may only be heeded when they hit the media. Governments can and should try to provide every avenue for public employees to first make their disclosures internally, or to regulatory or integrity bodies. But in a democracy, there may always be situations where this cannot reasonably be expected or where these agencies turn out to be wrong. We know that in some such cases, as a society, we will continue to be grateful that a diligent public servant was prepared to go outside. Such a public servant should have at least some chance of protection from defamation action or criminal prosecution.

Nothing is likely to be more successful in making public sector managers realise they need to manage whistleblowing better for themselves than the dual risks of seeing their problems splashed on the front page, or of being forced to fork out compensation to the employees they have allowed to become damaged.

Legislative practice in places as diverse as Whitehall – the home of official secrets – South Africa and Japan now seeks to maximise these 'drivers' of changed organisational behaviour. They form just two of the thirteen principles for best-practice legislation, which as yet do not come together in any Australian jurisdiction. The time is now ripe to make these changes across the board.

Fortunately, federally, there has been a big shift in approach. In the lead-up to the 2007 federal election, the incoming Rudd government's policy statement on 'Government Information: Restoring Trust and Integrity' promised 'best-practice legislation to encourage and protect public interest disclosure within government to an integrity agency', with the added commitment that, 'where a person has exhausted all legitimate mechanisms and avenues of complaint, and still finds that through the force of extreme circumstances they are obliged to disclose information to third parties such as journalists, protection by a court may still be provided dependent upon the circumstances'.

In July 2008, the Rudd government referred a range of key questions on the design of its public-interest disclosure legislation to the House of Representatives Standing Committee on Legal and Constitutional Affairs, chaired by Melbourne QC Mark Dreyfus. Its report in February 2009 showed a lot of the way forward. There is still much to be finalised in the drafting of the legislation. What is going to be the most effective way to ensure the workplace rights of whistleblowers are enforced? What threshold of 'seriousness' will be set for the types of whistleblowing that will be covered? Is the threat of 'immediate serious harm to public health and safety' the only time that whistleblowing to the media should be recognised as justified? (The short answer is 'no', confirming the Commonwealth still has a way to go.)

However, on many of the major issues needed to put in place a new legislative approach, Australians have good reason to be optimistic. The challenge lies squarely on the federal government, opposition parties, Green Senators and independents as to whether these reforms will move public accountability forward. Best-practice legislation that drives new organisational commitment to the management of whistleblowing, and sets up realistic mechanisms for oversight and compensation, will have many positive effects. Most state governments are watching to see what the Commonwealth does before implementing their own legislative reform. The next steps will be important for determining when, and how, more comprehensive whistleblowing regimes are extended to the private and civil society sectors.

But if it is achieved, best-practice Commonwealth legislation will also send much wider signals. Australia is a society where citizenship and the quality of democracy matters. Australians know they can participate in affairs of government in many ways but, ultimately, their control over the quality of the government that serves them is reduced to a trip every three or four years to the ballot box.

In between those events, the guardians of the public interest, in the way our governments go about their daily affairs, are each and every holder of public office. How the rights and duties of any employee are recognised and protected is a vital issue. But nowhere is it so vital as in the rights and duties of public employees to speak up about the things they suspect might be going wrong. Every public official, or public contractor, or employee of a public contractor is the ordinary, day-to-day custodian of every Australian citizen's interest in seeing government work effectively, honestly and responsively for our society. When they speak up, they do so for all of us. The least we can do is support them in the process. ■

References available at www.griffithreview.com

A.J. Brown is Professor of Public Law in the Griffith Law School, Griffith University, and was project leader of the Australian Research Council linkage project, *Whistling While They Work: Enhancing the Theory and Practice of Internal Witness Management in Public Sector Organisations*. His essay 'The states we're in' was published in *Griffith REVIEW 19: Re-imagining Australia*.

Essay:

Been there, done that, still hoping for more

Author:

Peter Shergold

Image: Fran / Skills and experience being dragged down by bureaucracy and protocols. / www.cartoonstock.com

Been there, done that, still hoping for more

Let the reader beware. Whilst this essay is, I hope, objectively written, it is committed. By that I mean two things. First, it is aspirational. It is driven by a fervent hope – and by far more cautious optimism – that Australia can develop as a participatory society. That goal, in its diverse manifestations, seems to me to be the holy grail of public and social innovation.

History does not seem to be on my side. Trust in governments and politicians is at low levels. A Roy Morgan Research Poll undertaken in 2008 showed that only 23 per cent of respondents gave Federal MPs, and 20 per cent state MPs, a high or very high ranking for ethics and honesty – although it's worth noting that both groups scored a paltry 7 per cent back in 1998. Confidence in public servants was not much better, at 29 per cent. Meanwhile, membership of traditional organisations such as churches, trade unions and political parties has been declining significantly.

Trust and engagement are the twin pillars of a participation society. In their absence, the ties that bind – the networks of 'social capital' that underpin civility, respect for others and a collective sense of mutual responsibility – are loosened. In Robert Putnam's wonderful metaphor of American individuality, citizens end up bowling alone.

Second, I have form. The manner in which I marshal my evidence reflects two decades as an Australian public servant. If I had been a former minister, the ex-chief executive of a not-for-profit organisation (or even a real academic), I like to think I would have come to similar conclusions. The way in which I would have prosecuted my case, not least the emphases struck, would almost certainly have been different.

In 1987 I took leave from my position at the University of New South Wales. My absence lasted rather longer than I had expected. For twenty years I worked at senior levels for four prime ministers and eight ministers across the political divides, often on matters that were the subject of fierce Parliamentary contest and media scrutiny. When I look back on the main issues to which I contributed policy advice or administrative oversight, it's a pretty eclectic list. Chronologically, it begins with the Hawke Government's commitment to a National Agenda for Multicultural Australia and ends with the Howard Government's commitment to the introduction of an emissions trading scheme. Between lie the legislative enactment of native title legislation in response to the *Mabo* High Court decision, the writing of a values-based *Public Service Act*, implementation of the *Workplace Relations Act* and changes to the higher education system. I held positions of authority during the response to Aboriginal Deaths in Custody (on the one hand) and the Northern Territory intervention (on the other). I was there during the waterfront dispute, the war in Iraq and Australia's response to the Asian tsunami. I was deeply involved in welfare-to-work initiatives and in the establishment of the Higher Education Endowment Fund.

I served during the early months of the Rudd government, taking some pride in the seamlessness of the process of democratic transition. I left at the end of my contract not because I was pushed. I confess that my departure was not 'to spend more time with my family' but because, in spite of finding great reward and value in public service life, I had come to believe I could now derive more satisfaction outside the public service than within.

To many of the academic colleagues I left in 1987, I had displayed the political instincts of a chameleon and, at least to some, the morals of a lizard. Worse, by far, my career as a mandarin could be typified as that of an economic rationalist – a distinctively Australian term of abuse. I comforted myself by seeking to display the professional qualities that I thought were required of a traditional senior public servant within Australia's version of the Westminster system of government.

I was secretary of a number of departments of state. Secretaries, I should note, are no longer permanent. In 1994 the innocuously named *Prime Minister and Cabinet (Miscellaneous Provisions) Act* effectively removed continuing tenure. Yet, in spite of having fixed-term 'contracts', their influential role remains. Their powers, however, are appropriately limited by the structures of governance. Today, as in the past, public service leaders have a significant capacity to persuade the government of the day but their advice is usually hidden from view. It is for governments to set political directions and take decisions and, whether bureaucrats like them or not, it is their responsibility to administer them with dedication and commitment.

This, to me, is a foundation upon which a more participatory democracy should be built. My palpable frustration is not with this political substructure, but with how the edifices set upon it have remained so unimaginative. There are forms of architecture governance that can enhance the development and delivery of public policy by engaging more citizens in more engaging ways. By doing so, opportunities are provided to create a more inclusive and civil society, strengthened by new manifestations of social capital and marked by renewed interest in diverse varieties of social innovation.

The obstacle, curiously, is not politics. The virtues of participation can be argued across the political spectrum. Although there are rather unconvincing attempts to establish new ideological distinctions between 'conservative' and 'radical', and between 'neo-liberal' and 'social democratic', the aspects of political participation which interest me straddle the old left–right divide. Doing my best impersonation of Sir Humphrey Appleby, I find that I can argue the case for greater citizen engagement equally convincingly from the perspectives of shifting power from the state to the individual (right?) or of building a more inclusive and caring society (left?). I can base my rationale either on the democratic rights of individual citizens (left?) or on the civic responsibilities that they bear (right?). I can posit the benefits of greater involvement of non-government organisations either from the perspective of creating competitive markets for the delivery of public goods (right?) or from that of enabling greater community engagement (left?). My point is simply this: the politics of participation is complex but not fatal.

Rather, the problem is a lack of imagination, insufficient courage and too great an abundance of caution. Too many good things have happened in the delivery of government services only for their beneficial potential to be stymied by being argued for the wrong reasons and/or undermined by a failure of political nerve or bureaucratic inflexibility.

Let me get personal. I enjoyed immensely the opportunity to administer the newly-established Job Network in the late 1990s. I was somewhat surprised but delighted at the capacity of community-based organisations to scale up and or create consortia to deliver labour market services just as effectively as the private sector businesses against which they successfully competed. I remain convinced that the quality of services delivered to jobseekers was better, and the outcome costs lower, than under the Commonwealth Employment Service's government monopoly.

Yet my enthusiasm has been progressively diminished by the blinkered vision brought to the administration of Job Network members, reflected in an extraordinarily intrusive contract management. If the Commonwealth Government is paying providers on the basis of outcomes (essentially, success in placing people into work) then there is little justification for prescriptively determined micro-management by bureaucrats. All that is required is for public servants to ensure that the conduct of outsourced providers is ethical and that their aggregated expenditure is publicly accountable.

The difficulty has become clearer to me with the wisdom of hindsight. The establishment of Job Network was argued almost exclusively in terms of cost savings and, to a lesser extent, service quality. The implicit danger was that contracted providers might behave in ways which brought political controversy. Indeed, I remember well the media storm about one community-based organisation spending 'taxpayers' money' funding haircuts for job applicants.

The most exciting potential advantage of outsourcing – that competition would generate social innovation in assisting jobseekers – was lost. Instead, well-intentioned public servants have felt the need to get themselves involved in the internal management of the providers. Many providers, and particularly not-for-profit organisations, feel that they are being moulded to become little more than the government agencies that they replaced. I don't believe that this is the inevitable outcome of such initiatives.

A few days ago, as I was finishing up this essay, I enjoyed the opportunity to share a cup of coffee with Chris Hall. Chris bears testimony to the old adage that if you want a job done well ask a busy person. He is the Chief Executive of UnitingCare West, the President of the Board of the West Australian Council on Social Service (WACOSS) and the Co-chair of the Community Employers' Forum. He has been at the forefront of the relationship between governments and the not-for-profit organisations who increasingly deliver public programs and services under contract.

UnitingCare in Western Australia runs about thirty funded programs from sixty-five different cost centres across such diverse areas as disability, mental health, independent living, residential accommodation, drug and alcohol rehabilitation and child sexual abuse. (At the national level, UnitingCare Australia has a close relationship with Wesley Uniting Employment, a successful Job Network provider that has a commitment and ethos that I continue to admire.)

Chris and I were talking about the regulatory burden of bureaucratic red tape that increasingly weighed down on not-for-profit service delivery. 'Governments can't purchase a service from us and then tell us how to run it,' he argued. 'It won't happen when we've built Australia as a participation society,' I replied. Actually that's not true. I just thought it or, more accurately, hoped it. My job, I knew, was to try to write it down.

Back in November 2008 I was asked to deliver the Spann Oration to the New South Wales branch of the Institute of Public Administration Australia. To an audience of the converted, or at least sympathetic, I extolled the new and exciting changes occurring in the processes of governance, which had profound implications for public services. Let me reprise a few of my arguments.

I think it is a good thing that the provision of policy advice is becoming more contested. The views of officials (such as my old self) now compete with those of political advisers, lobbyists and policy think tanks. Community-based not-for-profit organisations advocate with increased professionalism. The implementation of policy is increasingly contracted out and delivered through the private and 'third' sectors with the public service retaining responsibility for oversight, evaluation and accountability.

At the same time, and significantly extending these developments, new configurations of policy influence are emerging. All demand new ways of doing things and new forms of leadership behaviour. At the heart of these changes lies the growing importance of collaboration – both across government agencies and jurisdictions, and between the public, private and not-for-profit sectors. In most instances, governments and their public services remain as a hub, with spokes of community-based delivery. More occasionally, genuine networks are emerging, with interconnected webs of political authority.

Until now, the traditional structures of Westminster have continued to frame the relationship between Australian governments, public services and the community sector. Recently, more complex institutional structures of governance have been emerging. They take many forms. Some challenge the premises of representative government by embracing – albeit in a rather inchoate and somewhat reluctant manner – the idea of joint responsibility for public policy. What I mean by that is the opportunity for those outside the formal structures of governance (individual citizens, community groups and contracted providers) to help design and deliver publicly funded programs and services. Instead of being recognised merely as 'stakeholders', to be informed and consulted on government policy, there is the possibility for non-government players and third-party agents to work together in the construction and implementation of public good.

Private sector and community institutions already deliver services to and on behalf of the government outside the traditional structures of governance. The key characteristics involve the allocation of government business, by public service tender, with conditions set by contract. The goal is to harness market competition. Payment is made on the basis of outcomes and tenders awarded on the criterion of performance. The contracted organisations enjoy greater autonomy with respect to delivery processes than is normal in public sector agencies. Crucially, public services (the purchaser) remain accountable as managers for the use of public funds by the contracted body (the provider) for the delivery of government programs to the citizen (the client).

In aggregate, not-for-profit organisations (particularly in the area of social welfare) have become more reliant on government funding. More importantly – and this is often the reason for their increased financial dependence – the form of government support has changed. Governments are now relatively less likely to provide submission-based grants to not-for-profit groups to support artistic endeavour, community sport, social welfare or the environment. Rather, they increasingly are attracted to awarding competitive contracts for the delivery of their programs. Instead of providing funding to organisations to pursue community goals which governments agree to be in the public interest, governments are now more likely to tender out to community organisations the delivery of public services.

Outsourcing by the Commonwealth and state governments began in the early 1990s as a competitive form of procurement. It used the market to secure best value for money and better quality of service in achieving government outcomes. It required public service contract management to guarantee required standards and to assess performance. It is time that this rationale for third-party delivery took on a more adventurous form. Increasingly – it has become evident to me – the success of outsourcing depends on ongoing collaboration between public service and delivery agents. It calls for relationship management, in order to facilitate social innovation and ongoing improvement over the long term.

A contractual relationship, initially based upon rigid compliance to prescriptive administrative guidelines, has the potential to be transformed by collaboration. Third-party delivery, particularly through third-sector organisations, has the capacity to evolve into partnerships in which public and community goals and values become not only more similar but more creative in delivering public benefit.

I hope that these are not vain dreams. A variety of new network arrangements, many still in the early stages of development, suggest to me that an evolutionary process is underway. Government, it would appear, is being transformed into an 'enabling state'. Sources of authority and influence are becoming more diffuse. A 'shared power world' beckons. This is not to suggest that I see any indication of a diminution in the desire of government to shape society. Indeed, government appears to be embracing new interventions. It now seeks to extend its influence to private behaviour in areas such as smoking, use of alcohol, sexual conduct, obesity and respect for the rights of others. The present financial crisis has brought renewed interest in forms of government regulation, intervention and even ownership.

What we may be witnessing is the evolution of a far more participatory 'centreless society' in which public policy is made and delivered by an interdependent mix of government, markets and networks. The traditional hierarchical procedures, formal organisation and rules, procedures and conventions are being replaced by institutional relationships in which sources of influence are fragmented. The exercise of power is becoming more diffuse.

More players get to play a part, including a diverse variety of social enterprises. More organisations are engaged with the political process, even as the number and influence of individual members of political parties wanes. Community-based organisations are accorded a greater role. It is a new process of governing, involving non-state actors, in which the boundaries between the public, private and third sectors are becoming more porous.

This is exciting. It opens new prospects. Not-for-profit organisations have the chance to play a more influential role. But I do not want to exaggerate the speed or substance of change. Public services remain central to coordination. They retain positional authority. In exercising government, the bureaucracy continues to dominate.

Public services are still at the political heart of governance networks. They retain extensive powers. There are many reasons: their resource capability; their collective experience and knowledge; their legislative and regulatory authority; the financial control they wield through grants, loans and contracts; their access to influence; and their exercise of covert power (by which I mean nothing more sinister than the provision of advice to governments on the basis of confidentiality).

The processes of public sector collaboration often continue to reflect implicit hierarchical relationships between the players. Their structure is often externally imposed by governments. To a significant extent, they decide the form and extent of third-sector representation. Their public services can exert power through access to information and their capacity to marshal resources. They benefit from direct access to government ministers.

Structures tend to maintain public service dominance. The real work of collaboration is generally done in committee or through secretariat, usually organised and dominated by the bureaucratic 'host'. Decision-making continues to reside with governments. While neither public services nor governments operate within the networks of governance as 'just another organisation', the environment in which they wield their influence is changing. Public services are playing out a traditional role in contemporary circumstances. Increasingly – outside or within government – their power is that of persuasion.

I am not naïve. There is a long way to go. The reality is that the integration of and innovation in the delivery of government programs is unlikely in traditional bureaucratic arrangements marked by hierarchical authority, administrative rigidity and a strong culture of control. The better alternative, as Jim Hyde has noted in examining the requirements for health system reform, is a 'pulsating organisation' which can reduce or increase its own role through collaborative contact, external interaction and facilitation of joint responsibility. Jim works in Victoria's Department of Human Resources. He illustrates the extent of thinking which is going on within public services. Yet the reality is that the integration of and innovation in the delivery of government programs is unlikely to come easily to many of his colleagues.

My intuition and experience suggest that public services, and the governments they serve, still exercise their persuasive talents in an environment characterised by asymmetrical power. It is not yet, and perhaps cannot ever be, a partnership of equals. Community-based enterprises negotiate from a position of disadvantage. The obvious question is whether not-for-profit organisations should avoid entering into contractual relationships with governments, knowing that – no matter how politically protected they are by a compact or charter of civil engagement – they remain relatively weak when bargaining with the formidable strength of public service agencies speaking with the authority of government.

Community enterprises will always struggle by virtue of the fact that their values-driven ambitions have an infinite capacity to outstrip the resources available. A not-for-profit organisation, committed to community benefit, will find it difficult to harness voluntary labour, raise donations, collect fees or earn interest payments on investments that are sufficient to meet its expanding goals. As the global financial crisis transforms itself into a worldwide economic downturn, the challenge of raising sufficient funds to meet growing demands will preoccupy many social welfare institutions.

Australian not-for-profit organisations have a long history of successful commercial operations. Many have embraced the market to raise funds that can be ploughed back into community benefit. That explains in part why, when governments started to contract out the delivery of their programs, not-for-profits were so successful in winning and retaining business. They are now substantial players in governance.

However, the extent of their success intensifies the challenges that they now face. Community-based groups define themselves in terms of their vision. Values underpin the ambitions that are articulated in organisational mission and goals. Values are their reason for being. Unfortunately, in the relentless pursuit of the resources that can make their mission manifest, there is a danger that collaboration with funders – and particularly governments –can progressively undermine social intent.

The danger I see (and fear) is that in a world in which access to the levers of democratic power are palpably unequal, not-for-profit enterprises may find themselves being reduced to minor partners in contracted governance. Their wonderful strength – devising community-based, socially innovative approaches to the delivery of public benefit – may be dissipated if their potential for critical insight and new approaches is undermined by the welcoming embrace of governments. At worst, they may come to resemble arms of government.

Let me be clear. Now, as when I was a public servant, I am attracted to these new forms of government. In an era in which party political affiliation has declined, a robust and raucous squabble of community enterprises gives life to democratic process. In their influence on public policy, however, not-for-profit organisations need to be provocateurs as well as partners. Individually and collectively, they need the inner strength of conviction that builds a civil society. They need to preserve the knowledge and belief that they can make their own futures without government funding and irrespective of government support. It would be a disappointment if, for the very best of reasons, the capacity of social enterprise to influence governance was lost. It would be a tragedy if contractualism stymied opportunities for genuine partnership.

Collaboration in governance involves a recognition of interdependence across a network of institutional structures. It depends upon accepting mutuality of interest. It should not unthinkingly assume consensus. The parties will often come to the table with competing interests. Their different perspectives will only be resolved – indeed, they will only properly be understood – by honest interaction and genuine negotiation. The entire process of seeking solutions needs to be iterative: not just reaching agreement on answers but jointly framing the questions and identifying the problems. That ethos should lie at the heart of the National Compact to which the Rudd government is committed and on which the Parliamentary Secretary, Ursula Stephens, has so widely consulted.

A culture of collaboration between the state and the third sector is crucial to the creation of a shared-power world. Building that represents a daunting task. Yet there are even more exciting possibilities on the governance horizon. Opportunities are emerging for citizens, as individuals or local groups of shared interest, to influence significantly the form in which public support is provided to them.

One option is to fund small-scale, bottom-up social initiatives that are community based. Instead of trying to fit the proposals into a government-constructed agenda, or fund them from within the existing range of prescribed government programs, people need the opportunity to identify and resolve local problems.

This is what I, at least, had in mind when I enthusiastically embraced the notion of Shared Responsibility Agreements with Indigenous communities a few years back. My idea was to focus negotiation between public servants and community leaders on specific concrete problems for which both sides would take responsibility for finding a solution. The goal was for ownership of projects to arise from inside communities and be financially supported by the Commonwealth government from relatively small amounts of discretionary funding. By building on the resourcefulness of those within the community, it offered a greater chance of success.

In modest ways and for short periods, they worked. The Commonwealth website is still up. The Agreements, it emphasises, were to be entirely voluntary:

the 'community decides the issues or priorities it wants to address, how it wants to address them and what it will do in return for government investment'. There is even a map, 'current as at August 2006', of the communities that had participated.

SRAs (for acronyms give a false sense of public service permanence to the fluctuating moods of governments) taught me that which I would have preferred not to learn. The experience revealed to me that, even with the genuine goodwill of many public servants, the UK's School for Social Enterprise is correct: 'valuable initiatives can lose many of their potential benefits by being put through conventional governance aims and processes'. Bureaucracies (and larger community organisations) find it hard to think local. I observed a constant pressure to make the community initiatives greater, to link them to broader government programs, to 'roll out' to communities that were not ready and to 'scale up' to wide-ranging Regional Partnership Agreements. There was an obsessive interest, from some Indigenous organisations as much as public servants, with governance structures. Small is rarely beautiful (or sufficient) in government.

I am chastened but not disheartened. I find hope in new dimensions of participation focused on the delivery of governance to individuals. New forms of partnership are evolving between people who rely on publicly-funded programs (such as jobseekers or those in need of disability, aged care or health services) and the governments, public services and contracted providers who deliver them. It's known as 'co-production'.

To the extent that citizens are allowed to contribute to the design of their own services to meet their own needs, the various initiatives are often articulated as 'Consumer Directed Care' programs. They allow recipients of government programs to participate in the design and control of their own 'individual budgets'. Funding can take the form of direct government payments, 'cashed-out' programs, service vouchers or – less boldly – active involvement in tailoring a package of existing programs in ways that best suit them. The watchwords are self-advocacy and empowerment.

As so often in public policy, the theory (and the terminology) have run ahead of reality. Yet, at both the Commonwealth and state government levels, there are emerging new approaches which are premised upon providing Australia's citizens (in which I include, of course, permanent residents) with greater opportunities for participation in accessing the public services that they need. Centrelink is now trialling personal services brokerage for young refugee jobseekers in Fairfield in Sydney and Broadmeadows in Melbourne. Billed as 'a genuine collaborative effort to take a fresh look at the way Centrelink and the local community have been servicing young refugees', the object is to give the jobseekers ownership of their goals and allow them to take responsibility for achieving them. The challenge is whether the government broker providing personalised assistance, or indeed the community workers and organisations who lend support, have the sensitivity to hand over sufficient power to make the venture a success.

More broadly, jobseekers are being offered increased flexibility in negotiating individualised 'Activity Agreements' with their Job Network provider (which may well be a contracted not-for-profit organisation). Supported by a pool of money called an Employment Pathway Fund, individual jobseekers are now given the opportunity to tailor for themselves a mix of vocational and non-vocational work experience, educational and training activities to help them secure employment.

At the state level, the Western Australian government has introduced an Intensive Family Support program for families who are seeking respite to continue caring for a family member and for families with a child under eighteen with a disability. The Victorian Transport Accident Commission has initiated an Individual Funding Agreement that allows those who have sustained severe injuries to self-purchase programs. Clients directly, or through brokers, can make their own plans on the attendant and support care they require.

The range of opportunities to increase the participation of government service recipients in the design of the programs they require is wide. I was recently talking to an erstwhile colleague of mine, Gavin McCairns. We continued a conversation we had begun when we worked together on welfare-to-work. Presently the State Director of the Department of Immigration and Citizenship in NSW he had, before I knew him, worked for the New South Wales Department of Housing. In examining how best to manage public housing estates, Gavin had explored ways to increase tenant and community involvement through neighbourhood boards. Community renewal, as he noted, is dependent on building partnerships which involve residents in decision-making. While public services need to retain responsibility for ensuring appropriate accountability for the expenditure of public funds, they must also base relationships with community organisations on trust. The goal is not to 'give power away' but to collaborate.

A somewhat disheartening reflection on the challenge of public service reform is that only a couple of weeks back I received a visit from an enthusiastic young man from the NSW Department of Housing. He was seeking examples of social innovation. He was unaware of the thought-provoking Discussion Paper put out by his own department nine years ago. I gave him my copy. How many good ideas in public policy lie neatly stacked at the bottom of unopened filing cabinets?

Perhaps the greatest progress in the area of individualised funding in Australia has occurred in the provision of government services to people with a disability. I'm presently a member of the Western Australian Economic Audit. My particular interest is in how service delivery might be improved. It's given me the chance to meet with Ron Chalmers who heads up the state's Disability Services Commission which, for two decades, has embedded the principles of partnership and co-production into the Local Area Coordination support strategy. Coordinators help people with a disability and their families and carers to plan, select and receive the services they need. Small amounts of direct funding are also available. In Ron's view, providing personal choice and control has been highly valued both by those with disabilities and their families. Certainly the approach has now been taken up by other states and territories.

The Victorian government, which has also been a leader in the provision of individual support packages for disability services, makes it clear that recipients are able to choose and change service providers. Indeed, more radical reforms have been foreshadowed. While recipients of disability services can agree to have their funding go directly to a combination of service providers and financial intermediaries, there are also options (presently limited) for individuals to sign a deed of agreement directly to purchase the support they require. A Direct Payments project is being trialled which will transfer an agreed amount of funding directly to a person with a disability, a family member or carer. They can then purchase support in line with an agreed plan and, if they wish, administer their own funding.

By promoting a market for disability services in which program users are treated as informed clients, while advocating social justice through the active participation of citizens, individualised funding can make its pitch to both ends of the political spectrum. It rejects the 'one size fits all' approach to service delivery which, far too often, has served to turn not-for-profit providers into arms of government or extensions of public service bureaucracy in delivering programs to citizens.

As Charles Leadbeater has extolled, on the basis of UK experience, 'personal budgets and self-directed services mobilise the intelligence of thousands of people to get better outcomes for themselves and more value for public money'. The 'self-directed services revolution', Leadbeater enthuses, offers a transformational approach to public service delivery. Yet to fulfil its revolutionary potential will require public servants committed to revolutionary intent, willing to share power with the communities and citizens that, through their ministers, they serve. It requires governments, their public services and their outsourced providers to comprehend that the power they wield has in effect been ceded to them by communities and individuals. This, at its heart, is the 'contractual' basis of democracy.

The welfare state often envisaged needy citizens as clients of a patrimonial state. Traditionally, service users were perceived as grateful recipients. More recently they have been portrayed as informed shoppers in a market for public goods. The co-productive state, by contrast, conceives all citizens as active users and designers of publicly funded services. Whilst they can call on the knowledge and expertise of brokers, facilitators and case workers inside and outside of government, they are in control. Indeed 'In Control' is the name of a British program that gives force to these ideals. The right of citizens to access individual budgets is premised on the right to self-determination: they 'should be able to decide how the money that pays for (their) help is used' and 'decision-making should be made as close to the person as possible'.

I am an enthusiast for the opportunities for political and community participation offered by co-production. In the words of Vern Hughes, who is National Director of Social Enterprise Partnerships in Melbourne, co-production opens the door to 'demand-side', 'person-centred' care and support. It can provide a lifeline of self-reliance for those who too often feel helpless victims of a system over which they have no control. It offers the chance to replace dependence and isolation with dignity and involvement. The people who rely on government services get the chance to participate in defining the problems that they face and, to varying degrees, in developing and implementing solutions. They have an opportunity to choose how, when, where and by whom they will receive the services they need.

Where Vern Hughes and I perhaps differ on 'the empowerment agenda' is in his view that governments should cease funding peak bodies and advocacy groups and direct the savings to consumers and their intermediaries. Perhaps because I view personal budgets and self-directed services through the prism of participatory governance, I continue to see a continuing and important role for not-for-profit organisations at both the national and local level. I don't see that position as exclusive, not least because new hybrid forms of social enterprise are emerging whose commercial orientation and community ambition can help drive innovation and reform. Nevertheless the role of community-based organisations as service deliverers, brokers, professional advisers and advocates needs to be built into models of co-production.

There is an understandable apprehension amongst many not-for-profit organisations that individualised funding will be used to undermine their role. The New South Wales Council of Social Services, for example, is wary of the transition from a 'welfare state mode of service support into a market based approach'. To more vehement critics – and I've met a few – 'choice' and 'consumer demand' are just illusionary fig leaves to cover an agenda of 'welfare on the cheap'.

More moderate is the position put forward by Aged and Community Services Australia in August 2008. It carefully articulated the mixed views in the industry 'with some embracing a choice and rights approach while others have serious reservations about the potential impact it would have on the care delivery system'. In the same month, National Disability Services, whilst acknowledging that the rise of individualised funding was driven by attractive values such as personal empowerment, expressed concern that 'if poorly implemented [it] could actually restrict individual choices and service flexibility'.

Certainly there are those in the not-for-profit arena who see the potential benefits of Consumer Directed Care. Glenn Rees worked alongside me at the Aboriginal and Torres Strait Islander Commission in the 1990s but is now the chief executive of Alzheimer's Australia. Rees believes that the pilot programs have already been shown to 'provide better outcomes than those that rely on mainstream agency delivered programs'. Many others share similar views. Count me in.

I recognise that the move from consultation to collaboration to co-production poses complex and contentious issues, not only to the individuals and communities who have the responsibility to determine their own services, but to the not-for-profit organisations which are often the chosen service providers. The citizens' flexibility and choice in deciding from whom they wish to purchase services can also be the community providers' risk and insecurity. The self-directed services revolution, to which I look forward as an opportunity for a more inclusive and participatory society, makes not-for-profit welfare agencies worry that their greater involvement in delivering government services will be reduced significantly. Professionals, many of them relatively poorly paid case workers, may feel uncomfortable as they perceive that they are losing their power to control services. The move towards individualised services may be portrayed as undermining the role of existing providers.

My earlier experience of outsourcing ensures that I share these concerns. There is an ever-present danger that co-production will be implemented as just a new form of contractual managerialism. Already the benefits of individual budgets are being argued in terms of effectiveness and efficiency – personalised budgets allow the delivery of government services to be re-engineered, reducing transaction costs and potentially lowering the financial burden of welfare dependence.

Whilst these are worthy considerations, the truth is that most human services are under-resourced and the capacity of self-direction to build a more participatory, socially inclusive society will be constrained by the funded services available. People need not only a real voice in shaping the government services they want but sufficient money to back it up.

That's why I see the need for not-for-profits to be integrated into structures of co-production. Designing one's own programs may not be a practical reality for some support recipients. Some will be able to enlist the assistance of relatives and other informal caregivers – a resource often disregarded. Others will need the professional help, experience, empathy and care that are the hallmarks of the not-for-profit ethos. Individual citizens will still benefit from the advocacy of their interests.

Yet in truth, while I am concerned to ensure that the transition to co-production of government services is implemented with care, I worry more that bold initiatives will founder on timidity. There is a risk that governments will be too cautious and that public services and contracted not-for-profit providers will unwittingly create a collusive inertia in the name of protecting individuals from themselves.

Just as competitive outsourcing has failed to deliver the ferment of social innovation that might have been hoped, so individualised budgeting may fail to give citizens the capacity to determine the structure of the services governments provide. Progress has been slow. Too often, at present, only parts of the service are available for discretionary spending. Too often recipients are restricted to choosing from a limited suite of program options. Too often the need for transparency and accountability risks commoditising recipients into 'units of funding'. Too often central rules and regulations inhibit local initiative, individual discretion and risk-taking.

There lies before us the chance to build far more open structures of Australian governance. There is an unparalleled opportunity for much greater levels of political participation. It also involves dangers. It requires shifts of power. Decision-making needs to be less bureaucratic and more citizen-centric. That requires far more flexible organisational structures and delivery systems and more collaborative leadership cultures. It demands that governments embrace social innovation and that public services are willing to manage the risks that inevitably accompany it. It needs to be recognised that too much 'accountability', too much public service process and too much 'professional' expertise kill creativity.

The question is whether the institutions which presently deliver the state – governments, parliaments, public services and contracted providers – have the capacity or will to seize the moment. Will they act, through fear or lack of imagination, to block change? Or, as I hope, can they accommodate the structural innovation and build the cultural collaboration necessary to create a participation society? I saw plenty of change during my two decades as a public servant. In truth, I'm still hoping for more. ■

Peter Shergold is the Macquarie Group Foundation Chair at the Centre for Social Impact, a collaboration of the business schools of New South Wales, Melbourne and Swinburne universities.

Essay:
A woman's place ...
Author:
Megan Davis

The federal government's commitment to establish a new Indigenous national representative body provides Indigenous Australia with a unique opportunity to galvanise the potential of liberal democracy to reshape the way we do business, both with the state and with each other.

We know that establishing a representative body for Indigenous Australia is aimed at ameliorating the tendencies inherent in ballot box democracies, where politics are dictated according to the greatest good for the greatest number. But the task of designing a new representative structure is a rare opportunity to reshape Indigenous politics. This presents a chance to reflect upon the successes and flaws of the Aboriginal and Torres Strait Islander Commission (ATSIC), and allows us to reassess the way we do business and make decisions, especially in relation to women.

Indigenous women comprise just over half the population; within their communities, women are the primary nurturers and caregivers, and they hold important cultural and leadership roles. Yet for decades they have borne the brunt of violence. The evidence-based crisis of endemic violence committed against Aboriginal women in urban, regional and remote communities undercuts the claim that women are valued members of Aboriginal society. We must move beyond the rhetoric of the 'separate but equal' idealism in traditional communities and focus on how communities that routinely commit and permit violence against women will work to respect them and their children.

One way is to ensure that the unique experiences and needs of women are addressed in an institutional way by equal representation on the new body. The opportunity to design a new organisation is a time to consider how we can push the envelope on democratic representation. The report on the new national representative body produced by Mick Dodson and prefaced by Tom Calma noted that no particular structure or design had been contemplated. As this essay argues, this is why women's representation is so important.

Regardless of one's view of the motivations or impact of the Northern Territory intervention, the reality is that it has profoundly shifted the way in which Indigenous affairs are conducted. An unexpected consequence is that the absence of a national representative body has opened up a space for the voices of Aboriginal women. The challenge facing those designing the new national representative body is whether this will continue or cease.

The idea of equal mandated representation provides us with an opportunity to create a new inclusive narrative of who we are. Most importantly, it could be a narrative unconstrained by the fear of abuse – the type of lateral violence Marcia Langton discussed in *Griffith REVIEW 22: MoneySexPower* and that Bess Price described at the Indigenous Family Violence Forum – the bullying that many Indigenous women receive when they speak out.

While a universal Indigenous narrative has been crucial to political advocacy and strategy, it has in effect stifled Aboriginal women's voices and advocacy. Women may feel less inclined to voice opinions perceived as being in conflict with the central political message of organised advocacy – land rights and racial discrimination. But respect for critique and dissent is crucial to developing a more sophisticated conception of Indigenous concerns, one that fights tooth and nail in Australia and all the way to the United Nations for women and children's rights in the way that we do for land rights.

The idea of a separate representative body for Indigenous peoples is not novel. Most liberal democracies have tinkered with the structures of their public institutions to accommodate Indigenous peoples permanently within their constitutional system. Canada has included Indigenous rights in its constitution and is currently engaged in belated 'post-colonial' agreement-making with its First Peoples. New Zealand has the Treaty of Waitangi which, for all its flaws, provides Maori with a legitimate and sustained legal and political place.

In Australia, Indigenous interests have been accommodated in the most temporary way, by statute. What the state gives, the state can take away, as has happened with ATSIC, the *Racial Discrimination Act* and native title. ATSIC was a statutory body which had its flaws. Like most public institutions it would have benefited from improved design and processes; this much was suggested by the ATSIC Review panel. Instead, it was simply repealed by the Howard government. Its evidence-based knowledge of what works in Indigenous governance and its Indigenous public servants with expertise have all been lost.

A national representative body is vital to navigating the complexities of Australian federalism and achieving national commitment to closing the gap. Michael Dillon and Neil Westbury, in their excellent book *Beyond Humbug* (Seaview Press, 2007) identify the inertia of governments when it comes to law and policy reform in Indigenous communities. They argue that the vastly varied conditions and needs of Indigenous communities across the nation confound policy-makers. Indigenous communities clearly defy the preferred one-size-fits-all approach.

Having said that, a new national representative body must recognise the way Indigenous politics has adopted its own one-size-fits-all approach to gender. In doing so, we fail to recognise that in the context of self-determination, 'self' for Indigenous women is not always the same as 'self' for men. The right to self-determination is not only about the way we collectively exercise control over the economic, social and cultural aspects of our community life; it is also about the right of every individual to have the opportunity to participate actively and equally in those decisions.

The unsophisticated mainstream discussion about the strengths and flaws of ATSIC means that we cannot engage in an open and serious debate about how we can best learn from its mistakes. Yet the experience of ATSIC provides us with important signposts for improving Indigenous women's participation in decision-making and policy formulation. Originally ATSIC was to have equal representation of men and women, but this was absent from the final design. It was a hybrid institution of administrative functions and democratic representation with regional elections from which the national board was elected. A study conducted by the Centre for Aboriginal Economic Policy Research found that 'women do not seem to be successful in being elected ... nor in attaining higher elected ATSIC office'. Although women participated more at a regional level, there was a gradual decline of their participation. When Geoff Clark was re-elected chair in 2002 he declared 'a victory for the Aboriginal community' and thanked 'all those Aboriginal females' who had voted, saying, 'You've given us a mandate, you've returned the traditional role to Aboriginal men.'

The low level of participation could be explained because ATSIC elections were not compulsory and therefore not representative of women. Anyone who identifies as being Indigenous and is recognised as such by his or her community could vote or stand for election. There were many structural deficiencies and limitations that had the practical effect of limiting women's participation. These deficiencies included isolation and marginalisation of women as leaders and decision-makers; the impact of traditional beliefs and values about the role of women on their confidence; the absence of female role models; and a lack of access to training and education. Yet these structural barriers were overlooked; the lack of women's representation was dismissed as a simple issue of choice. The former Indigenous Affairs Minister, Philip Ruddock, reinforced this by supporting Geoff Clark's statement: 'Indigenous people [were] given the opportunity to choose whom they wanted to represent them in a free ballot. [They] chose to elect sixteen men and one woman'.

Ruddock was echoing the great mythology of liberal claims to neutrality and equality of institutions. It is important for us to continually scrutinise the impact of Western liberal democratic structures on our communities and our attitudes. Some activists would spurn the application of any model based on Western democracy. But we have a chance to temper the distortion created by male-dominated institutions by choosing a new direction. There is nothing wrong with allowing people to say who represents their interests. And, given the large urban population, I would expect there is an expectation of legitimacy manifest in a ballot box. It is fair, it is open and it is transparent.

Improving women's representation by mandated equal representation should not be viewed as a discriminatory act towards men, but rather a temporary form of substantive equality to help women achieve political representation. Whatever the outcome of discussions about a national representative body, decision-makers must be cognisant of the fact that any institution will have a different impact upon Indigenous men and women. ATSIC prioritised the advancement of the 'rights agenda' as a major platform which masked the gendered effects on women's already disadvantaged position. One example is the conflict between the right to sustain a customary practice and the right of women and children to live free from violence.

In the course of my doctoral research examining Aboriginal women's right to self-determination, I located an audit report that had been conducted and published almost ten years ago. *The Evaluation of the Effectiveness of ATSIC Programs in Meeting the Needs of Aboriginal Women and Torres Strait Islander Women* was conducted by ATSIC's

Office of Evaluation and Audit and was aimed at measuring the effectiveness of its policies, programs and representation.

It concluded that ATSIC programs and services had limited effectiveness in meeting the needs of women. Five hundred and fifty-five women were asked whether ATSIC programs had met their needs and those of other women, and only 5 per cent answered in the affirmative.

The report found that women had limited opportunities to contribute to the design of programs and services or participate in activities that impacted on their communities. The report identified procedural barriers and a strong view that programs needed to be changed to take into account the needs of women and children. Some women responded that because of these barriers they 'quietly go on about their own business, looking after their families and their communities'.

The women interviewed were especially critical of male-dominated leadership: 'Women consulted considered that some community government councils did not acknowledge women's needs – most are male-dominated. When women complained about injustices, they were intimidated and could lose their homes, etc.'

The audit report was an acknowledgement of shortcomings. ATSIC's ineffectiveness was a direct result of its reliance on the liberal state that excludes women from its politics. There were discussions of equal representation in ATSIC early on, and there was once a Women's Unit. But over time this unit was disbanded, women's issues became a part of the 'social justice' agenda and women were transformed from half the population to a marginalised 'special interest'.

The ATSIC review initiated by the Howard government flagged the same issue and found that the lack of women's participation affected ATSIC's capacity to govern; Indigenous politics were diminished because of the lack of women's leadership: 'This failure to recognise the role played by Indigenous women is accompanied by inadequate leadership development and insufficient recognition of, and a reluctance to talk about, issues related to families and women.'

This was manifest in ATSIC's failure to adequately deal with the problem of violence, especially violence against women, until the end of its existence when it developed a national policy about 'family' violence – but even that was rather opaque.

The review questioned whether there should be a mandated level of representation for women and whether a Women's Council should be established. The ATSIC Board responded that, while it was 'keen' to see women play a greater role in regional councils, there was no place for designated positions or mandated levels of representation for women. Yet the ATSIC women's committee, *Kungkala Wakai* – Our Women's Voice – submitted that there was a relationship between the paucity of representation and poor policy-making on women's issues: 'In our view, a key objective of any new arrangements should be equal representation of women ... one way of addressing the marginalisation of women.'

Other women's organisations supported this argument. Nevertheless, the panel decided against mandated representation of women. Jackie Huggins, the only woman and Indigenous person on the Review, was in the minority when she '[m]ade a recommendation which was not supported by my colleagues ... the recommendation reflected a belief I hold very strongly that Indigenous women must be represented at all levels of leadership and that this imperative must be enabled with the creation of designated positions throughout any future representative structure. Men and women have always shared responsibility in Aboriginal society, and if women are not supported in leadership roles today and in the future, our communities have no chance of becoming viable.'

The two white male members, John Hannaford and Bob Collins, rejected equal mandated representation.

In designing a new body, we have to consider why women's issues were marginalised in the past. And we have to be honest about the way in which colonising practices have influenced male attitudes towards women. While Indigenous scholars have been highly critical of feminist theory, feminist scholarship about women's issues is a useful tool to consider when redesigning a new representative body. The public/private dichotomy holds that, insofar as political issues affect the entire community, they are divided into two spheres. Issues like workplace, employment, politics and the economy are in the public sphere and heavily regulated. The private sphere, on the other hand, including child care, health and education, is considered the bastion of women. The effect of this dichotomy relegates the role of women as secondary. This entrenches gender inequality by influencing public attitudes to women's issues. All the evidence suggests that this paradigm existed in ATSIC; how do we now ensure that this does not occur in the new national representative body?

To make a new Indigenous politics more inclusive, we need more resources and greater flexibility in our imagination. We must seriously reflect upon the considerable barriers preventing women from seeking office. It is possible to arrest the potential division of issues into 'public' and 'private' by making women's perspectives and involvement crucial. This would entail a completely new and innovative way of 'doing business'. A women's council is not enough – especially if it sits alongside a youth council and an elders' council.

The suggestions I am making will be readily argued and bullied away as feminist, as Western, as academic.

But the reality is that if the perspective of Indigenous women is to be 'brought to the table' and normalised, equal representation is necessary to help achieve a more sophisticated approach to Indigenous issues than currently exists.

At this stage there is no preference for any model, but I am arguing for a gender balance because women make up more than half our population. The Indigenous population is aged predominantly under thirty, and there is a strong argument to be made that youth should also have mandated representation. There is talk of a youth council – and a Women's Council – but without decision-making power such councils would further marginalise women and young people from the central representative body.

Many will reject the new national representative body because it will be constructed in the form of a Western liberal democracy, and funded by the state. But the reality is that it is not just resources that are required to make these things happen – it is also our imagination.

When an opportunity like this is given we have to think boldly about who we are and who we want to be. Many Indigenous Australians reject the Australian state and continue to assert Indigenous sovereignty. This remains an important exercise in terms of protest and activism but few of us have the luxury of ruminating on this on a daily basis.

On the other hand, on a daily basis many women and children struggle to live their lives as full human beings free from violence in Aboriginal communities. If we believe in a more holistic narrative of Indigenous rights that extends beyond land rights and racial discrimination, addressing this struggle should be the starting point for a new national representative body. ■

Megan Davis is Director of the Indigenous Law Centre at the University of New South Wales.

Memoir:

Seeds of hope

Author:

Hilary McPhee

Image: Boys at Ruwward facility, Jabal Nathif, Jordan / Photo courtesy of Simone Salvo

Seeds of hope

When I first started going in and out of Jordan three years ago, my well-honed multicultural sensibility was shocked by what I could only hear as virulent anti-Semitism. Israeli and Jew and Zionist were terms of abuse used by all but the most cosmopolitan. But as mainstream Arab media and YouTube ran footage night after night of Palestinian olive trees being uprooted by bulldozers protected by young Israeli soldiers, elderly Palestinians being attacked with sticks in their own fields and the proliferation of checkpoints and settlements, what I had first heard as anti-Semitism began to sound more like rage and fear and hopelessness.

Nearly two-thirds of Jordan's population is Palestinian, most displaced from Jerusalem and the West Bank or from southern Israel and herded into Gaza during many years of illegal occupation. Since 2003 they have been joined by more than half a million Iraqis. Jordan throughout its short history has provided a safe haven for dispossessed people, some still hoping to go home. The people trapped in Gaza or those enduring daily deprivation and humiliation in the West Bank are their own people and they agonise with them.

By their own admission, many Israelis do not look on Palestinians as human beings. The latest war on Gaza had more than 90 per cent popular support. Israeli surveys abound that identify increasing fear and loathing of Arabs in Israeli schools and suburbs and illegal settlements. In a society that likes to proclaim itself the only democracy in the Middle East, apartheid is impeccably documented.

Now more than four times longer than the Berlin Wall and twice its height in places, the Wall of Separation, the so-called 'Separation fence', made of solid concrete and barbed wire and electronically monitored, snakes through nearly half of the West Bank. Despite the United Nations declaring its construction illegal when building began in June 2002, nearly twelve million square metres of agricultural land have been confiscated in its construction and more than a hundred thousand olive trees destroyed.

But Jordan and Israel are neighbours. Jerusalem is seventy-two kilometres from Amman. You can see Bethlehem and Jericho from Jordan's Mount Nebo, where Moses first saw the Promised Land. Some Jordanian and Israeli leaders work tirelessly towards understanding and cooperation. Amman does international conferences these days – interfaith, business and marketing – and Israelis are welcome and attend. The borders between Jordan and Israel have remained open since the peace process in 1994 and young Israelis with the latest camping gear and new boots head for the glorious *wadis* around Petra and are sometimes billeted in villages. Farmers have been known to exchange views on crops on either side of the Jordan River despite the vastly disproportionate use of water for irrigation. Israeli efficiency and scholarship are admired.

Business propositions across the divide in recent years have been promoted by some people as more likely to succeed than peace talks. Shimon Peres and others claim that 'economy will defeat war', while the problems of the poor remain intractable and signs of hope are infinitesimal. But in Amman, before the outbreak of war in Gaza in January, a small community initiative that seems to some like the beginnings of a big idea was starting to spread.

When I first told friends here last year that I was returning to Amman to spend some time with a community that had begun as a Palestinian refugee camp in 1948, some went rather quiet. We tend to harbour a fairly undifferentiated image of the Arab world: of ideologically inspired terrorism, AK47s, veiled women unable to speak for themselves, damaged children, angry victims of war and displacement, all hell-bent on revenge. And a visceral loathing of Islam, with its own echoes of anti-Semitism, seems at risk of taking root here. My pleasure in the Prime Minister's Apology to Indigenous Australians was spoilt shortly afterwards by his inexplicable omission of the suffering of Palestinians and the failure of the United Nations to enforce its own resolutions when he led the parliamentary celebration of Israel's sixtieth anniversary. Only the courageous and well-informed MP Sussan Ley challenged this, but Australia's one-sided gesture was widely reported throughout the Middle East.

When I arrive in Amman and tell my Jordanian friends I am going to be based in a poor suburb called Jabal Nathif, many of them do not know where it is and none of them has been there. One or two remember a government survey a few years before that had found Jabal Nathif to be the most deprived neighbourhood in Amman with unemployment 50 per cent above the national average and access to tertiary education more than 50 per cent below. I am warned that I am in for a shock and that no cab will venture into Jabal Nathif, that I'll be assumed to be an Israeli or an American. I practise saying *Ana min Australia*.

The unmarked entrance to Jabal Nathif is only seven minutes drive from Abdoun, a new suburb where the very rich live, opposite the two new showpieces of modern Amman, the grand King Hussein Cultural Centre and City Hall, up one of the steep and narrow streets that wind above old downtown and the *souq*. There is the usual jumble of rubble, grey ramshackle houses, children playing in the road, skinny cats on rubbish heaps, plastic bags billowing – like poor settlements everywhere.

This one began life in 1948 as a camp for Palestinian refugees – on what was then private land, which precluded the United Nations Relief and Works

Agency from providing assistance and gave the government a reason not to. After the Six Day War in 1967, when hundreds of thousands more Palestinians were displaced from the West Bank, the camp and others like it became permanent. Apart from a couple of terrible schools, there had been no services or official recognition for sixty years, not even a police station.

Today, a flash of green paint on a low wall marks a turn left into a street where sparkling yellow, green and blue buildings proclaim themselves – a library, a post office, a children's workshop and a meeting room for tertiary students. Greenery hangs over a pink wall where a bunch of bright-eyed children wait to show the way. We follow the murals down a long alley to a shady playground and crowded upstairs offices. This is Ruwwad, the new heart of Jabal Nathif.

The timing was right in 2005 when the process of confidence-building and consultation began here. Urgent solutions were being sought in Jordan and elsewhere for neglected areas made vulnerable to extremism and manipulation. In November that year, the Al-Qaeda suicide bombings at three international hotels in Amman aimed at Westerners killed fifty-seven mainly local people.

Corporate philanthropy, any kind of philanthropy, was new to the Arab world when the Jordanian global transportation and logistics company, Aramex, selected Jabal Nathif as the community with it wished to engage. Repairing the run-down primary school had been identified by the people of Jabal Nathif as their first priority. Materials were donated, labour volunteered and, importantly, the process was documented and filmed. By February 2006, when the film was shown to thirty business people, some joined Aramex to form a foundation. The idea that companies could have a role in encouraging impoverished communities to take responsibility for themselves and their children was quite new. Ruwwad is now funded by ten local and regional companies and individuals, the only Jordanian organisation to neither solicit nor accept donor funds which have agendas and strings attached.

In much of the Arab world, the affluent are inclined to view the poor as stupid. Where petitions are still the norm, where *wasta*, knowing the right person, is everything, the poor's perception of themselves as victims is endlessly reinforced. Occasional handouts and favours do happen – oranges in Ramadan, jobs and scholarships for the well connected, visits from the Queen. The dozens of glossy magazines for middle-class women provide photo opportunities and gestures of generosity are well publicised.

Impoverished people used to seeing themselves as victims in Jabal Nathif were quite unused to being consulted. The people here are Palestinians mainly, but also Iraqis displaced by war who have moved into Jabal Nathif, a few Bedouin families from the rural areas and Egyptian labourers who queue each morning hoping to get work on Amman's innumerable construction sites. Government agencies had always failed the area – and Ruwwad's motives were at first queried. But today, where once people struggled to raise children in makeshift housing without services, there is a health centre and a clothing depot, a police station, a new employment agency, a nursery, a ceramics workshop, a computer centre – run by local people to suit what they perceive as their urgent needs.

Pivotal to it all is the Mousab Khorma Youth Empowerment Fund, created by Ruwwad in November 2005. Mousab Khorma, then Deputy Director of the Cairo Amman Bank, was one of those killed in the Al-Qaeda hotel bombings, but the ramifications of his legacy of community activism already run deep. In less than three years, more than 350 young people have been awarded full or partial tertiary scholarships in a wide range of fields that they choose for themselves. They are encouraged by Ruwwad to think big. One boy chose art history, another veterinary studies, many girls do engineering. All must contract to repay in kind, with four hours a week of volunteer work in their community. Students choose from Jeeran, the neighbourhood program, to repair and improve houses, to help the housebound, and Shababeek (Windows), the children's program, where they share their talents and pass on some of the skills acquired through study by mentoring younger children.

All volunteer work is expected to be delivered with respect for the people being helped. Lateness is not tolerated. Nor are mothers' intercessions on behalf of recalcitrant sons. Volunteers are formally assessed each semester as a condition of the continuation of their scholarships – a crucial component often lacking in programs elsewhere. Here, a sense of entitlement is avoided and young people learn the satisfaction of reciprocity in their own community. Volunteers and staff told me again and again that this circle of interdependence was their most valuable lesson.

In the first year, Raghda Butros, founding director of Ruwwad, came across a boy leaning on the banister of the stairs leading up to the newly established children's library, still the only place for children to spend time outside school and their crowded homes. The library attracted a hundred and fifty kids a day even before the sign went up saying what the place was, and when it only had a few books on its shelves. Word of mouth drew the children and this little boy.

He could not speak well enough to say his name, or where he lived, and he looked as if he had not been washed in quite some time. He was left to fend for himself all day in the street while his mother and father worked long hours and his siblings went to school. The other kids called him retarded and knew him as The Boy Who Pushed his Sister Down the Well. The story circulated that, as a young child, he had pushed his sister into a well – whether accidentally or in an act of sibling fury or whether it happened at all, no one knew. But he became an outcast, said to be a stunted nineteen-year-old not a normal-sized child.

Raghda took a shine to him and discovered his name was Suhaid, and that he had a disability that no one had bothered to identify. By the time I was told his story a few months ago, he was sitting in her office playing with a plastic puzzle. Suhaid spends time there whenever he can after coming back from a school for the mentally challenged, sponsored by one of Ruwwad's many volunteers. It was not difficult to encourage him to open up, Raghda said. He's a gregarious, lovable boy and his smile and energy have now made him somewhat of a celebrity in the community that once shunned him. He takes choir classes at the Children's Museum, taekwondo classes at a local martial arts school and has attended theatre, musical and other performances which he re-enacts for Raghda and the other staff and community members with great enthusiasm and skill. His speech has improved remarkably and so has his demeanour. In many ways, his story encapsulates the philosophy of Ruwwad: first, build authentic relationships with the community and then together resolve the challenges its members face.

In the house with the pink wall opposite the library, Awad and Manal keep an eye on Suhaid too, as they do on the rest of the community. With its public room lined with rubber mattresses and cushions, their house is a place where people come to talk or rest and be served coffee and Manal's almond cakes. She grows vegetables in pots from seeds sent by her family who live in an agricultural district in the mountains. Awad drives the old community van all over Jordan delivering people and goods. He has recently bought himself a computer and is now teaching the local children and some of their parents how to email. Manal coordinates Ruwwad's Sharabeek program where hundreds of children from the community are helped and workshops are run by volunteers who have skills to share. One of the most popular is Bisatall-Reeh (Magic Carpet) where kids dream up places they want to visit and learn how to look them up in books and on the internet. I am asked, of course, about kangaroos and try to explain about the *baran kteira*, the many wild camels in Australia, and struggle to describe Alice Springs' Camel Cup. Then a young boy finds films of it on YouTube.

Ruwwad's genius is that it is homegrown. Instead of one size fits all, like so many aid-based projects, there is human interaction, skills exchange and the minimum of paperwork. Juggling the community's priorities and extremely modest budget depends on the knowhow of locals. Families once crippled by drug dependency have been helped by the volunteer medical program. Children who could not read now gravitate after school to the sparkling library with its blue tables and full bookshelves. A volunteer who describes himself as a poet teaches a complex spelling game he has invented to a group of boys.

Almost all of Ruwwad's staff come from Jabal Nathif and everyone has a story to tell. Rabeea, a librarian and distinguished writer, established the library three years ago. Local women now read stories here and help children select books. Telling children stories and reading to them is the most important work of all, Rabeea says, because it releases their imagination and helps them deal with difficulties and trauma. Libraries are safe places, without hierarchy, that create a spirit of impartiality, she insists.

Rabeea tells me about an impoverished municipal library with empty shelves that she was trying to help a few years ago in a large northern city. One day the town was to be honoured by a visit from a member of the royal family who had asked to see the library. The day before the visit, the Ministry of Education delivered several truckloads of books so that the Prince, an intellectual and a reader, would not be embarrassed. Rabeea threatened to tell him, and the books were allowed to stay. Now she works to establish an outreach children's library program run by volunteers in villages where the schools often have no books.

The room at the top of the stairs is packed as it always is for Dardashaat, the chat room session, where young students share their quandaries and ideas each Saturday morning.

The girls sit together. They wear long-sleeved blouses, jeans and trainers, white scarves covering their hair. The boys, who have made an effort to look cool, stand at the back. These are students from some of the poorest families in Jordan, most of them recipients of Mousab Khorma scholarships. Only one boy and girl sit together, side by side, rather self-consciously. 'They would be punished if they did that outside,' the translator whispers. She tells me the girl's name means 'revolution'. The group discussion a few weeks ago was about men and women respecting each other and being friends.

Ramadan has just ended. This Saturday morning the question put by one of the coordinators is, 'What happened to you in the last week that made you think again?' First there is a few minutes silence and everyone is encouraged to close their eyes.

Then a young man, a sharp dresser, slick black hair, pointy shoes, a neck chain, takes the floor. He speaks with great feeling and breast beating. He has been crossed in love, the translator says in my ear. The girl promised to him three years ago has left him because his studies are going on too long and she wants to get married now and start a family. A widowed man in his fifties with money has approached her father who has agreed that the older man is a better bet. The boy is distraught.

Everyone listens intently: the girls with downcast eyes, the boys nudging each other and making comments. Then a young woman stands up and goes to the front and says firmly that the girl did the wrong thing, she should wait. A young husband with qualifications is worth waiting for.

You are living in a dream, another woman contradicts her. If the girl can marry now she should. This boy will be two more years studying, then he'll have to find work in another country, send money back home, to support his brothers and sisters, as well as a wife and children. What kind of a life is that?

The boys seem to think the young man was badly treated, that the girl must be no good. She must have done something to encourage the offer. You're well out of it, they tell him. Some of the girls disagree angrily. The last to speak is a boy in a blue tee-shirt who sells roasted corn cobs on the streets of old downtown day and night. An orphan, he lives in a hut nearby and is being taught to read by a student volunteer. He never misses a session, the translator tells me. You must stick to study, he tells the room, and trust that the right wife will come. *Insh'allah*. Everyone seems to agree.

The issues raised that morning range widely. The girls' questions are mainly about friendship and fathers. One thinks her friends all want something from her. One realises her father can never change but she loves him and doesn't want to defy him. The boys are more open. One weeps when he describes the death of his grandmother and how she had cared for him in Jabal Nathif after his parents had died in the First Gulf War. This is a small community driven by loss and rage, who know each other's stories and the calamities that have brought them here. Many have relatives in Gaza.

Often Dardashaat is about manners, about treating people with dignity, why modesty matters, and coping with change. Western values come up in Saturday sessions – which ones are good and which must be resisted. How parents and brothers can be helped to understand that a girl can be both virtuous and out in the world. There is a real sense in the room that the girls are strong. Later I am told by one of them: 'All girls know how to be strong and brave. Boys have to be encouraged.'

Wounds run deep in this poor community as wave after wave of displaced and struggling people arrive here. But something else is happening that runs counter to the despair and poisonous ideologies that are fuelling extremism all over the region. The young participants in the Ruwaad programs know they have been given a chance that they would not get elsewhere – and there is hope. Ruwwad's programs tackle victimisation head on. Attitudes and aspirations are being changed, opportunities created and the first steps towards creating a meritocracy have been taken in ways that seem to many to have every chance of lasting.

What has happened in just three years in Jabal Nathif is remarkable and inspiring. Just as the now widespread micro-credit movement has begun to enable the poor to improve their living conditions by their own efforts, Ruwwad seems to many people to be the start of another big idea that can counter ideology and extremism and start to soften identity politics by giving the people the hope they need. Recently, plans were taking shape for similar communities in other parts of the region: in Gaza and the Occupied West Bank and East Jerusalem. The hope now is they will not be on hold for long. ■

Hilary McPhee, a writer and editor, is a Senior Fellow of the University of Melbourne.

Essay:
Dark times
Author:
Susan Varga

This is to let you know that I have arrived safely in Australia and am being detained in immigration detention. I am currently unable to telephone or write a letter to you but as soon as I can I will be in touch. I am in good health and being looked after. Return faxes will not be accepted.

– Standard fax and only communication allowed to asylum seekers on arriving in detention.

One of the pluses of living through dark times is that people get angry; they are stirred to put pen to paper, begin email campaigns, to get out on the streets. They write books. They try to make change. Thankfully we live in a country in which those forms of protest are possible and the punishments and sanctions for citizens who rebel are relatively subtle.

But when the dark times seem to be over – when, as now, the Rudd Government has ameliorated or abolished the worst features of the asylum seeker system initiated in 1991 by the Keating government and made more terrible by the Howard government – there is a tendency to forget, to say 'oh well, that's all over, back to the beach'. Unaccustomed to oppression, Australians tend to lose vigilance very quickly. We prefer to think that *Tampa* and its aftermath were mere glitches in our generally sunny democracy.

Let's not fool ourselves. Australia's refugee regime was a very dark time indeed and there are lessons to learn. One is that resistance and protest can work. When the *Tampa* sailed into Australian waters, over 85 per cent of Australians agreed with the government's refusal to allow the asylum seekers it rescued to land. Seven years later, there has been no magical turnaround, no heartfelt embrace of the men and women who made it onto these shores and threw themselves on our mercy. But the size of the opposition increased dramatically and it was well organised, varied, vocal – and hugely influential for change.

It's hard to pinpoint exactly what brought about change. Was it the few brave journalists, writers and musicians urging us to feel, to think differently? The activists and demonstrators? The far left pushing a middle-class agenda? Or was it really the rebel rump of the Liberal Party which eventually forced the prime minister's hand? They all combined in a mysterious alchemic way to alter the national consciousness.

A recent spate of books explains some of the mystery and the key players and factors. These books will be excellent material for future academics and historians, and stand up in their own right as well. The books are very different, their variety a sign of how complex this subject has become, touching as it does on law and jurisprudence, bureaucracy, and ideas about ourselves and who counts in this society. They are the 'second wave' of recent refugee literature. During the first wave, David Marr and Marian Wilkinson wrote their brilliant *Dark Victory* (Allen & Unwin, 2004) and former diplomat Tony Kevin tried to bring the tragedy of the *SIEV X* to attention with *A Certain Maritime Incident* (Scribe, 2004). Books by Peter Mares, Julian Burnside, Eva Sallis, Mary Crock and Linda Jaivin, a couple of terrific plays and some pretty awful CDs all added to the debate.

In this post-Howard wave, four good books have emerged – two on the individual stories of asylum seekers, one on the various activist groups who formed the 'resistance', and one on the testimonies of the survivors of the detention system. Together, they illustrate a complex and terrifying picture; they begin to join the dots

Margot O'Neill's *Blind Conscience* (UNSW Press, 2008) traces the trajectory of the very different but interconnecting groups in the asylum seeker movement. After a gripping account of how the rebel Liberals first decided that 'enough was enough', she follows some key figures in the movement – from psychiatrist Louise Newman to long-time street campaigner Ian Rintoul.

O'Neill also talks about Rural Australians for Refugees (RAR). I was one of the women who began RAR. We named it out of wild hope; at the time there were only three of us. We lived outside a capital city – where all the bleeding heart activists were supposed to live. We acted on a hunch – that this issue went beyond city/country divides and the usual party politics. The first proper planning meeting of seven or eight people in someone's home included Labor and Green supporters, and a woman from the National Party. That's when I thought we were on to something. I knew we were when five hundred people turned up to the first public meeting in conservative Bowral just before the 2001 election.

And the next day I was certain. We had made sure we had good publicity and that morning emails started flooding in from towns all over the country: 'Thank God you're here'; 'How can I join?'; 'I thought I was the only one in my town who felt this way – how can I find others?; 'What can I do out here in Girilambone?'

For the next couple of years there were more than ninety active RAR groups throughout the country. The city activists loved us. We were living proof that the pro-asylum seeker movement could reach beyond a tiny minority.

O'Neill was one of many journalists who were initially sceptical of the activists. Surely their claims were mostly exaggeration and hysteria. The shocking stories told by advocates made emotional by what they had heard and witnessed were simply not believed. Kate Durham, artist and wife of Julian Burnside, told O'Neill that a newspaper editor later admitted that he'd torn up her letters as they came in. He thought she was a nuisance, a nutter.

The media was so mute, so tame for a couple of years partly because of the unhappy alignment with September 11, and the pervasive shock and hysteria in its aftermath. The government's media management – including the initial success of the 'children overboard' lie and the sensational reports of riots and lip sewing – combined to create a virtually impassable barrier against good journalism.

For O'Neill, the sheer amount and patent truthfulness of what she was seeing and hearing caused a reassessment. For the editor of *The Daily Telegraph*, David Penberthy, it was the gentle and genteel Ngareta Rossel who, instead of immediately denouncing his sneering article describing detention centres as luxury hotels, waited four months for tempers to cool and then persuaded him to come with her to visit Villawood Detention Centre in Sydney's west. Penberthy, to his credit, then wrote a series of very different articles. It was a real turning point. Middle Australia was beginning to think again.

I remember talking to Linda Briskman in a small room at Melbourne's RMIT University about a project she had started with her social work students. She took us to another small room where we met a few shy young students eager to find out more about RAR. The idea was to initiate a People's Inquiry into Detention along the lines of the Truth and Justice Commission in South Africa. It seemed a hopelessly ambitious idea, and yet …

Briskman needed money for translators and transcripts, and we found it for her. She cobbled together some other funding and from that tiny beginning grew *Human Rights Overboard* (Scribe,

2008), one of the most ambitious and important books of recent years. Briskman and her co-authors, Susie Latham and Chris Goddard, have not been content just to publish the testimonies they collected from the People's Inquiry; they draw on other material for background and context. They document the whole saga: the journey to detention, the processing of the claims, detention itself, life after release, the impact of the Cornelia Rau scandal, and finally, the Rudd government's reforms and their limitations.

But the heart of the book is the People's Inquiry, which created non-government spaces into which ex-detainees and others could bring their stories. The 'others' who participated were the guards, nurses, administrators, doctors, psychiatrists and visitors caught up in the detention regime. There was an inquiry in every capital city and some towns, and many, many testimonies were gathered.

An extract, almost at random, gives the flavour: an asylum seeker who had spent years in Baxter described the 'management unit' to the People's Inquiry: 'Almost soundproof, there is no window, twenty-four hours there is a light, there is a video camera, there is no privacy. If you go for toilet or shower they will see. There is female officer there watching everything and this is called humiliation. I been [there] only a couple of times. But I have seen people there twenty, thirty times, so because of that treatment I believe people become mentally insane or abnormal.'

Human Rights Overboard is confronting reading – I have not read anything as painful since I made myself read a sample of Holocaust literature some years ago. And while neither the scale nor the consequences can be compared, the litany of cruelty, ignorance, mismanagement and duplicity was such that I couldn't read more than thirty pages at a time. But it's worth the effort and emotional cost.

What strikes me now about the pro-refugee movement was its great diversity. Many of the activists were, of course, the usual suspects: RAC (Refugee Action Collective, now Committee) with its Trotskyist roots, the Greens, the rebel Labor Party types, the social-justice Catholics. Then there were the middle-class groups with very particular and intensely felt agendas – the 'doctor's wives' phenomenon as the media objectionably called it. There was Chilout, dedicated to getting kids out of detention. Chilout was begun by a Singapore-Australian woman, Junie Ong, who lay awake at night thinking about bringing up her young son in a country that could lock up kids. Chilout attracted Trish Highfield, early childhood worker and wife of broadcaster John Highfield, who had never had radical inclinations.

She became one of the fiercest and most tenacious advocates for children in detention, willing to ring ministers and bureaucrats any time of day and night, shaming and berating them into action. Another was lawyer and journalist Jacquie Everitt, who began visiting Villawood and met the Badraie family and their nine-year-old son Shayan, who had been rendered comatose and mute by what he had witnessed inside the razor wire. She became an advocate for the family, and put herself in danger by smuggling a video camera into Villawood to film Shayan. So began an epic legal and propaganda struggle. One result has been her moving, illuminating book of the Badraies' life before they came to Australia, their experiences in detention, their long fight for permanent residence and compensation for their damaged child.

I spoke to Jacquie Everitt about her book *The Bitter Shore* (Pan McMillan, 2008) before its publication. She bewailed the mountain of material she had to deal with – the letters to and from departments, press releases, court cases – literally thousands of pages of documentation. This was the experience of many advocates – interminable, frustrating encounters with bureaucracy. The Department of Immigration and Multicultural and Indigenous Affairs was gripped by a culture that sat ill with some staff, a culture in constant crisis-control mode, rife with double-speak.

A visitor to Baxter told the People's Inquiry: 'When I first got involved I used to say, "We'll do it the right way, we'll contact the right channels." I think the time I really learnt was when they had some people in isolation. They left them for weeks, no phone, newspapers, TV and I knew they were going to hurt themselves. I rang DIMIA in Canberra, DIMIA Baxter, ACM Canberra, ACM Baxter, HREOC, Amnesty, the Ombudsman, the minister's office, the opposition's office, telling them all to do something. No one did anything. Then the people cut themselves and a few days later they were out of there – it's just honestly the only way you achieve anything in Baxter.'

It was hard to deal with the information coming from the detention centres. Even though I was involved, I often could not bear to read the constant flow of emails detailing specific cases of mistreatment and injustice. A visitor to Maribyrnong Detention Centre told the People's Inquiry: 'I remember one man telling me that the thing he liked that they got for food was a boiled egg, and every now and again they would get boiled eggs and he would take an extra one. An officer took this boiled egg and held it above the rubbish bin and said, "You beg me for this."

He wouldn't and the officer threw the boiled egg into the bin.'

At times I wondered if some advocates were going a little crazy; they had become so obsessed with the cause. Yet they were just attempting to humanise the detainees, to publicly give them names, histories, personalities – the guards used only numbers at roll calls – and counter the negative image-making fostered by the government. What *Human Rights Overboard* and the other books do, is put these stories into a context, enabling us to trace a narrative and begin an analysis.

It was, admittedly, very difficult to give the crisis a human face, far less analyse it, at first. Access was restricted and public interest limited. *The Rugmaker of Mazar-e-Sharif* (Insight, 2008) is a splendidly readable example of redemptive humanising. It should now gain the wide audience it could not have had a few years ago. Najaf Mazari, an Afghan Hazara, is a delightful man, lacking all pretension, full of wisdom and resourcefulness. In Robert Hillman he found a skilled and empathetic writer to help him tell his story. Hillman retains Najaf's voice, but imposes discipline and a cunning structure.

Najaf's deeply humane take on his religion pervades the narrative, revealing more about a moderate interpretation of Islam than a dozen more learned texts. He does not dwell on the misfortunes that befell him, nor talk with bitterness of his life in detention. His dream, which sustains him throughout, is that one day he will be reunited with his wife and child and that he will open a successful rug shop. And this came to pass, with the help of some good Australian friends.

Many Australians tried to help. Some used polemic and lobbying, some visited detention centres, others concentrated on freeing the kids, the 'Pacific Solution' in general or Nauru in particular. Some hounded the minister, Phillip Ruddock, some hid escaped detainees or helped those on temporary protection visas. Some joined movements, others worked alone.

This movement broke down the usual barriers of political, religious and class alignment in a way that hadn't happened since the Vietnam marches. Women like Ngareta Rossell and Trish Highfield found themselves working with far-left activist Ian Rintoul. Members of his inner-city RAC and our rural-based RAR found themselves in a room together, planning tactics. Chilout members, mostly middle class and apolitical, got on the clapped-out buses organised by young radicals to the desert where they tried to penetrate the razor wire surrounding remote Woomera and Baxter. A Just Australia linked people like Phillip Adams, Malcolm Fraser and the cricketer Ian

Chappell. The Liberal rebels – Petro Georgiou, Judy Moylan, Bruce Baird, Judith Troeth – were overwhelmed by grateful emails and phone calls from refugee supporters who would previously never have been seen dead with a Liberal. National Party MP John Forrest, the Federal Member for Mallee, had a change of heart at a RAR regional conference in Victoria. In Bowral and many other country towns, RAR members stood on street corners and saw former friends cross to the other side or throw their leaflets to the ground. They were still on the streets two years later, when the tide began to turn and people began to take their leaflets eagerly and sign the petitions. Sometimes they were the same people.

Email was a huge factor in getting RAR off the ground so quickly. Distance suddenly meant nothing – and in a country as vast as Australia the change this made to campaigning and lobbying was stupendous. RAR had none of the sophisticated apparatus and techniques now used by organisations like GetUp! But it rode the email wave. Every email was answered, every fledging advocate encouraged. We urged members to adopt the older techniques – arrange a meeting, go out on the streets and talk to people, lobby your local member, write to your local paper, visit the detention centres, raise money. Don't let up.

The effect this had on ordinary lives was often galvanising. The pro-asylum seeker movement was, as O'Neill and others have pointed out, a movement of middle-aged, middle-class women. Most had never been interested in party politics or political issues. I remember the first rally RAR organised in front of Parliament House in Canberra. A group of grey-haired women, all past fifty, mostly grandmothers, all wearing their RAR tee-shirts, almost ran towards me, beaming and excited. 'We've never been to a demonstration before! This is wonderful!' These women worked hard. They had the time or made the time, their passion fuelled by a simple anger with injustice and inhumanity.

The movement required, and won, an unusual degree of flexibility. Ian Rintoul, O'Neill reports, was not only willing to work with organisations like RAR, but he broke from his founding organisation because of his view that the asylum seeker campaign was more important than the spread of international socialism. That rift has since been healed, but it was a sign of how this campaign demanded new ways of doing things.

We should know that, even with the Rudd government's saner and more compassionate approach, the dark times could return very easily and quickly. A sudden sharp increase in boat arrivals, this latest economic downturn, unexpected global events, a political crisis or opportunity … What politician would not be tempted to blame the weakest and most defenceless? The detention centre at Christmas Island has not been dismantled, nor has the legislative framework. The majority of Australians have not ceased to think of asylum seekers as alien, and inferior – and impudent in attempting an unorthodox arrival to this promised land.

So the watchwords for successful campaigns in the twenty-first century are flexibility, informality, sophisticated use of email and the internet, constant contact to keep people motivated and aware, and issues that break down old barriers.

There is also a new emphasis on pragmatism. There is little comfort left in ideology. We seem to be entering an era where political and social theories may still form the backdrop of ideas and actions but they are no longer the bedrock. People will work together if the issue and the times demand it. Surely that is no bad thing. ■

Susan Varga is an author and activist. Her novel, *Headlong* was published by UWA Press in April. Her essay, 'Opting out', was published in *Griffith REVIEW 17: Staying Alive.*

Books referenced in this essay:

Blind Conscience, by Margot O'Neill, University of NSW Press

Human Rights Overboard: Seeking Asylum in Australia, by Linda Briskman, Susie Latham and Chris Goddard, Scribe

The Bitter Shore, by Jacquie Everitt, Pan Macmillan Australia

The Rugmaker of Mazar-e-Sharif, by Najaf Mazari and Robert Hillman, Insight Publications

Essay:

From me to we

Authors:

Mehrdad and Roya Baghai

HIGH RESOLVES INITIATIVE
"Be the change you want to see in the world" - Ghandi.
I learnt that there are many things that you need on your journey. These include, passion, vision and values. My passion is science. The way everything revolves around this phenomenon that shapes the world.
My vision is that I want to use science in a way that can provide service to the community. And my
include integrity, freedom
love.
www.highresolves.org
HIGH RESOLVES INITIATIVE
I would like to be remembered as someone who has made a very positive contribution in the global arena. I would like to be an ardent advocate of issues such as global poverty, human rights, gender equality and climate change. Above all, I would like to make a difference in helping to improve the lives of people in society. Nothing would give me more personal satisfaction than putting a smile on someone's face.
www.highresolves.org
this postcard is printed on 100% recycled paper
HIGH RESOLVES INITIATIVE
Follow your principles and your passions. Have courage and take initiative. Make a choice and follow it. Reflect - take the time to do so. One person can make a difference
LEGACY -
www.highresolves.org
HIGH RESOLVES INITIATIVE
Surging through my heart, I found the burning desire, fiery passion to solve global issues. I feel like a caged bird, yearning to be let out of my cage and FLY
www.highresolves.org
this postcard is printed on 100% recycled paper

From me to we

Imagine the Great Hall at the University of Sydney, packed row after row with teenagers, being asked to write on a postcard what they want most for their lives and the world they are inheriting from their parents. The pens and pencils in their hands capture the capacious vision of a world that embraces a desire for an inclusive family of mankind with equal access to justice and opportunity. Their words are significant, but what is more important is the personal intent in their statements: these students are not indulging in a superficial, feel-good exercise. Their statements are inspired yet pragmatic; optimistic yet grounded; confident yet realistic; courageous yet reasoned.

These young people are committed to becoming agents of change, to initiate it, to link the measure of success in their personal lives with the success they see in the lives of their fellow man. These postcards from the head and heart represent the voices of Australian high school students who have been systematically exploring the theme of global citizenship through the High Resolves Initiative (HRI).

We founded HRI four years ago because we believe that any hope of responding to the increasingly complex challenges of our world requires a critical mass of future leaders with the desire, skills, vision, creativity and confidence to accomplish what previous generations have failed to do: acting with solidarity in the collective interest of humanity. HRI's mission is to motivate high school students to view themselves as purposeful global citizens and to acquire and practise the skills they will need to lead their communities, and the world, to a brighter future.

Obviously, mere intentions and good deeds will not suffice: the problems are too intractable and the time too short. New capacities and unprecedented creativity, born from years of disciplined training, will be required. Today's students will need to be inoculated against the automatic and blind imitation of the past and be trained to tackle the myriad problems facing our civilisation.

Unfortunately, as Sir Ken Robinson, the internationally recognised leader in the development of creativity, innovation and human resources has noted, education systems have not been designed to cultivate most of these traits. In fact, the rigid approaches of many schools do exactly the opposite. Fresh new approaches are needed to break from failed formulae.

When we speak with people who have successfully incorporated a path of service into their lives, they frequently refer to some peak experience during their youth that transformed the way they thought about the world. We designed the Initiative to offer an experience of awareness and self-discovery that can materially change the life trajectory for thousands of students.

The HRI curriculum is delivered through a creative mix of interactive simulations, role-playing exercises and small group discussions in a growing number of Australian schools. Participatory learning is central to the design of all modules. Facilitators and undergraduate recruits guide the students through five modules – collective identity, justice, conflict resolution, collective action and leadership – that give them the skills to design and launch initiatives to improve their schools and to serve their communities. Feedback from the schools has been extremely encouraging.

'Students are more acutely aware of their rights and responsibility as global citizens and more aware that their individual choices and individual actions do indeed make a difference,' wrote Robert Phillips, principal of Hornsby Girls' High School; and Mary Ann Das Neves, prinicipal of Girraween High School, noted, 'There is no doubt that this program has a life changing effect on students … it takes them from being helpless observers of the world's problems to being leaders who have a conviction that they can bring about change.'

The contribution of HRI can be measured by the change in the life path trajectory of its participants and the many projects spawned as a result. But we believe these measures will pale in comparison to its contribution to creating a community where a critical mass of its leaders is trained to think and act in the collective interest.

Although the HRI experiment is only four years old, it has already generated valuable insights about the transformation of this generation. We recognised that it was essential to build the mindsets and capacities to drive constructive social change in the real world, provide provocative experiences which trigger a response, develop a staged learning process and provide opportunities for real-world involvement.

Schools prepare students to enter universities or the workforce, not to engage in social change. Yet there are specific mindsets and capacities that are needed if one is to be effective at engendering such change.

Starting with mindsets, we identified five frames that are critical to understanding and dealing with the challenges of the twenty-first century. First and foremost, it is critical for young people to view themselves as global citizens belonging to one united human race. They also need to view the world's issues through the lens of justice, because it is difficult to foster unity without justice and to have the integrative mindsets necessary to analyse and resolve conflict. They need to learn the dynamics of how to enlist others in collective efforts and to see leadership as service, which is the domain and responsibility of all.

Having isolated these mindsets, the challenge quickly became a pragmatic one of breaking each down into the capacities that need to be developed. We were inspired by the long list of capacities critical to development that were identified by the Institute for Studies in Global Prosperity – collective identity, justice, conflict resolution, collective action and leadership.

Much has been written about the different learning style of Generation Y. Traditional teaching techniques are not very effective with them. Students cannot be taught the skills of engagement through lectures or readings and the subject matter does not necessarily lend itself to electronic or digital media. Learning takes place most effectively through participatory techniques involving simulation and interactive exercises.

One must eschew the very notion of trying to 'teach' these skills, and design experiences that allow the specific learning to take place naturally. The HRI Justice module draws on the principles elaborated in John Rawls' masterpiece *A Theory of Justice* (Harvard University Press, 1971). At the core of Rawls' theory is the concept of the veil of ignorance. Fairness is defined as what you would choose if you did not know which share you would receive. As compelling as Rawls' argument is, no lecture on the theory of justice is likely to capture and hold the attention of teenagers for more than a few minutes. It is possible however, to devise an experience that does. We begin by dividing students into pairs instructed to split a cupcake or a chocolate bar. In the first round, one person cuts the cupcake and chooses who eats which piece. In the second round, one person cuts and the other person chooses. Typically, the division is much more likely to be 50–50 in the second round. With this simple exercise, the students gain an initial intuitive understanding of Rawls.

The learning is then deepened through a discussion of how to divide $100 in various scenarios. Those who 'flip a coin' need to understand that procedural fairness does not necessarily result in substantive fairness, but how do you help them learn that? Oxfam has designed a 'hunger banquet' where students are randomly assigned roles – about half are designated low-income and given only a bowl of rice for lunch; a third are middle-income and receive beans and unlimited water as well as the rice; and the others are high-income citizens who are served lasagna, chocolate cake and juice. In this case, random selection may seem like a fair process, yet the outcome is definitely not fair. The lesson is not easily forgotten, especially for those who have only the bowl of rice for lunch.

The Collective Action module is based on a theoretical construct about the choices facing two prisoners, which explores the tension between short-term individual interest and long-term collective interest. The prisoner's dilemma is at the heart of many global problems from global warming to the financial crisis. Scholars like Robert Axelrod, the author of *The Evolution of Cooperation* (Basic Books, 1984), have used computer simulations to model the dynamics of this class of problems.

The trouble is that many teenagers do not find the academic work in this space accessible, yet understanding the nature of the implicit tradeoffs is absolutely critical to their development as future leaders. To help them learn this lesson, HRI uses a role-play simulation exercise where students are ambassadors from thirty countries negotiating their carbon dioxide emission reductions over fifteen years. The problem is structured so that they all benefit from lower emissions, but prefer other nations to carry the burden.

As you would expect, the simulation usually results in an undesirable macro-outcome as emission reductions are abandoned by country after country and students realise how hard it is to cooperate. Over time, some learn how to forge, and sustain, a coalition. Most struggle with the challenge of how to react to those who continue to free-ride despite all the eloquent or passionate speeches that occur in the room.

The insights triggered by these simulations are far more visceral and lasting than those generated by scholarly discussion alone. We are convinced that participatory learning is a more powerful way to build these capacities.

In most schools, citizenship and leadership education takes place through a series of disconnected workshops and experiences without a thoughtful overarching design for capacity building. Interestingly, this is in stark contrast to the way the core curriculum is approached.

Consider the way mathematics as a critical knowledge system is taught in schools. Over the years, the constituent subsystems of mathematics – arithmetic, algebra, geometry, trigonometry, calculus – have been thoughtfully arranged over the curriculum. A student would not be taught calculus before mastering the basics of arithmetic and algebra: subjects are taught systematically and in a logical progression.

Our experience suggests that the study of citizenship should be similar, that specific capacities and frames need to be mastered and there is a natural and progressive sequence to learning them. This can be represented as a staircase, with progressive mastery which helps students develop certain capacities, and build on them as they move through the modules.

In order for students to become purposeful global citizens most need to reset their frame of reference to see the human race as one single (yet diverse) race and to develop the capacity to have a positive relationship with people from other cultures. Thus, the first module on Collective Identity helps students develop the capacity to interact with other cultures in a way that leads to the advancement of all cultures and not to their degradation. Building on that capacity in the second module, students begin to explore the concept of justice as fairness through simulations that force them to see situations from a different perspective and approach distributive issues with greater objectivity and compassion. In short, the students first develop a general sense of solidarity and follow that by learning how to act on that through justice. These are the introductory modules for all Year 8 students in each HRI school.

About thirty students are then chosen to continue with the advanced modules on Conflict Resolution and Collective Action, as an intensive two-day workshop at the beginning of Year 9. At the end of this workshop, they are asked whether they would like to continue as part of a Leaders Group for the next two years. The turnover rate is negligible at this stage – almost all students choose to continue, often very enthusiastically.

The focus is then on putting the learned capacities into practice in real projects. Even in this final phase, the learning is progressive. Students begin with lunchtime sessions on leadership, learning from great thinkers and writers. Then they are trained to facilitate the Year 8 modules to further assimilate this knowledge by teaching the skills they have learnt. Over time, they begin to arrive at a sense of their passion and a clearer picture of where they wish to engage. By Year 10, they design and execute a project in their school and finally the crowning activity project which delivers real value to a selected community organisation.

The holistic and progressive nature of the curriculum makes the learning extremely effective. Capacities continue to build on each other and the learning from service projects in later years reinforces the earlier years. The HRI experience has demonstrated that engaged high school students crave real-world opportunities to apply their energy and skills to make the world a better place.

These lessons are interesting in their own right, but they suggest an even more important overarching insight: it is possible to be systematic in kindling the desire and building the capacities needed to become a purposeful global citizen. HRI functions as a human resource engine for many other worthwhile agencies and organisations in Australia. Students begin a journey in Year 8. Experiences build important new capacities and awaken the motivation and desire to make a contribution to the world. The newfound passion channels talent into a range of new and existing activities, organisations and community networks that benefit from this fresh new injection of energy.

There is no doubt we can be as systematic about leadership and citizenship education as we are about the mathematics or science curriculum. And, given the state of the world, we have no choice but to do just that.

The high school teenagers crowded into the Great Hall and writing down their hopes for the world at the Sydney High Resolves Annual Summit last year are already on a journey to make the world a better place. The postcards on which they inscribed their intent will arrive in their mailboxes later to ask the question: Did your words become your reality? ■

For footnotes and more detail on the curriculum, modules and student projects see www.griffithreview.com

Mehrdad and Roya Baghai founded High Resolves Initiative in Sydney in 2004.

Sydney Writers' Festival, 18–24 May 2009

The world, in words

Add your voice to Australia's best conversation.

Join Griffith REVIEW at the Sydney Writers' Festival where contributors tease out ideas from ***Edition 23: Essentially Creative*** and ***Edition 24: Participation Society***.

Speakers include:

- Robyn Archer, Nicholas Jose, Nicolas Low and Elizabeth Ann Macgregor on *Building Resilience into the Arts*
- Frank Moorhouse, Robyn Archer, Helen O'Neil and Geoffrey Atherden ask *For Whom the Arts Serve*
- Cheryl Kernot, Hugh Mackay, Susan Varga and Alan Attwood look into *Creating a Participation Society*
- Megan Davis, Sarah Maddison and Wesley Enoch debate *Terms of Engagement*
- Ann McGrath, Ann Curthoys and Maria Tumarkin consider *Projecting and Finding History*

Full program and ticketing information available at www.swf.org.au

SYDNEY WRITERS' FESTIVAL

Essay:
Must film be fiction?

Author:
Ann McGrath

Image: Aboriginal actor David Gulpilil as King George / www.australiamovie.com

Must film be fiction?

'Primarily, we historians write books – and academic articles,' Yale historian Dr Jay Gitlin said in a history documentary we made together in 2006 called *A Frontier Conversation*. On our 'Exchanging Histories' tour in the Northern Territory, the high-achieving American historian grew hostile to the camera. She said it made her uncomfortable; she could not see its purpose and vowed to have nothing to do with film again. Most academic historians are trained to research and deliver in text. Although many have been developing innovative websites, most teach students to critique and deliver only by writing. Film and history courses are popular, but they are more often taught in art history, communications and media studies than in history programs. Most historians have had nothing to do with film and television productions. Those who have are still licking their wounds – usually because their advice was unheeded. Film fictionalisations made them feel that their professional integrity had been cheaply compromised.

In late 2008, after a conference in his honour at the National Library, Professor Henry Reynolds was invited to respond. Reynolds writes bestsellers. His books are so readable that I admit to having raced through one of them in an airport bookshop. Yet, reflecting back on a brilliant and highly influential career that framed significant national debates, he regretted not being more involved with television. He had been a key speaker in various documentaries, including *Frontier*, the 1997 television documentary inspired by his work. But he had not been an initiator, or a maker. Reynolds, with his clear agenda of getting a message to a wide audience, had been struck by the revelation that even a badly rating television program could attract an audience beyond the reach of all his books combined.

Australian history is recognised as an area of national importance. Visiting overseas academics are amazed to see Australian historians being quoted on the front pages of our newspapers. Once upon a time, historians loved 'debates'. Over the last decade, history has been framed as a more adversarial, violent combat. Our historians are now warfatigued. When John Howard launched the National Museum of Australia – the only 'big thing' to come from the Centenary of Australia in 2001 – his pained expression said it all. At stake was the nation's identity. 'Howard's war' deteriorated from a gentlemanly game to a pie-throwing competition. As the 'war' dragged on, it was waged over the long-dried ink of aging footnotes. Its protagonists almost forgot that there might be Aboriginal people alive and willing to comment on the legacies of frontier violence. The media often seemed unaware of Aboriginal historians in the academy. As footnote fetishism reached its climax, the public switched channels and the 'history wars' were taken off prime time.

The peace did not last long. A more literary, and more politely conducted, 'war' quickly erupted – this time over genre rather than political intent: the relationship between history and fiction. Kate Grenville had paddled down the *Secret River* (Text, 2007) to 'discover' that novelists could write better history than historians. After the elegant twirls of *Dancing with Strangers* (Text, 2003), Inga Clendinnen stepped on to the dance floor. This debate is not new; novelists often claim to have 'discovered' documents historians have already used, and to be the only ones who can make history come alive. A book by Ann Curthoys and John Docker, *Is History Fiction?* (UNSW Press, 2004), exposes the long dynamic story of narrative and history – from Herodotus to the Smithsonian Institution's Enola Gay exhibition and the recent 'wars'.

A lot of historians use fiction to teach history, for books can spark interest in reluctant readers, and explore feeling, emotion and intimate relationships often not backed by archival evidence. Kate Grenville's *Joan Makes History* (UQP, 1988) was brilliant in the way she imaginatively recreated female perspectives during Australia's convict era. Similarly, historical films are often used in teaching.

Using drama, character, colour and evocation of sound, novelists and filmmakers can appeal to many senses. The late Greg Dening thought historians could too, by inviting them to explore the theatrical nature of historical writing as embodied performance. Historians should be reflexive, delve deep, and transcend the ordinary; they should excite, perform and 'fly'. The best historical ideas and interpretation will be based on careful research, innovative analysis and good writing. As a profession, however, historians may need to learn to fly with new equipment. To some historians, non-text media is viewed suspiciously – as something with glitter and excitement, but as ephemeral as fireworks. Younger historians are more interested, but they will need to have a lot of energy to have an impact on the history delivery required for film and television.

The blockbuster movie *Australia* was touted as an opportunity for Australians to find out about our history. A Tourism Australia poll revealed that many Australians did not know that Japan attacked Darwin during World War II. Many believed that the Japanese had attacked Sydney, while 80 per cent of those surveyed thought more bombs fell on Pearl Harbor than Darwin. Northern Territory Minister Marion Scrygmour had educational hopes: 'The film will lift the curtain for many Australians, particularly those from younger generations, on this important moment in our nation's history.' Tourism Australia's marketing promised self-learning for an international audience: 'Lose yourself in the movie. Find yourself in the country.' The unpleasant 'Pom' Lady Sarah Ashley is supposedly 'transformed through a combination of the incredible beauty of the Australian landscape and the Australian people'. In this, Lady Ashley becomes slightly 'Aboriginal' and the land becomes truly her own; 'our' country, as the King proclaims.

As the movie mixes political sincerity with tongue-in-cheek, the Wild West with 'Down Under' Crikey! cartoonishness, it is easy to be cynical. *Australia* makes some strained efforts to avoid cultural insensitivity, but I loved the feisty horsemanship of the female drovers, the stampede, the cinematic and boyish magic that stopped the beasts in their tracks, and the non-English speaking power of David Gulpilil's enigmatic King. Perhaps the movie's huge box office and the pulling power of sexy Hugh Jackman and accomplished Nicole Kidman have increased Australia's northern exposure and alerted people to the fact that we have a history. Movies can be powerful – even the primary purveyors of history education. While you don't go to a Hollywood-style movie and expect historical accuracy, *Australia* fused the real and the unreal in a fashion that will further confuse Australians.

As well as the official hype, the film creates its own historical credentials. Bringing the child removal policy and the Japanese attacks of World War II together, it opens with 'factual' newsreel style captions and footage. *Australia* is book-ended with reference to factual policy and the reassuring statement that the Prime Minister, Kevin Rudd, had 'offered an apology' to the stolen generations. The lead boy went back to Arnhem Land. Kevin apologised. History finishes. The difficult, complex questions are omitted.

In the fictionalised *Australia*, the Japanese targeted 'Mission Island', the kind of island 'half-caste' home to which Nana Fejo and others mentioned in Rudd's apology speech were sent. Residents of Melville and Bathurst Island sighted the bombers overhead, and Father John McGrath fruitlessly radioed Darwin. Both islands had missions for children of mixed descent who were not evacuated until after the bombing. Japanese Zeros dived on Bathurst Island and hit it with machine-gun fire, but only Hagime Toyoshima landed – when he crashed on Melville Island on his return journey. Tiwi man Mattias Ngapiatilawai captured him and Toyoshima became the first Japanese prisoner of war on Australian soil.

Luhrman opted to make the goodies and baddies clear-cut. The Japanese only appear as enemy soldiers, not the pearl divers, fishermen and skilled boatmen who were living in and around Darwin. In the late 1930s, about a hundred and fifty Japanese-owned pearling vessels worked around Bathurst and Melville Islands, and the men had children with Aboriginal women. In the movie, the missions, police and government were baddies because they collaborated to steal children; the Japanese landed and tried to kill the stolen kids. Fortunately for Japan's reputation, they did not kill the young Aboriginal star or Hugh Jackman.

Some Indigenous leaders have approved *Australia*'s rendition of the stolen children history. Kathy Mills (nee McGinness), long-time activist for Territorians of mixed descent, went to the Darwin premiere. She really liked it, and felt that, although it was obviously fiction, it captured the essence of the child removal story. Marcia Langton celebrated the film while Germaine Greer was appalled. Many of my friends liked it a lot.

Most troubling to me was the heterosexual white couple ennobled by their willingness to take on an Aboriginal child. Celibate missionaries? Stay away. Glamorous romantics? Don't let the government stop you. After their many ordeals, the couple finally gain the reward of parenting an extremely cute, clever and musical child. Sexual tension between the main actors, wistful looks and emotive music build the thrilling excitement of screen romance. Once achieved, it is as if the racism-crossing past love of the bronzed Drover and the pure white love of the barren Lady Ashley exonerate them both from the 'child stealer' label.

On first viewing, I was quite impressed that some of the settings and characterisations seemed historically based. The Drover's life story was a little like Bill Harney's. Bruce Spence's government man was well cast as the awkward-looking Chief Protector of Aborigines Cecil Cook. They must have employed a historical adviser, I reasoned, or some kind of archival researcher who did their homework well. In order to find out, I conscientiously read *Australia*'s voluminous and commendably egalitarian rolling credits. But I could see no mention of a historian or historical adviser. I spotted an Indigenous liaison officer, an Indigenous costume advisor, but no historian. Then, on the fuzziest roll, I finally saw the small 'inspired by' acknowledgment to Xavier Herbert's *Poor Fellow My Country* (Collins, 1975). With this, my assumptions about a historical adviser collapsed. Now the film's 'historicity' made sense; Herbert's 'historical novel' provided a prefabricated northern history with a cast of 'factional' characters and multi-sensory moments that traversed World War II. After all, fiction writers write histories better.

The origins of several key characters, as well as Herbert's pre-painted 'historical backdrop', can be found in this novel. Herbert's depiction of the war was closer to fact than the film. Herbert sought advice on useful books on Aboriginal legends, finding out about the Rainbow Serpent from Baldwin Spencer's writings on the Arrente. Ever since, hybrid myths of serpentry have circuitously permeated contemporary popular culture.

Drawing on fiction for a dramatic film may well be superior to using a history book or an expert. We might get a good movie out of a good novel, but not good history. Imagine the eye-opening educational potential of a well-researched documentary or a docu-drama telling the story of Darwin and Bathurst Island's actual war. This might include how Aboriginal people, who in these parts often spoke some Japanese, responded when Japanese pilots parachuted in desperation onto their land.

Some people have tried to move Australian historians along. Bob Carr tried to bring filmmakers and historians together and also encouraged documentaries with prizes. Carr invited archival doco-maker Ken Burns to Sydney, and his New South Wales Premier's History Prizes included an audio-visual category. The prime minister's history prize also invites audio-visual entries. The rules do not require a historian to be involved.

When she was head of television at the ABC, Sandra Levy initiated a major push to connect with leading historians to scope ideas for television. With proven public demand for historical themes, including archaeological digs and historical 'reality TV' shows such as *The 1940s House*, a series of meetings brought together some of the most innovative historians around the country. The Humanities Research Centre's Iain McCalman was enthusiastic and started to think of broader ways that humanities scholars might engage with media, film and digital media experts. The Council of Humanities, Arts and Social Sciences was to move this forward, but has not yet made the anticipated headway in building bridges between academics and screen industry.

One such history effort was *Rewind*, a magazine-show with 'history detectives' pretending to single-handedly 'discover' new facts about history. SBS followed with Hilton Cordell's *The Colony*, a reality-TV series that threw people into 'first settler' mode. Unusually for Australian television producers, they worked closely with historians at all stages of production and took what they had to say seriously. And now we see the highly successful (celebrity) family history formula of *Who Do You Think You Are?* Alex West, chief executive of Screen Australia, arrived fresh from producing this series for British television. *Constructing Australia* was a prize-winning Film Australia initiative with Richard Evans in which West worked collaboratively with senior historian Dr John Hirst.

Hirst has served as a Board Member for Film Australia (now Screen Australia), as well as on the Council of the multimedia oriented National Museum of Australia. Leading film history expert Professor Jill Matthews sits on the Board of the National Film and Sound Archive. The new CEO of the National Film and Sound Archive, Darryl McIntyre, has a doctorate in history. While all this seems promising, historians in the academy are not driving what television buys as history. Thinking nobody wants to hear them, they are politely staying away. At the 2005 Film Australia 'Making History' workshop, Hirst called for historians to take on film as a medium: 'I don't think that the academy is the enemy of this project. I think the academy can contribute a lot to it. More than that, film might find new ways of exploring our history. It is a hard history to penetrate and I don't think the historians in their books can say they've said all that has to be said.' Tessa Morris-Suzuki's *The Past Within Us: Media, Memory, History* (Verso, 2005) argues that students of history need to understand film and how its 'rolling narrative of moving images' creates emotional impacts and shapes 'shared feelings of identification'. They also need to understand how different media co-exist and interact with each other. Historians in the academy need to be better educated viewers and collaborators.

Peter Weir's historical adviser for *Gallipoli,* Bill Gammage, objected to the casting of Mel Gibson because his height would have precluded him from the army. While height presents little problem in filmed warfare, Gammage was correct to be concerned about the accuracy of the landings and other issues. He lamented that his big *Gallipoli* credit as 'Historical Adviser' was ludicrous, as he only advised on the biscuit tins; another version has it as the bootlaces. Gammage's tale has become a fable where film becomes the big bad wolf.

Historians can certainly offer more than the 'facts'. Their trade encompasses sophisticated research, insightful historical conceptualisation and path-breaking interpretation. Historians get frustrated that producers prefer simplistic, 'true' or 'false' style storylines – for example, 'Is this really Ned Kelly's skull?' – rather than the more expansive, revealing historical questions. Scripts are inclined towards clichés rather than fresh ways of seeing.

This doesn't mean that historians are allergic to projects involving new media, including participation media. A number are making history accessible via digital history sites, developing valuable by-products of their archival research. So why can't this happen in the film industry, especially historical documentaries?

Some historians and numerous cultural theorists are critiquing film and teaching about the place of history in film. But relatively few Australian historians are actually involved in *making* them. Late in 2008, a Film and History Association conference was held at the University of Otago called 'Remapping Cinema, Remaking History'. At least a hundred and fifty papers were presented, but only three people, including myself, offered papers on films they were making. Rather than being integrated into relevant topic themes, we were shunted into a panel entitled: 'Makers Comment on Their Practice'. Like curiosities at a large zoo, we had been placed in the special exhibit category.

As a profession, Australian historians are humble about what they can offer in the field of public history generally. There are some boundary crossers, including Ned Kelly expert Ian Jones. Producer and director Andrew Pike of Ronin Films, with whom I am working on several film projects, is an accomplished historian. Indigenous filmmaker/historian Frances Peters-Little and filmmaker Rachel Perkins bring a strong historical knowledge to Indigenous history. ABC radio history programs such as *Hindsight* and *Rearview* have done exceptionally well, using highly trained historians as producers who in turn draw upon the best expertise to produce entertaining and informative programs. A promising development is that some students are now incorporating film in historical PhDs – albeit in interdisciplinary departments.

When I was in first-year university, my cousin Michael Hasson enrolled me in a filmmaking course in Brisbane; the technology was complicated and I let him hold the camera. Ten years ago, ethnographic filmmaker David MacDougall told me everyone could learn how to make a film, but I still wasn't ready to jump in. Clearly, DIY participation is the way ahead. In their writings on history and film, both Paul Smith and Charles Geshekter argue that if historians wish to avoid frustration and disappointment, they must know enough to be their 'own producer'; historians should be identifying and evaluating not just the text, but all the components of the visual and aural message.

The screen industry could adopt best practice models to enable more of this to happen. 'Factual filmmakers' such as Michael Cordell routinely ask their researchers to consult with the top historians, but others are openly disparaging. Nial Fulton, producer of the Irish-Australian cannibal historical drama *The Last Confession of Alexander Pearce,* which he dubbed a 'factual drama', commented: 'It's just a cracking story and I didn't have to hire people with big beards to tell me all the difficult stuff.'

Historians have appallingly little impact in shaping the history content on our screens. Australia has received a lot of criticism for its taxpayer funding, but the whole industry is heavily subsidised, as are the public broadcasters buying Australian history content. Yet, in all the boxes that must be ticked for film funding, there is no requirement for 'factual' or historical filmmakers to engage a historian. Nonetheless, many historical docos are touted as 'educational', 'realistic', 'historically accurate' or 'based on a true story'. Despite the government subsidies, there is no quality control on 'history'. Medical shows employ medical specialists; police dramas employ psychologists and forensic experts. Kids learn history from film and television, yet there is no quality assurance for historical content and no incentives to enhance quality. Expertise, knowledge, the latest research breakthroughs are not getting into Australian history films – dramatic or factual. Except as talking heads, the historians undertaking the latest research are rarely consulted. This reveals an arrogant undervaluing of historical expertise, and raises serious questions of quality control over public spending.

The 2020 Summit of 2008 held the promise of a more innovative Australia that would break down the old binaries. A cloud lifted, and academics and industry experts were meeting for an exchange of national benefit. Now the recession is darkening the skies, the days ahead can be a building time for culture, not just for skyscrapers.

Kim Carr's portfolio as Minister for Innovation and Research sounded forward thinking and holistic. Its *Venturous Australia, the National Innovation System* report recommended 'knowledge connection', and a strategy that aimed: 'To build concentrations of excellence, encourage collaboration and achieve better dissemination of knowledge', including building capacity for research organisations to 'partner with each other'. Current ministerial portfolio divisions don't help. University history comes under both Kim Carr and Julia Gillard as Minister for Education while film funding is under Peter Garrett's Arts umbrella. History is 'research'; film is 'arts/creative arts'. Screen is apparently not research, so what can be done?

While innovation involves unusual match-making and risk-taking, key funding bodies like the Australian Research Council and quality review bodies readily become hostages to the most conventional training, measuring and gate-keeping. Except for the 'creative arts', Excellence in Research in Australia has made stifling assumptions that 'quality' humanities research products are best ranked by the stiffest text formats.

By ensuring that the knowledge creators in the humanities and social sciences are linked with the creative arts industries, the power and punch of creativity can be enhanced. Until this happens, we are left behind. Academics and the creative arts people are forced into separate spheres with few incentives to encourage collaboration.

If the Rudd government is serious about education, history and innovation, it needs a new script for its funding and qualitative mechanisms. Screen Australia's funding guidelines are inward-looking; they repeatedly emphasise 'screen professionals' and the 'screen industry', mentioning nothing about pairing with knowledgeable experts in the humanities or elsewhere to enhance content, concept development and innovation. The Australian Research Council funds research in the history discipline, but not the production of history in diverse formats. If its rules won't allow, some kind of 'Screen History Making Grant' scheme should be developed under somebody else's umbrella. After all, we are talking about a national history problem.

In the US, filmmakers can apply for funding to make historical films. Grant approval requires carefully prepared assessments from leading university-based historians. The National Endowment for the Humanities then gives out tiered grants for historical documentaries: smaller grants of up to US$80,000 for planning and scripting, and large grants up to US$700,000 for production. This provides an excellent funding stream plus an imprimatur of educational quality that is valuable to teachers. Worthiness can clash with entertainment, but this provides a national system for educational history films, thus enabling strong expert collaborations and quality content.

Digital humanities grants in the US have similarly brought together academic and technical expertise, knowledge and innovation. While it's difficult to spot in the documents, the Australian Academy of Humanities' John Byron reports some policy progress in this direction. American digital humanities grants encourage a whole variety of digital delivery modes, but they insist that the outcomes 'should rest on *sound humanities scholarship* and *enhance the project's humanities content* for the general public in ways that take unique advantage of the proposed format'.

We need *genuine* history products to 'construct Australia' for television and film.

Australian universities produce cutting-edge historical research, yet there is a troublesome gap between knowledge creation and dissemination. We should be looking to how to share expert knowledge to much better effect. If historians must fight another 'war', I suggest it should be over what passes for history on Australian film and television. To get started, both historians and filmmakers might get together to develop a series of pilot projects of national significance and of high research, innovation, entertainment and historical quality. This would be a great national infrastructure project: a jobs boost and a knowledge boost.

In my view, there is no need for filmmakers to cannibalise history. Big beards are irrelevant. Historians should not be allowed to make television boring, or pedantic. Rather than being at war with the camera, historians need to learn *what* to shoot, and *how* it should be shot. History experts and screen experts could learn to collaborate. If they don't, Australia's history films will always be fiction. ■

References available at www.griffithreview.com

Ann McGrath is Professor of History at the Australian National University and head of the history program in the Research School of Social Sciences.

Essay:

From an unconscious state

Author:

Maria Tumarkin

Image: Roots / Photographer: Johan Joubert / Image courtesy of the artist / www.redbubble.com/people/mugsy

From an unconscious state

Something is missing from the debates about teaching history in Australian schools, even though their explosive, raw and at times distinctly personal quality must surely be a good sign. If we are not prepared to shout and bang on tables over history and kids, then surely we are, in those all-knowing words of Tom Waits, 'pulling on trouble's braids'.

Yet just like school history curriculum itself, the debates about teaching history have become tedious. On one hand, we have those who believe in history as a tool of nation building and civic pride and who decry agenda-driven, ideologically coloured, dogmatic history, infected, in their minds, with a singular contempt for the facts. The counter-argument, of course (the one I resent having to subscribe to because it seems so bleedingly obvious) is that teaching history should essentially be about developing historical consciousness. It should be about giving kids the all-important skills of analysis, critical reflection and tolerance for difference – the skills they need, first and foremost, to live good and engaged lives in the present. Untill recently I had nothing to add to these debates, except that nagging feeling that something central was consistently overlooked in them. Then, in October 2008, while on a trip in Russia, I met with several historians working at Memorial, the international historical and human rights society with active branches right across the country. It was at that point, far away from the Australian goldfields, that I had my very own Eureka moment.

Since 1999, Memorial has been running a highly successful national competition of history research papers for high school students. For the past seven years, this competition has been part of EUSTORY – a European network of twenty countries, which hold regular non-governmental history competitions. In Australia, we have something of this ilk – the National History Challenge for high school students in Years 9 to 12. Just like its European counterpart, the History Challenge emphasises the research-based approach to history and an active engagement with primary sources, yet there is a profound gulf between the philosophy and the real-world effects of these two initiatives. Perhaps most critically, the EUSTORY's objective is not simply to get students interested in history, but to foster historical awareness as a powerful tool of civic engagement and as an antidote to the selective, ideologically driven and cynical uses of history in the public sphere. In Australia, this all-important emphasis on civic participation through independent historical research is completely lacking. In Russia, the student papers have been regularly published in the independent media not in the name of charity or of the increasingly untenable dream of democracy but because many of them are original, powerful and good. By now

I have read over a hundred of them and I am filled with awe. The astonishing thing is not simply that today's fourteen- or sixteen-year-olds are capable of thinking and writing like this, but that the forty- and fifty-year-olds in charge of this competition have managed to get it so right.

The fundamental idea is for teenagers to engage with their local history – the story, usually never told fully, of their family, their street or their town. Many entries are sparked by children coming across a monument to god-knows-who, by stepping accidentally on a grave in a neglected cemetery (and recoiling in horror), or discovering that not that long ago the church everyone goes to was used as a horse stable or a wheat barn. The competition's focus is squarely on private, everyday lives and the way they have been lived through the two world wars, mass repressions and deportations, the wholesale destruction of the Russian village, famines, poverty and just about every imaginable calamity that could be thrown at human beings.

In the introduction to her paper, Darya Tkacheva – a Year 7 student from the city of Astrakhan and one of the competition's youngest participants – writes, 'I cannot agree with those adults who say, "You are too young to get involved with this. Wait till you are older." But who can really determine when it is too early or too late? I keep on hearing the argument – children should not be allowed to rummage through this stuff. And perhaps we do not always understand all of the processes that took place in our country but we are more than capable of letting the lives of other people through ourselves and of figuring out what is just and what is not.'

To let the lives of others through ourselves – an expression that does not translate well into English, presupposes not merely a quick sprint in someone else's shoes. Instead, you open yourself up to the fate of other people so that they are no longer the moth-bitten exhibits in the museum of history but human beings whose suffering will hurt you, whose powerlessness in the face of injustice and indifference will enrage you and whose heartbreaking choices will feel, for a moment, like your own. It is essential that by letting these people and their stories through you, you consent to being changed by them. 'What can the story I tell you now add to "Archipelago Gulag"', writes Polina Reutova from the town of Perm, but 'coming across this story "added" something to me if you understand what I am saying.' If we don't, Polina, we are the fools, for this unquantifiable, transformative something you describe with such gentleness is precisely the historical consciousness that we should be desperate to foster in our kids.

Unsurprisingly, Memorial research papers do not look anything like essays or extended homework assignments. The majority of them are serious and original pieces of historical reflection and analysis that engage with the undocumented, the unknown or the largely forgotten, that venture into places well off the map of official historiography. As such, they are small but all-important acts of defiance in a country where the clock is clearly ticking on any independent historical research. All across Russia, both regional and state archives, which started opening up in the late 1980s, are becoming more and more unwelcoming to historians. The access to many historical documents is disappearing in front of researchers' very eyes. Independent historical organisations, such as Memorial, concerned with the preservation and transmission of historical memory, are raided, kept under constant surveillance and repeatedly threatened. As to history curriculum at schools, it finds itself, tragically but by no means unexpectedly, at the vanguard of the government-led 'rehabilitation' of the Soviet regime and, most cynically, of the figure of Stalin. At the same time, in various regional centres, government-run history essay competitions use the name of the Memorial initiative in the attempt to deceive school kids and their teachers and to displace the Memorial competition altogether. In keeping with the Putin-Medvedev revisionist stance, their agenda is diametrically opposed to that of Memorial. The fake competitions are peddling the patriotic Soviet history complete with visionary leaders, great victories and unprecedented achievements. The fate of millions of people shot, made to rot in camps, displaced and exiled as well as of their families are yet again presented as the inevitable 'excesses' of the country grappling with enormous challenges of bloody wars and swift industrialisation.

'Our saving grace,' says Irina Sherbakova, a well-known historian and the competition's organiser, 'is the work we do with teachers and the focus on family history.' Family history, as uncovered and documented by the new generation of today's adolescents, may just be the most powerful antidote to the current falsification and fabrication of historical narratives, even when it comes to the event central to the revisionist push – World War II. Known as the Great Patriotic War, World War II is widely regarded as the one resounding victory in a century of senseless suffering – if you are prepared to disregard its cost, of course. The cost was astronomical – twenty million is the official number of lives lost, close to thirty million is what more recent estimates suggest. Yet the memory of the war is consistently being substituted with the memory of the victory as a way of legitimating the figure of Stalin and the seven decades of the Soviet regime more broadly. Personal histories of the war act as a counterforce to this born-again patriotism because they essentially humanise the war. Gradually, organically, we see in students' papers pathos and zealotry replaced with empathy and understanding.

This is not say that family history and oral history in general should be seen as some kind of pure, revolutionary force that speaks truth to power, even if in a little person's voice. There is little purity in people's memories – they are not only selective and deeply flawed but also particularly sensitive to societal pressures and fear. Sometimes people unconsciously replace their own experiences with newspaper headlines. Sometimes, equally unconsciously, they do the opposite, assimilating things they have read or heard about as their own experiences. Sometimes (actually quite often) they struggle to speak in their own voice, slipping into the endlessly repeated idioms and incantations. And yet in today's Russia, where there are virtually no memorials or plaques to the millions who died in Gulags, where so many of the dead have simply been thrown into the ground like dogs, people's memory remains the most precious currency. 'What could people take in memory of their past,' writes Sherbakova, 'what could they save and keep, these special deportees, Gulag prisoners, evacuees and those who were bombed or forcefully taken to Germany? … What family relics are kept in millions of Russian families that had "24 hours to pack" and were shipped to Siberia, what valuables? Whatever tiny little bits and pieces, a letter here and a scarf there, what remains first and foremost is memory alone.'

Today's adolescents in Russia are the last generation still able to encounter and speak to the living witnesses and carriers of the memory of Lenin's and Stalin's legacy. And for many of these witnesses, their moment of truth has finally arrived. As they near the end of their lives, finally, their need to share stories and documents is stronger than their fear, the trauma of re-immersing themselves in the past and their deep reluctance to speak. These are the last conversations of this kind and they carry a profound significance. Memorial receives more than three thousand entries each year. In 2007–08, for instance, students from twelve hundred towns and villages took part in the competition. Organisers have been surprised not only by the success of the competition but also by the largely regional nature of the entries received. The expectation was that children from Moscow and St Petersburg would dominate the competition. In reality, most of the entries came from regional centres, small towns and villages. Interestingly, the same pattern is replicated in most countries involved in EUSTORY. The further away you get from metropolises, the more pronounced, it seems, is the hunger of children for history.

Ekaterina Remezova, a Year 11 student from the Russian town of Vladimir, was able to reconstruct the fate of her family on the basis of extensive conversations with her grandmother and the fragmented but unexpectedly fertile family archives.

'The only task I have set myself,' she writes in the introduction to her work, 'is to attempt to tell about those who, having unwillingly been turned into toys in the enormous and cruel social experiment, were simply human beings desperate to make a life for themselves, desperate simply to survive, in those years.' Reasonably prosperous merchants before the 1917 Revolution, Ekaterina's family endured a swift confiscation of their business and property under the newly-formed Soviet regime and the sudden homelessness that came with it. And then, ever so swiftly, there came hardships, relocation in search of livelihood, the arrest of her great-grandfather on the fabricated charges of the anti-Soviet activities, camps and, perhaps most poignantly, the daily struggles endured by the family left behind.

The most powerful part of Ekaterina's paper describes the decision of her great-grandmother, Valentina Mikhailovna, to divorce her repressed husband in a desperate attempt to keep herself and her baby daughter, Ekaterina's grandmother, alive. 'It took a very long time for Valentina Mikhailovna,' writes Ekaterina, 'to finally go ahead with the divorce, even though it was fictitious. She struggled because of her upbringing, and because the marriage was not only listed in the Marriage Registry but also consecrated in a church.' For a long time Valentina Mikhailovna could not forego the oath she gave to stand by her husband in sickness and in health. Yet it was her husband who, before being taken away, begged Valentina to divorce him in the name of their young daughter. This is what Ekaterina Remezova writes about her great-grandmother: 'Alone, with a tiny child, without a roof over their heads, with no money or work, humiliated and cornered by circumstances, she had no choice but to file for divorce.' This level of understanding and compassion is humbling. To get inside the nightmare faced by your great-grandmother, to reconstruct it so vividly, to know that it, in all its poisonous, soul-destroying power, was replicated in the lives of millions of wives and children of the enemies of the people – this is what the emphasis not merely on teaching history, but on developing historical consciousness, can produce.

What happened is really simple. A grandmother and granddaughter talked like they had never talked before. A grandmother said things she had never said before – fundamentally important things. A family history that so easily (with the passing of the grandmother) could have remained filled with shadows and ghosts was rescued from the oblivion. The chain of transmission remained unbroken. Ekaterina is now the guardian of her family memory.

These are the words of Polina Gerasimenko, a Year 10 student from the town of Ulyanovsk: 'While my eighty-three-year-old grandmother is still alive, while her children who know so much about their parents and grandparents are alive too, while there are things that testify to the past, I believe it is important to engage with that past so that my children and grandchildren can draw the strength of spirit and character from the generations before them.' Polina's is a beautifully rendered description of memory transmission – it is not merely information that is traveling from one generation to another, but strength of spirit and character.

There is no question that history should foster skills of critical and compassionate reflection and analysis. But it is not enough to get students to pull documents apart and question the 'received wisdom'. The Memorial competition lets us peek into what happens when kids step into memory's circle, when they get to connect with history that is both personal and heartbreaking. We watch them become crushed by the weight of this history and then struggle to rebuild themselves and their faith in the world. We watch them fight to save their souls from cynicism or apathy. And every time they win, we witness a small miracle. There is a great deal of talk about the importance of turning Australian schoolchildren into active, empowered participants. And this emphasis should, of course, be welcomed, except that much of the time it sounds like an affectation. 'Come on, kids, let's play history detectives, let's get down and dirty with primary sources.' Pretending that the opinions of these children matter apparently helps achieve better educational outcomes. There is nothing wrong with this concept, in theory. Yet the Memorial competition shows us what can happen when we stop pretending, when we start taking children and their opinions seriously and when we finally stop serving them diluted history.

Three Year 11 students from the village of El'niki in the Russian region of Mordovia came across two photographs of the man who, in the early decades of the twentieth century, had been their village priest and schoolteacher. 'In the first photograph,' they write, 'we can see a handsome, confident village teacher Vasiliy Ivanovich Kashin. His gaze is strict and composed. Thick hair is neatly cut and smoothly combed back … his face is smooth, without wrinkles. It is easy to think that a long and interesting life awaits this man in the photograph.' The second photograph is taken in 1930 after Kashin's arrest. In this photograph is 'a real old man: bags under his eyes, wrinkly face, hair hanging like icicles, uncombed grey beard. His gaze is dreary and anxious. He is wearing a peasant undergarment. His shoulders are slumped.'

This once proud, strong, self-possessed man has been totally defeated. How? Why? The three students were drawn into analysing documents, letters and eyewitness accounts of relatives and friends all in order to understand why 'a young, strong man has come to the end of his life in such a terrifying way'. At the end of the research, they organised a family reunion in their village for the relatives of Vasiliy. Scattered across Russia, many of them met for the first time with some previously unaware of each other's existence. Such an occurrence is not a rare outcome for the Memorial student papers. A significant proportion end up creating tangible effects in the real world. Some lead to the erection of memorials and plaques in small towns and villages, while others produce new historical exhibitions for the general public and occasionally force the pay-out of government compensation or the reburial of human remains.

A few years ago in the small town of Kotlas in the Arkhangelsk region, routine building works uncovered human bones and remains. The local adults were, of course, less than impressed but a lifetime of dissatisfied passivity meant they simply waited for authorities to do something about it. Meanwhile a group of high school students decided to take matters in their own hands and started collecting the scattered bones, which were being even further destroyed by passing cars. The adults asked, 'Aren't you scared to collect human bones?' The kids replied, 'We are not scared to collect bones, we are scared to walk on them.' The bone-collectors from Year 9 felt the need to find out who the bones belonged to and how they had come to be completely forgotten. And so their research paper was born. The bit of road where the bones were accidentally unearthed used to belong to a factory before being bought by a private company. But much earlier, in the 1940s, it had been a makeshift cemetery, the final resting place for many prisoners from the nearby corrective labour camps and special settlements who were brought in to build a bridge over a river. The fatality rate at the construction site was extremely high due to food shortages, harsh physical conditions, disease and lack of medication, and constant industrial accidents. The dead were buried in trenches right alongside the site. In the 1950s when the makeshift cemetery was about to be swallowed up by a new industrial site, the residents of Kotlas were given the opportunity to re-bury their relatives. It was an unabashedly cynical offer since Gulag prisoners were never local. The graves were violated, built over and finally forgotten. As a result of the students' research, the remains were re-buried and an exhibition about the history of the bridge and its construction was put together by the students themselves. This is how the local chapter of the little-known history of the mass use of Gulag labour made its way into the psyche of the little town of Kotlas. This is how children succeeded in stirring and awakening adult memory.

Timur Gaisin and Maksim Nazarov are students of the Magnitogorsk Technical College who went looking for information about a group of former students from their college who were arrested in the 1930s and sentenced to the labour camps. Initially Timur and Maksim turned to the local archives, where even a quick peek revealed countless innocent lives ripped to shreds on the basis of cynically fabricated cases. Even at this early point the boys wondered long and hard about whether it would be best to leave the sordid business of the past alone. But memory, they discovered, cannot be artificially contained. It cannot be shoved back into a box. 'It is there and that's it,' they write. For a couple of young men born in the cynical, history-for-hire era, to recognise historical memory as a kind of an uncontainable force, not simply a benign resource, is a profound discovery. 'We need to tell this terrible truth,' Timur and Maksim decided. Why? 'Because the evidence is hidden behind the steel frames of the archives. Nothing can be checked out. Nothing can be proven.'

In the 1930s, Magnitogorsk was one of those young industrial Soviet cities that could never meet its need for high-quality technical specialists. More and more technical colleges opened, churning out engineers, metallurgists and electricians. At Magnitogorsk Technical College, two of the students studying to meet the demand were Iosif Tkalich and his friend, who Timur and Maksim refer to only as 'G'. They were the same age but had markedly different characters. Iosif was modest and reserved, while G was extroverted and intent on becoming 'one of the guys'. Distinctly mediocre in his academic achievements, G was hungry to be noticed in all kinds of extra-curricular activities. Iosif, on the other hand, was one of the best students in his year. Unrivalled in his mastery of mathematics, he helped G with his studies. Fast-talking, always visible and on fire, G desperately wanted to lead, to be noticed and promoted. Yet it was the tongue-tied Iosif who was invariably singled out by his peers for various leadership positions.

G ended up denouncing Iosif. In those years it did not take much so he came up with some wild anti-Soviet activity and soon Iosif was arrested and sentenced to years of hard labour. Iosif managed to survive the labour camps but spent the rest of his life fighting against the prejudice encountered at every step by the 'former' enemies of the people. He never had a 'normal' life and was never even able to start a family. As to G, he did finish college but, lacking in technical expertise and a general level of education, never became even a mediocre specialist. Instead, as Timur and Maksim discovered, he spent the rest of his life being a Party activist. He fought in World War II before being wounded. He went on to sit on committees, distribute funds and tirelessly carry out the 'ideological' work. And so it seemed that he did become 'one of the guys' after all. 'Who knows if he remembered the past,' write Timur and Maksim, 'especially since it is unlikely that anyone at his factory knew anything about what he had done. But he was deeply mistaken if he believed that the distant past had sunk into oblivion and no one could now accuse him of anything.'

I read and marvel at the boys' contempt for G. We are quick to denounce contempt, but I am not so sure we should. Not with these boys. They earned it. They did the work. Besides, if we are to explain to kids how totalitarianism works, how dictatorships are built and sustained, they need to be able to smell guys like G, men who represent that grey army of functionaries and bureaucrats who always claim to just 'follow orders'. As an ageing man, Iosif wrote a letter to G telling him of his life after the arrest. Timur and Maksim chose, very wisely, to include the full text of the letter in their research paper. Profoundly dignified and clear-sighted, the letter lacks both pathos and any lust for revenge. It is – and this fact is not lost on the boys by any means – a remarkable historical document, which they have brought to light.

From what textbook could Timur and Maksim have learned so vividly that, in Stalin's Soviet Union, a single denunciation, no matter how unsubstantiated or fantastical, could provide sufficient grounds for arrest, camp internment, a broken life, even death? What better story to make them see that not everyone behaved in the same way and that especially in the 1930s a certain category of people used the machinery of the state terror to settle their personal scores? A neighbour from a communal flat wanted an extra room. A scorned lover wanted revenge. Mediocrity wanted brilliance squashed. One moment of human weakness, parasitism or jealousy held enormous consequences. By painstakingly piecing together the story of Iosif and G, Timur and Maksim have come to see that under Stalin, petty, gutless functionaries like G had the upper hand until most of them too were squashed by the machine. Perhaps it can be argued that the Stalinist society cloned Gs en masse. Yet, no matter how hard the system tried to turn people into embittered lone wolves interested only in their own survival, it did not succeed. In the end, G was hardly an exception, but neither was Iosif.

Historians speak of the labour of memory or memory-work. Remembering, they say, is not some recreational pastime. It is hard, confronting work. In the end, every generation, every person has to make a conscious choice about whether or not to take on this arduous task. I suggest that we begin to speak of 'tolerance-work' because tolerance is not a starting point, handed to kids in a series of sexy slogans, but a destination. Real tolerance cannot be arrived at without a bitter struggle against our own and our peers' urge to condemn, judge, dismiss or mythologise all that is different from us, including the experiences of previous generations. The promotion of easy, ersatz tolerance is antithetical to the development of genuine historical consciousness. This thoughtless, ready-made kind of tolerance is little more than a glorified extension of ignorance as bliss. Under its guise, we are teaching our kids the joys of complacency, of the great Australian 'middle of the road', the virtues of eyes wide shut.

Aleksey Evstratov, a Year 11 student from the town of Borisoglebsk in the Voronezh Region writes about the shock of coming across his town's Jewish history. A non-Jew in a small Russian town in the country, where the Holocaust is largely forgotten, Aleksey travels a truly immense distance in reconstructing the fate of Borisoglebsk's Jewish community. 'For ten years I have been going to my school past a Jewish cemetery, paying no attention either to the condition it was in or to the barbaric behaviour and vandalism that had been taking place there virtually round the clock ... And only three months ago I found out that all the time I had, in the words of my teacher, been walking past the cemetery in "an unconscious state" ... Now I walk past it with a sense of unease and shame ...'

The cemetery lies neglected and vandalised. The graves are desecrated. Everywhere you look there are piles of rubbish and syringes and, of course, graffiti. Aleksey finds himself nursing a million whys. Why didn't someone stop him when he played 'war' in the cemetery? Why didn't someone throw him out of what must be considered a sacred place for all people? Why did the authorities ignore all the barbaric behaviour at the cemetery? Why do the Jews of his town, of whom there are around a hundred, allow this to happen to the final resting place of their people? Are they too walking around 'in an unconscious state'?

Ultimately, the Memorial competition is about children illuminating and beginning to counter this unconscious state, a state in which most of Russia now walks past its desecrated cemeteries. Yet to do so, they must first learn a fundamental fact about history. History passes through people's lives like a series of electrical currents – or, perhaps more aptly, electrical shocks. People's lives, in other words, are not merely shaped by history (the little 'pretend' word we like to use in Australian schools and universities), but are charged and convulsed with it. No matter how many decades have passed, this kind of history remains burning, radioactive. You engage with it at your own risk, yet by really engaging with it, you may just be able, tiny bit by tiny bit, to start changing the present.

In the seminar he gave last year at the University of Melbourne, one of the world's most distinguished and innovative contemporary historians, Dipesh Chakrabarty, raised the question, which (thankfully!) refuses to go away – 'In what sense and under what conditions can history be a public good?' Beyond political debates, beyond politics of representation, beyond blame and claims of victimhood and entitlement, there are ways in which historical awareness and knowledge must underpin any culture of genuine civic participation. This is precisely the philosophy behind the Memorial competition and behind the EUSTORY in general. And it really works. This is the idea that seems conspicuously absent from most of the debates about teaching history in Australian schools – the idea of Civic Participation or Engagement. Is it too much for us? ■

Maria Tumarkin is the author of *Traumascapes* (MUP, 2005) and *Courage* (MUP, 2007). Her essay 'Life in translation' appeared *Griffith REVIEW 19: Re-imagining Australia*

Memoir:
Welsh rarebit

Author:
Raymond Evans

Image: Police attacking union demonstration outside Brisbane Central Station on St Patrick's Day, March 17 1948. Source unknown.

Welsh rarebit

The past in maiming us, makes us. – Frank Bidart

On most days when I was very little I would be pushed in a pram past a massacre site on the way to my grandmother's house. Or perhaps it was the site of a stand-up battle. It is sometimes hard to tell with these things. The place was the Castle Inn, situated on the High Street in the slate-grey industrial town of Merthyr Tydfil, spread untidily along the Taff Valley, bordering the Brecon Beacons, the Vale of Glamorgan and the Black Domain, South Wales: vast coal deposits below ground and belching iron and steel works above.

Here, on June 3, 1831, soldiers of the 93rd Foot, the Argyll and Sutherland Highlanders had opened fire from the street and the upper windows of the Inn on a huge concourse of Welsh workers – 'ironstone miners, colliers, puddlers; women and shouting children'. The vast throng were demonstrating against unemployment, lowered wages (they were paid in tokens not money), the higher prices of the employers' truck-shops, ballooning debt, sequestered belongings, ongoing disfranchisement and semi-starvation. The mostly English coal owners and iron masters, who had come in from their opulent mansions and mock Tudor castles to collude that day, were meeting inside.

The demonstrators, seven to ten thousand strong, were grouped behind their banner – a cloth dyed red with calf's blood at Hirwaun some days before. It was the first defiant display of the Red Flag on British soil, held aloft that day by a certain William Williams. Beside it was raised a loaf of bread on a long, sharp stick. The crowd was chanting *'Caws gyda bara'*– Welsh for 'Cheese with the bread' – just before the soldiers opened fire. Welsh people have this talent for fine theatrics. There were few Ghandians in such a crowd. As the most enthusiastic of the physical force advocates among them went to work, trying to seize the soldiers' muskets with their bare hands, the troops continued firing and plying their bayonets. Hundreds of shots rang out and the High Street was littered with bodies. In the fracas, sixteen soldiers were injured – six seriously. But over a score of protesters were killed and more than seventy wounded: all that carnage in the narrow street that my pram bumped along more than a century later.

If you look for information on this conflict in *Cassell's Chronology of World History* or even *The Oxford Companion to British History* you will be disappointed. It is as though it never happened, even though more were killed here by British military than during the well-anthologised Peterloo Massacre near Manchester a dozen years earlier. In 1978, Welsh intellectual Raymond Williams suggests the Merthyr Rising is less well remembered than Peterloo or the transportation to Australia of the Tolpuddle Martyrs from Dorset in 1834 not just because the latter were English incidents and the former Welsh.

Those peaceably assembled at St Peter's Fields or quietly organising their trade union at Tolpuddle chanced their hand, it is true, but when the authorities struck, they did not fight back. Merthyr was different, for the bloody riot was just the start of it. It merely inflamed the workers there rather than subduing them. Over the next four days they contained the military and, using their seized guns and other weaponry, drove back or held down other detachments sent in to re-secure the town. The agitation had moved from reformist to insurrectionary. Raymond Williams calls it convulsive, for out of the struggle a united working-class consciousness was forged. Gwyn A. Williams, the historian of the Rising, observes that the defeats 'repeatedly inflicted by armed workers on regular and yeoman troops seem without precedent in the history of civil conflict in eighteenth and nineteenth century Britain … Not to mince words, the Merthyr Rising was a local attempt at revolution.'

So best to keep a lid on this one, I suppose. It might give plebeian readers ideas. The bold initiative was eventually quelled, the town retaken and the entire coalfields militarily occupied. By October, all resistance had been starved into submission. Twenty-eight activists were indicted and seven imprisoned, including a woman of sixty-two years. Five others were transported to New South Wales – four for life. One man, Richard Lewis (or *Dic Penderyn*) was executed for stabbing a soldier in the thigh, as an example to all belligerents. He was later found innocent of the charge. His statue stands in the centre of Merthyr Tydfil. He is so common a sight there that no one appears to think it odd that, whereas other town-squares normally commemorate statesmen and military leaders, this one remembers a hanged man – a martyr and, in the manner of his death, a working class hero. Being Welsh can take a lot of living up to.

These are the kind of origins that can creep into the blood. I was raised on the tale of *Dic Penderyn*; and several Evanses were also caught up in the Rising. There is also a vast hidden history here of shadowy night-riding vigilantes who, across several decades, attacked unscrupulous employers and their acolytes, 'scab' workers and toll-houses. There are innumerable anti-enclosure and anti-eviction disturbances as well as a long tradition of food riots and embryonic trade union organisation. Merthyr was the centre for Jacobin and Chartist activism in South Wales and in the mid-nineteenth century returned the Welsh pacifist and anti-slavery campaigner Henry Richard ('The Apostle of Peace'), an early advocate for a League of Nations, to the House of Commons.

Merthyr was then the largest population centre in Wales, and its huge, surrounding coalfields were an epicentre of the Industrial Revolution. Its nine iron and steel mills led the world's production of pig-iron – some 40 per cent of Britain's output. Thomas Carlyle and Lord Melbourne concurred that Merthyr was one of the most squalid and dangerous places on earth. Over three thousand miners were killed in these valleys in industrial accidents. Following the great coal strike of 1898, Merthyr's political representative was James Kier Hardie, the legendary socialist/pacifist leader. Sylvia Pankhurst wrote on his death that Hardie was 'the greatest human being of our time'.

Hardie died of a broken heart in 1915, my father would always say, crushed by the workers' enthusiastic acquiescence to the Great War. The wreath sent by the Queensland Labor Government of T.J. Ryan arrived too late for the funeral. On August 6, 1914, at Aberdare, south-west of Merthyr, Welsh jingoists drowned out his anti-war appeals with their raucous 'Rule Britannias', finally pouring boiling water on him from above as the meeting broke up in disorder. It was probably the last straw. Hardie's repudiation – and especially the boiling water – are remembered in my family as South Wales's day of shame.

The interwar years bring disaster to the Welsh valleys and my parents are raised in the thick of it. Unemployment skyrockets as mines and ironworks close down and the young and fit migrate eastward in droves, leaving the elderly, dependent and less adventurous behind. Merthyr Tydfil is hit especially hard. In Britain, peak unemployment of insured workers reaches 22 per cent in 1931–32. Though matters have improved somewhat by 1934, the terrible official statistic is still 62 per cent for Merthyr, second only to the doomed shipbuilding centre of Jarrow, 'the town that was murdered'.

My family's fortunes, never too flush, fall with the town's. My father's father, a veteran of the Western Front, where he served as an overworked stretcher-bearer, is out of work for fourteen years from 1924 due to pit closures. My father and his three siblings are raised almost entirely 'on the dole'. A Christmas parcel of handouts, left on the doorstep, brings only tears of shame rather than relief and is returned unopened. I look at my father then. The rare photos display a threadbare little fellow, malnourished, with matted hair. And in his eyes, a disturbed and haunted look. It is the face of privation – a face no child should have. Unlike most of the others in his Class Five school photograph, he wears no overcoat, only an ill-fitting and patched old pullover. He appears ready at any moment to take flight from the frame.

Yet dissent with gusto matches deprivation throughout this difficult period. Merthyr and its surrounding towns contribute the largest regional contingent in the world of militant idealists to the International Brigades, fighting Franco's Falangists in the Spanish Civil War. The first song I ever learned in full was a music-hall number entitled *The Spaniard Who Blighted My Life*, taught to me by a close family friend, Dan Harrington, whose brother Tim had been prominent in the Spanish fighting. In Merthyr itself there are running street fights with members of the British Union of Fascists; hunger marchers setting out from as early as 1927; Marxist orators prolific in their number and their passionate, lilting rhetoric; hymn-singing strikers and pacifists galore – with an emphasis on the fists. In early 1935, after Chamberlain's new *Unemployment Act* threatens to reduce dole payments by a rigidly imposed Means Test, over half a million protest across South Wales, marching in inclement weather, often in their Sunday best. The day after some three thousand men and women raid the premises of the Unemployment Assistance Board in Merthyr, Baldwin's ministry acquiesces and withdraws the Test: 'It was a great victory, the only time in the 1930s when direct action caused a government to change its course.'

'Struggle or Starve' is the motto for such times: 'We paid our dues before the rent' is the unionist boast and 'One man victimised; every man out' is the promise. There are Communist mayors and town councils. Communism in these valleys is as respectable as the Eisteddfod. Welsh travel writer Jan Morris observes, 'The red flag, which had first been seen in these islands up the road at Hirwaun a century before, flew defiantly in the Rhondda in the 1930s.' Rhondda novelist and playwright Gwyn Thomas adds, 'We suggested a possible definition of Wales as a non-stop protest with mutating consonants. Navels distended by resting banner-poles became one of the region's major stigmata … [O]ne could have sworn that the very blood of the place was on the boil.'

Families migrate but seem to carry the spirit, like anthracite, in their pores and veins. 'Little and good like the Welsh,' they will say; and 'Don't worry, boy bach; though we lose today, there is always tomorrow.' Even those with forbearers who have had the Welsh tongue knocked out of them with the 'WELSH NOT' rod, following the 1847 British educational reforms, still memorise the talismanic words, *Cymru am byth* (Wales forever), expressed with more of a republican and anti-colonial inflection than an aggressively nationalistic one. My grandfather teaches me the small phrase before my family leaves for Brisbane in late 1948. 'And when you are saying it, don't forget to make the fist,' my uncles add. The fist is important. It is as though they are saying to this little boy: 'We give you this shred of your culture to hold tightly on to. Don't forget us. Don't forget who you are.'

Queensland is more of a culture shock to my family than a pleasant surprise. Australians seem unduly pleased with themselves and eager for praise. 'It's easy enough to think it's all wonderful here when you've got nothing to compare it with,' my mother complains. The very expansiveness of the place suggests social and cultural dilution. The take-it-or-leave-it friendliness of the locals is dispensed with an easy, glancing dismissiveness. Life here lacks the intensities of Wales or any of the passionate depth. This is not only because relationships appear far removed from the close (and sometimes cloying) intimacies of Merthyr, but also because there is little sense of a directly experienced or lived-in past, other than a laconically boastful confection of clichéd swaggies and diggers. It hardly seems to reflect any proud tradition of struggle in which everyone, more or less, has a stake. And of course they can't sing to save themselves. People go about their individual business, caught almost absent-mindedly in the preoccupations of the moment or perhaps focussing all attention forward rather than back. Things just happen here and life goes on.

The one saving grace for us is a small smattering of Welsh families already living in the outer western suburb of Bardon who help to cushion the stresses of our initiation. May Collins – my great-aunt May – is at the hub of this circle and has sponsored us as 'ten-pound' migrants. We are officially in her care. She is an intense and vital person, looking somewhat like Bertrand Russell in a fox fur and floral dress. She has been in Australia since the 1920s. Her husband, Dave, met soon after arrival, was a collier and Communist union official. He has already died from the common miners' complaint, pneumoconiosis ('dusted' in the lungs), before we arrive in early 1949. Dave and May travel from New South Wales to the Mount Mulligan Mines, inland from Cairns. Here, in September 1921, a pit explosion killed seventy-five miners – every worker on the site that morning in a township of three hundred. Things happen. Life goes on. Dave and May move into a one-room galvanised-iron humpy that they have to bend almost double to enter. 'You wouldn't expect even a black gin to live in there,' other workers commiserate with Dave.

Auntie May eventually leaves Mount Mulligan full of stories about the general rough and tumble of the place. For a time, she works as a barmaid in the local pub. One day a drinker at the bar says to the proprietor's wife, 'Bess, there's a hell of a strong smell in here.' Down on the floor, the woman's naked baby is playing with a bunch of kittens. 'God, Bess,' the man persists, 'The kid has shat itself. Do something about it, will you?' Without a word, she walks from behind the bar, picks up the baby in one hand, picks up a kitten in the other; wipes the baby with the kitten; returns them both to the floor and goes back to washing the glasses. Then there is the one about the man whose tapeworm has become so large and voracious that it pops its head out of his mouth when he is eating dinner and takes the piece of meat clear off his fork. She swears up and down about this but no one will quite believe her. Another miner's index finger becomes so infected and rotten that he simply plucks the bone clean out the top of it while sitting, talking with her.

I wish I had communicated with Auntie May a lot more than I did. She had a flair for archiving the gothic and absurd aspects of working-class culture.

May and Dave travel next to Collinsville in the Bowen Basin, another militant coal-mining centre and arguably the place in Queensland most like Merthyr in relation to its class activism. Dave is a keen boxer and teaches his two sons, John and Arnold, the manly art. These two are larrikin tearaways, not backward in making their radical views known and using their fists against local councillors and policemen. During World War II, they are both under military surveillance. As they become deeply involved with the Collinsville branch of the Communist Party, they are caught up in the ultimately successful campaign to elect Rhodes Scholar, Fred Paterson – 'Red Fred, the People's Champion' – to parliament. Standing as an Independent Socialist candidate for the Bowen electorate in 1941, Paterson comes a very creditable second; and then, in 1944 and again in 1947, he is actually elected, to the surprise and chagrin of the mainstream parties: the only Communist ever to win an Australian parliamentary seat. My uncles are among the dedicated campaigners who help to get him there.

In March 1948, less that a year before we arrive in Queensland, Paterson is savagely battoned from behind on St Patrick's Day by an Irish-Australian plain-clothes detective named Mahoney, who had allegedly been drinking before the assault. The assault occurs during a small peaceful march of a couple of hundred Communists and other unionists from Brisbane Trades Hall, protesting the suspension of civil liberties by a Labor premier who was once himself a union leader and strike organiser. Some three hundred baton-wielding police conduct 'the Bash'. The trouble has been caused by the government's new low-wage industrial policy to attract foreign investment and the outbreak of a massive railway strike, of which this violent event is a part. Paterson is not even one of the marchers. As a leftist barrister, he is simply present as a legal observer, busily scribbling in his notebook when he is felled. The baton in this case is mightier that the pen. 'I was in town that day shopping with a couple of women from Collinsville,' Auntie May later tells me, 'and we were coming out of Barry and Roberts when the word came up Adelaide Street from mouth to mouth that the police had fractured Fred Paterson's skull with their clubs on the bridge near Central Station. The Collinsville women I was with both burst into tears, and so did I.'

In the aftermath of all this, we land in Brisbane in January 1949 to face fresh gusts from the industrial and political headwinds. Premier Hanlon introduces a Special Branch into the Queensland police service to spy on left-wing militants while Catholic 'groupers', facilitated by the Australian Workers Union, undermine Communist influence in the local workforce. In March, the *Electoral*

Districts Act outrageously ties up the voting system in Labor's favour. Paterson's Bowen seat disappears. In mid-year, a national coal strike is smashed by the gaoling of union officials and military intervention as, under pressure from Britain, the Australian Secret Intelligence Organisation commences its covert operations, vetting 'subversives' in the Canberra public service. In December, the Chifley government falls, instituting the long reign of Robert Gordon Menzies, who, impelled by the conviction that a third world war is imminent, almost immediately begins to implement his plans to outlaw the Communist Party.

So the development of something approaching a siege mentality in Auntie May's little white weatherboard home on Outlook Crescent, Bardon is understandable. Her sons are both now very active in the Waterside Workers Union. Some time in late 1950, I return from school one day to find a gang of blue-singleted men busily digging several deep pits with long crowbars and shovels under the house. My cousin Harvey and I are warned to 'keep right away' but manage to spot a pile of large packages wrapped in bright blue plastic, waiting to be buried in the holes. 'Now you kids go out and play somewhere else,' Uncle John tells us: 'There'll be big trouble if I catch you digging in this dirt.' There is a tone of seriousness in his voice I haven't heard before. 'Perhaps they're hiding Christmas presents,' I tell Harvey hopefully.

But they are actually hiding union documents, left-wing literature and part of a printing press, following the passage of the *Communist Party Dissolution Act* in late October. This legislation, however, falls victim to a High Court ruling in March 1951, precipitating a long counter-campaign. Menzies wins a tumultuous 'red bogey' election in April (with a reduced margin) but then narrowly loses a bitterly fought anti-Communist referendum in September. Brisbane's citizens vote more resolutely in favour of 'ousting the reds' than even those in the Queensland countryside, but a 'No' majority in the more level-headed southern capitals of Sydney, Melbourne and Adelaide carries the day. So while, for a substantial period, we are figuratively located in Bardon on the front line of resistance to the Conservatives' draconian plans, one day Harvey and I find the mysterious burial mounds have been emptied and only partially refilled with earth. Just a few shreds of that enticing blue plastic remain.

The Cold War continues unabated despite this comforting blip of reactionary miscalculation. I am only seven years old in 1951 but am aware enough to overhear customers in McMahon's local grocery store discussing 'commos' and 'dirty reds' and to wonder if they mean my relatives. I am alarmed when I discover a small pile of red-covered magazines with inexplicable political cartoons on the floor of the backyard 'dunny'. I try to hide them in the sawdust box, little knowing that they are actually copies of the right-wing *Bulletin,* still wrapped in its famous 'Red Page' of literary anecdotes and book reviews.

Before leaving Merthyr, my father has been encouraged by the mirage of Australian Labor in power at both federal and state levels into believing that he is travelling to a leftist haven. He is nonplussed by the rapid political shifts to the right, the reactionary nature of Labor in Queensland and the comparative gormlessness of most of the Australian workers he meets. In Wales, he has served as Secretary for the Dowlais Branch of the militant National Union of Railwaymen; now he becomes just another rank-and-file member of the luke-warm Amalgamated Postal Workers Union. He cannot comprehend the vapid nature of conversations during lunch-breaks and smokos, and the sudden silences when he tries to talk politics, religion or world affairs. If he persists, he is branded a 'whinging Pom'. 'I'm not a bloody Pommie. I'm Welsh!' he responds to no avail. 'They know bugger-all,' he tells my mother in genuine amazement, remembering perhaps the great workers' libraries in the Welsh Miners Institutes, and the avid reading habits of the men: 'And what's more they don't want to learn. Where is their sense of commitment, I'd like to know.' Poorly affecting an Australian accent, my mother will then chime in, 'As long as they've got their "footie" and their "four-exes" and their "sheilas", then "she'll be roite, mate". "Four-ex" they call it. They can't even spell beer.'

Dad is most bemused by the praise heaped on Prime Minister Menzies' silver-tongued anglophonics. It is lauded by the Australian media as great oratory. My father has seen and heard Welsh speakers holding huge concourses indefinitely spellbound – oceans of words delivered in cadences to pierce the heart and fire the blood. 'Now those men could speak,' he will say. 'Even the most mediocre spruiker in Merthyr could outdo Menzies. Menzies is definitely not a great orator. Menzies is not an orator's back-side.' Just as my mother misses the fish and chips in Merthyr – 'a nice piece of hake with chips from Thomas the Fish on the way home from the Castle cinema' – my father misses the political spirit and the mass participation that was part of life's essence.

When we first go to 'the pictures' in Brisbane, my parents are taken aback as the entire audience springs to its feet and remains at rigid attention during the mandatory rendering of the British National Anthem. When played at the end of programs in Wales, this is the signature tune for patrons to choreograph a rapid exit. But here my father is angrily prodded and admonished about his 'loyalty' by those around him when he does not stand 'for the King'. 'What the hell is wrong with these people?' he asks.

Middle-class probity jockeys with Imperial homage for public favour. One hot summer's day we go to Sunnybank on Brisbane's southside to swim at the fabled watering-hole, 'The Oasis', set in lush, tropical gardens. It is a long way to travel from Bardon – two trams and one bus-ride. We have barely entered the water, however, when my father is called out by a vigilant attendant. Apparently, he is committing an obscene nuisance and must leave immediately by a side-gate. His swimming trunks (from Merthyr) do not have the regulation skirt across the crotch to camouflage the male bulge. And so the attendant lectures him as he stands there dripping, with the more demurely attired bathers all listening in. Dad has again been publicly mortified – and all in the space of several weeks. We leave 'The Oasis' in disgrace, never to return, with him muttering audibly 'They're all bloody mad!' as we exit.

In May 1950, I am taken to watch my father, marching with his union in the Labour Day procession. I am expecting exciting scenes – chanting, singing throngs, tumultuous cheering – as befitting such an occasion in Wales. Instead, apart from several heavily-worked Scottish pipe-bands scattered through the passing ranks, it is a rather desultory affair. We stand near a street-corner in Fortitude Valley, in front of the Pig and Whistle Café. The happy pig on its signage is the most cheerful part of the festivities. Spectator ranks are spread thinly along the footpath and there is hardly a peep out of them. When are all the others coming? I keep thinking. As my Dad swings past to a reaction of near silence, I am deterred myself from cheering him. Admiration here is reserved for military heroes rather than working-class ones. The atmosphere is low-key, apologetic, nervous even, as if these people are all collaborating in something shameful merely by taking to the streets on their day of celebration. He never marches again. The following year, hundreds of police actually surround Trades Hall to prevent more radical unionists from staging a rival May Day procession.

These are fearfully conservative times. The tiny Welsh enclave in Bardon has less than a score of members, including offspring, but they hold together as best they can against the cheerless tide of right-mindedness. Auntie May arranges periodic singalongs in her living room or, on hot summer nights when the sky is clear, on the concrete slab behind her house. Most of the participants are relatives, so there is sure to be a lot of uninhibited vocalising.. With throats moistened by a few beers or a little drop of whiskey, they sing in unison and with a swelling resonance such favourites as 'Underneath the Arches', 'When I Grow Too Old to Dream' and 'A Shanty in Old Shantytown'. Without any accompaniment, their voices blend in a confident unity, drifting out into the Bardon night. Then, one by one, they are enticed to their feet for a solo turn. Uncle John always does:

> Mexicali Rose, stop crying.
>
> I'll come back to you some sunny day …

While my father, with his beautiful tenor voice, favours more challenging numbers, such as 'Old Man River', 'Donkey Serenade' or 'That Lucky Old Sun'.

Then, after much coaxing, my mother gets up and, with a shy proficiency, sings:

> It's just a little street
> Where old friends meet.
> I'd love to wander back some day …
> It's just a little street
> Where old friends meet
> And greet you in the same old way.

'Lovely, Maisie,' they say as she sits quietly back down and talk turns unerringly to Merthyr and battles lost and won, and those left behind. There are Welsh songs then – 'Sospan Fach', 'Calon Lan', 'We'll Keep a Welcome' (quavery voices on this one) and many others. And just when everything is verging on the maudlin, Auntie May comes to the rescue. Jumping on to a chair, she launches into a sprightly version of 'Knees Up, Mother Brown', in which they all join, as she lifts her long skirt above her skinny knees and kicks out giddily until she collapses, laughing hysterically, into someone's arms. Her brother, my Uncle Vernon, is red in the face and grinning widely, his cornflower-blue eyes bright with tears of pleasure.

One quiet Sunday afternoon, I am playing alone on top of a pile of sand, dumped across the street by council workers for road repairs, when I have a curious vision. I imagine Uncle George and Auntie Gladys, who live near the top of Outlook Crescent, coming out together through their front gate and advancing deliberately down the hill. As they pass each house, all the inhabitants issue from their front doors and fall into line behind them. Down come the Bennets, the Koraloffs, the Reeves and the Farleighs from the top road. Out come the Bridges, the Cochranes, the Triggs and the Legges; then the Copelands, the Collinses, the Evanses, the Cooks, the Murrays, the Longs and so on down the street. The adults are all singing and linking arms; the children skipping along delightedly beside them. Even Pat Keating, the shy loner with an iron on his leg is joining the march. Someone puts an arm around his shoulders. When they reach the bridge, another procession pours out from Barnett Road to join them. I have no idea where this swelling crowd is going or why its combined ardour is making me feel so euphoric. 'Nothing can stop them,' I remember thinking as I watch the cavalcade pass by: 'Not even the army. Not even the police …'

It is difficult to account for this unusual fancy of a six- or seven-year-old child; it is not so hard to assume that it is probably cast from some deep Welsh folk-memory, transmuted by a kind of generational osmosis. Listen, for instance, to this participant description of the march on Merthyr against the hated Means Test in February 1935: 'I remember us starting off from Pengarnddu with banners and all the rest of it, there was about thirty started … We stopped at Dowlais, there were people there with banners. By the time we reached South Street they were coming in from Pant, Caeracae, and all the rest of it. Then down the new road … they were coming in from all directions, well down through the town you could see it was a huge demonstration. Then when we reached Portmorlais, they came up from below, from Twym, Penyard and Swansea Road … Well the place was packed …'

This recollection and my little Bardon daydream carry the same sense of mounting exhilaration at the possibilities of participatory empowerment and direct action: that is, that people, acting together in the same spirit of fair play, moral economy, sound knowledge and careful planning, can sometimes overcome truly ominous forces and achieve great things. By their actions, they are less to be characterised as a fearsome mob and more as a noble engine of historical change and social advancement. My Welsh origins and upbringing have encouraged me from an early age to think this way. Such a faith may at times be seriously naïve or sadly misplaced. But when the promise of communal unity in a just cause is upheld, and goodwill and common decency prevail, then positive, indeed exceptional, outcomes may confidently be anticipated. ■

References available at www.griffithreview.com

Raymond Evans is a visiting fellow at Griffith University and the author of *The History of Queensland* (CUP, 2007). His essay, 'Done and dusted' was published in *Griffith REVIEW 21: Hidden Queensland.*

Fiction:
State of emergency: Brisbane 1982

Author:
Edwina Shaw

'What do we want?'

'The right to march!'

'When do we want it?'

'Now!'

'Joh must go!'

King George Square is crowded with hippies, punks, students, feral socialists and priests, all going red in the face. Yelling. About our rotten joke of a Premier: Joh, the peanut farmer who thinks he's king. He's just announced a State of Emergency for the upcoming Commonwealth Games, giving the police even more power so they can clear the streets of Aborigines, hippies and other unwanteds that won't make a good impression on visitors. Like me. Not that I'm a hippie or an Abo or even a student. I'm an average bloke, jeans and a plain tee-shirt, not a slogan on me. Finished high school last year, thank Christ, and started as a mechanic's apprentice.

Sure, I smoke a bit of dope sometimes, have a few drinks and see a band when I'm out with the boys. I'm young. That's what I'm supposed to do. But here in Brisbane that sort of stuff is enough to get you harassed by pigs every time you step out the front door on a Saturday night. All the big crime is controlled by the police bosses so the street pigs have nothing better to do than lay shit on anyone trying to have a good time. That's a crime in Queensland. If Joh had everything his way, he'd ban fun.

I'm not really into politics and that, they're all bastards. That's what Dad says anyway. But the other week when they tore down the best band venue in the city, like thieves in the middle of the night, I felt so angry I wanted to bash someone's head in. They can't just do that. Someone's got to say enough's enough. That's why I'm here today, really.

Well that. And her. She wanted to come.

That girl. The punk with black hair and too much make up, holding the 'Joh Must Go' sign. The one throwing back her head and laughing as if she knows what happiness is. That's Beck. She's with me. When we first started hanging out she laughed like that all the time and everything I did was cool and courageous. I was her hero, she said. But now, ever since she started uni, she doesn't seem to think I'm so great after all. The jokes that used to make her laugh aren't funny anymore. She yawns when I talk and there's a hard edge to her laugh that hurts.

I thought it would be great to change her. When we first met she was really straight – a goody two-shoes, 'straight A' kind of girl. I smiled and nodded approval as she took her first puffs on a joint, showed her how to draw back and keep it deep in her lungs to get the most high in her system with every toke. The first night she got pissed, I patted her back and kept her hair out of her face as she spewed into the garden. It was me who taught her there was more to sex than kisses and titty-feels. Maybe I should've kept her the way she was.

Beck's super-excited, her face blotched and angry as she screams, linking arms with all her new mates: 'Joh must go!' To tell you the truth though, I'm starting to get worried about the busloads of police unloading on to Ann Street. I've seen these demos on TV. I know how they end up. I hate Joh and his police thugs as much as anyone. But after what happened to my brother that night at the taxi rank, when the pigs decided his hair was too long and gave him some scars he'll have for the rest of his life, I stay as far away from anyone in a blue shirt as I can.

I give Beck a nudge and shout into her ear from behind, 'Let's get out of here, the pigs are just itching.'

'No way. You go if you like.' Then she mutters something under her breath that sounds suspiciously like 'Loser'.

That hurts. Not because she thinks I'm a coward, because maybe I am. I don't want to get arrested for this. I don't want to get my head beaten in. Calling me a loser really gets to me because lately I've been feeling like I am a loser. I'm losing her, I can feel it. Ever since she started university things have changed. Bloody big-word wankers with their fancy French cigarettes, books and bottled wine.

The hard part of me is steeled, ready for the end, but the underpart that's as soft as a turtle's belly under its shell wants to shout and cry and hold her to me. They'll have to pry my fingers from her one by one. A girl like Beck is worth fighting for. More than a knocked-down building and a rotten old man anyway. I grab her hand to wrench her from the line-up but she's so sweaty it slips from my grip. She's driving me crazy.

'Do you want to get brained? Come on!'

She whispers in the ear of the tall guy next to her and laughs.

She's laughing at me.

A witch in a short skirt with wild white hair and skinny legs shoves a piece of cardboard into my arms. 'No State of Emergency' is scrawled across it in paint that's still wet. I try to give it back but she's already moved on, handing out the rest she's got under her arm. Shit, now it really looks as if I'm part of this. It's like holding a target at shooting practice.

Up front a hippie with dreadlocks down to his bum is standing on the edge of the fountain, yelling and waving his arms, spitting as he shouts about the gerrymander and the right to march and join unions, about how Queensland is fascist, a police state. That part sure is true. Around the edges of the square, coming at us from all directions, a sea of police starts to flood inward. Wave after wave of heavy blue shirts surrounding our small island of protestors. I drop the placard on to the grass and reach for Beck.

'Come on,' I call over the chanting. 'We've got to get out of here. Now! I'm not joking.'

She turns and snarls. 'Go then. Piss off, you coward.'

Something in my guts cracks. I drop her hand and shove my way through the shouting freaks, my face burning.

'It's not worth getting bashed for,' I yell back.

She'll follow. She always does. Halfway out of the crowd, I stand on my toes and crane my neck to catch a glimpse of her, but she's not trailing after me as I'd hoped. She's not even looking in my direction. All I can see is the back of her messed up hair, like a toilet brush.

Already, on the outside of the circle to the front, protestors are being dragged away, cursing and screaming, getting gravel rash on their backs. Police laugh and encourage each other as they thump into protesters who lie curled like unborn babies on the ground.

Beck's going to be mincemeat once they really hit their stride and no one's stopping them. I try to look in another direction, force myself to keep pushing through, away from her. Let her bloody uni mates look after her. I don't care.

But I do.

I fight my way back through the writhing crowd, determined to bring her out before she's thrown into the watch house or whacked with a baton. Grunting and shoving, I struggle towards the front line, elbows ramming my ribs. I push past people who are ranting, sweating, their eyes wild with excitement and fear.

This girl is killing me.

I knew from the beginning she was a virgin. The way she kissed me that first night gave it away. So I took things slowly. Treated her differently from other girls I'd been with, the ones who knew their way around. Beck was special. I had to be careful; I knew what could happen. It would be easy to ruin everything if I made a wrong move. The other fellas warned me. 'Pop someone's cherry,' they said, 'and you're stuck with them for life. They chain themselves to your leg, want you to marry them.' Love makes things dangerous.

One night after school had finished, Beck and I made a bonfire in the backyard and drank red wine till our teeth were black. She smiled at me and reached up, soft and beautiful in the light of the fire. As I wrapped my arms around her, she started to say something but I put my finger to her lips and pressed her backwards on to the old dog rug. I lay down next to her and started kissing her, slowly. I kissed her eyelids, her forehead, her ear lobes, her chin, the curve of her jaw, the dimple at the bottom of her throat. I kissed the palms of her hands and licked between her fingers and up the inside of her arms. Inside her elbows. Till she was squirming and begging me to stop, though it was the last thing she really wanted me to do.

I rested my hands on her belly under her shirt, then lifted her so I could pull it off over her head. She looked at me half-frightened, half-excited and whispered, 'Are we? You know, are we going to … do it?'

'You want to?' I asked, undoing the top button of her jeans.

She nodded. 'Russ?'

'Trust me.' I leant over as she lay back down and kissed her hard on the mouth. 'Don't worry. You'll like it. I promise.'

I put my hand on her crotch outside her jeans, feeling the heat of her pussy under my palm as sure as I felt fire on my face. She was more beautiful than any girl I'd ever been with. Shining. I felt like a soldier, the hero she thought I was. Powerful. I wanted to roar and wave a gun in the air.

She lifted her hips and wriggled down so I could drag her jeans off, till she was just in her bra and undies on the dirty rug. As she stretched up for me like a little girl asking for Daddy, I wished the rug was velvet and that I was everything she thought I was. My dick was rock hard but I kept my clothes on. I lay down beside her and held her tight, kept kissing her till she didn't notice that I'd taken off her bra and that my hand was in her pants, exploring, looking for her bud. When I took my mouth from hers, she stared at me and I saw in her eyes, wide and black and full, something that made me stop cold.

I couldn't kiss her mouth any more, not with her looking at me like that. So I covered her nipple with my lips and then licked my way down to her pants, her hips rising up against my face, her hands pulling her panties off, wanting it. Wanting me.

'You can … put … put it in if you like. I … I want …'

I shook my head and buried my face in her pussy. Deep. She trembled and rocked under me and when I knew she was ready I pulled off my daks and went in. Slowly. Then fast.

When she came it wasn't with a whole lot of noise like some girls, no screeching like a cat or crying the way some of them carry on. She just sighed and shuddered and held me tight, her legs locked behind my back. Kissed me. And for a moment I let myself go, forgot that I wasn't the hero she thought I was, forgot about being careful, and came. Felt something inside me split open and glow.

'Did you like it?' I asked her later.

She nodded and wrapped her arms tighter, whispering, 'Oh Russ, I … I …'

'What?' I said, praying she wouldn't say it. That she wouldn't spoil everything.

'Nothing,' she said. 'That was great. Can we do it like that every time?'

'Sure.' I laughed and kissed her some more. But I'd gone too far. I loved her and that was dangerous ground. I felt as if I'd just stood on a landmine and couldn't move. Everything had to stay exactly the same, I couldn't lift my foot an inch, couldn't breathe too deeply, couldn't flutter an eyelash, or it would all explode in my face.

You can't count on things staying the same though. She doesn't look at me like that anymore. Not now that I'd like her to. Now she laughs with her uni mates, not with me. I'm not her hero these days. I'm her fool. I can't ever let myself go again like I did that night by the fire. My heart's in a stranglehold. One false move and the whole lot goes up.

I've lost sight of her in the tangle of bodies. The stink of sweat makes me choke as the sound of batons hitting bones gets closer. I force my way back through the crowd of protestors who are linking arms, preparing for battle, chanting, 'Joh must go! Joh must go!' Don't they know there are only a couple of hundred of us and three times that many police?

'Joh must go!'

Then I see her, her arm wrapped around the tall punk, but she's not yelling anymore. She looks pale, her eyes screwed shut, lips clamped tight as the line ahead of her falls under the batons.

'Beck!'

When her eyes flicker open and she sees me her face lights up.

'Russ!'

'Come with me.'

She nods and takes my hand, unhooking herself from the human chain. Leaning into my back, she hides behind me as I push a way through to the rear edge of the protest where another battalion of pigs is swarming, ugly as old footy players.

'Excuse me officer,' I say like I'm trying to weasel out of detention with a tough teacher. 'Can we get through?'

'Where do you think you're going?' he asks.

'Just leaving sir, don't want any trouble.'

'Desert your mates in a battle, do ya? Well get going then ya poof. Go get yourself a haircut.' He pokes me in the ribs with his truncheon as I wrestle through with Beck behind me.

'Pig,' she mutters under her breath as we squeeze past his bean-bag belly.

'Christ, Beck, shut up,' I hiss.

'What did you call me, freak?' says the pig reaching for his belt.

'Pig.'

'You'd better watch yourself punky. Rope your woman in would ya, mate?'

That really gets her going. 'Oh, go bash some hippie, you arsehole.'

She's got no sense. The pig raises his baton and lifts it high. I jam myself between them, forcing Beck behind me. 'Sorry officer, she doesn't mean it. Say sorry Beck.' I jab her in the stomach with my elbow. 'Beck.'

'Sorry,' she whispers. Then as we run off down the ramp to Adelaide Street she calls back over her shoulder, 'For nothing, you fascist pig!'

Before he can answer, I drag her after me. Fast. Across the road past the Tropicana to Queen Street where they're building the new mall. Her hand is sweaty but I hold it tight in mine. I'm not going to let her go.

'Was that fun or what?' she asks, throwing back her head and laughing.

For a moment I'm still pissed off but then I laugh too. I laugh and wrap my arms around her.

'My hero,' she says.

And there, right in the middle of the street surrounded by rubble and piles of bricks, with everyone watching, I kiss her. I can't help myself. Drinking in her softness, I let myself go and cling tight to her body, wishing that the heat of the sun could melt us together like pieces of metal in a fire. It's got to be us two. Together.

I lift my foot off that landmine.

Click.

Let it blow.

Let it blow.

She's mine. ■

Edwina Shaw is a Brisbane-based author and the winner of the 2008 Moorhouse, Most Promising New Writer, pen mentorship. Her stories have been published in *Griffith REVIEW 21: Hidden Queensland and 22: MoneySexPower, Island, Hecate* and *Idiom 23*. Her young adult novella, *Thrill Seekers*, will be released by Ransom UK in September 2009.

Reportage:

A story of the digital generation

Reporter:

Ellie Rennie

Image: Thornbury HS teacher, and creator of ClassTV, Paul Van Eeden proudly displays his Antenna award, while Year 10 students Jake Edgar and Steph Torre keep their eyes on the screen in the ClassTV editing suite. / Photographer: Timothy Burgess / Courtesy of Victorian Department of Education and Early Childhood Development.

A story of the digital generation

'You are listening to sin,' said the radio announcer. That was a few years ago now and I remember thinking I must have misheard. The music was also a bit odd, plunging into bad taste and then getting good again. As it turned out I had been listening to SYN, and not 'sin'. SYN, I discovered, is made by people between twelve and twenty-six. The only playlist is the 'sweet 16': a collection of songs they happen to like that week. The cheekiness of the name is deliberate. All their lives 'the SYNners', as they call themselves, have been told that the media is bad for them. And so they play up to it, taking SYN to be sin, knowing that they are in charge now.

SYN stands for the much-too-serious Student Youth Network; nobody can be bothered saying that on air. Audiences like the station because it has a child-like innocence – it has none of the polished, fast-paced, ad-ridden hype of commercial radio. If you live in Melbourne you can find SYN on the radio, television and the web. If you search hard you can also find a few old copies of its magazine, *Pecado* (which means 'sin' in Spanish), lying around its inner-city headquarters. SYNners will be listening to their peer-produced content in their rooms, watching it on television or downloading it to their iPods to take on the train. Some tune in and decide 'I can do better', so they call up and book in for a training program, others are online building the technologies, or in studios telling the newbies which buttons to press.

For all of the talk of a new communications paradigm there are very few stories of the people who are actually making it. SYN is a very small enterprise where people go to learn about, and become part of, the media. The high dramas of media dynasties, acquisitions and political influence lie pretty far from their reality. But the 'radical changes' occurring in the mediascape come from the sudden, wide-scale participation of ordinary folk in media production and distribution. New ideas and technologies are emerging out of non-market-based activities – friendship groups and hobbies – outside of professionalised industry. It is these stories that now need telling.

The life of SYN is also a story of digital literacy – a new literacy involving the ability to write, not just read, the forms and languages of digital media content. Through this poorly funded and only loosely organised institution, young people are planning their response to the hard questions: 'Where does new media participation lead to?' 'Who is it benefiting?' They are working out which structures will advance their capacity to communicate, get educated and compete in an increasingly competitive knowledge-based workforce. The policy-makers can't seem to keep up, relying on the private sector to deal with whatever major economic and social consequences digital communication throws up. The SYNners decided to figure it out for themselves.

There are different versions of how SYN started. The one that interests me most is the station's school days, before it grew up and became independent, so I visit Thornbury High, a large secondary school in Melbourne's multicultural northern suburbs. Two teachers, Paul van Eeden and Colin Thompson, meet me at reception in the late afternoon and guide me through the wide corridors, which would usually be crammed with kids, and into the heart of the school. Van Eeden's energy and middle-aged hippie vibe appeals to kids. Thompson, a former maths teacher with a drawl is a self-confessed 'sports jock'. When he starts speaking about the media, a deep and ambitious interest is revealed. The two teachers struck me as opposites, brought together by a shared passion and hours of hard work.

They lead me into a large room that has been converted into a television studio, kitted out with studio cameras and blue screens. A smaller room off to the side is filled with computers for video editing. This is the production centre of *Class TV*, a weekly television program screened on C31, Melbourne's community television station. The walls are covered with newspaper articles on *Class TV* as well as Thornbury High's first media experiment, Radio 3TD. The radio station is long gone, superseded by television, and by SYN. The two teachers are keen to tell their radio story and how SYN was the demise of everything they had worked so hard to create.

One of the school's brightest pupils in the early 1990s was Rorie Ryan. With the help of the Student Representative Council, Rorie raised money from the Education Foundation (then known as the Small Change Foundation) and was made the school's Junior Citizen for his efforts. He used the money to buy a mixing desk for the school, then set about creating some noise. Broadcasting on ten speakers, the Junior Citizen started a radio station that could be heard in the corridors and across the playground. The teaching staff were not impressed that their school had been turned into a massive ghetto-blaster. The students loved it. Two years later, Rorie was doing work experience at 3RRR and discovered that he could apply for a Temporary Community Broadcasting Licence, which is something like a test licence. Still only fifteen, he put together an application with the help of one of the English teacher aides. In 1996, Rorie's final year of school, Thornbury High became a licensed temporary broadcaster.

According to Paul Van Eedon, 'Rorie seemed to have this tremendous power over the school'. He had keys to everything. Although most of the teachers refused to supervise the radio station on top of their regular workload, Van Eedon, the facilities manager, was an early riser and didn't mind. Listening to and observing the early-morning broadcasts, he realised that radio production was actually good for the kids. They were learning things, having fun, becoming confident and getting to school really early. Van Eeden had been unhappy in his job and was looking for another school, but he stayed at Thornbury High because 3TD needed him.

Colin Thompson, the new maths teacher, had his office across the hall from the radio station. The first year kids kept knocking on his door looking for help when the big kids kicked them off air. Thommo, as he is known, became interested in the station and got involved in the licence application. 'The kids were really enjoying it,' he tells me, 'and they weren't enjoying my maths class.' Letting kids broadcast could have been a disaster and the teachers knew it. 'We were risk takers,' says Thommo. 'If we weren't then SYN would never have happened.'

The story of the radio station is heart-warming. But as I hear about it, I feel there is a subtext – a critique of the education system as a whole. If schools had been a satisfying place to work, if teaching had been all that teachers wanted it to be, if students were learning things that would make them interested in the world and able to be part of it, then 3TD would not have emerged. The students responded to 3TD with energy, engaging in a way that the school curriculum could not achieve. For the teachers, it provided a new kind of learning; students could express themselves on their own terms, resist conformity and understand the media from the other side. They witnessed the intangible lessons that came from learning by doing and public performance. The structure was simple: mostly the kids just played their favourite top twenty songs, or discussed topics from schoolbooks. This revealed the humorous, down-to-earth culture of kids from the working-class, 'ethnic' suburbs. Van Eedon and Thommo discovered a newfound passion for teaching. The way they tell it, 3TD was a little beam of sunlight in a system that was otherwise a bore for everyone.

3TD was also time consuming. Getting a temporary licence was the first step in applying for a full-time licence in a highly competitive process. With fourteen community media groups competing for four licences, the stations broadcast on temporary licences for short stints and shared channels. As a listener at the time, I remember being confronted with a sudden strange amount of choice. 3TD found itself alongside six other temporary community broadcasters in its first test transmission. Its frequency, 87.1, reached far across the broadcast spectrum. The shows were being heard as far away as the Mornington Peninsula. Eight other schools joined 3TD, providing programming for the test transmissions. Listeners from all over Melbourne called to say they loved it. One afternoon, Paul Van Eedon received a call from Nigel Slater who was running SUB FM, a station based at LaTrobe University. The tertiary stations were realistically thinking that there would only be one youth licence, if any. He suggested that 3TD join forces with a group of four university stations and together apply for a full-time licence. 3TD decided to join, but at a meeting with the tertiary stations, there was some hostility to the school students, who were offered bad timeslots and little input at the board level. After two years of negotiations, 3TD and RMIT University's SRA decided to form one station. They agreed to call it Student And Youth Radio, or SAY-FM. Jo McCarthy, who later became SYN's president, came up with a better nomenclature: the Student Youth Network. SYN was born.

In 2003 when SYN moved from being a temporary radio broadcaster to a full-time station, Craig Twitt was president. We meet at the pub one afternoon so he can give me his personal archive. Craig grew up in the country and moved to Melbourne after finishing school. He enrolled in a commerce degree at Melbourne University but felt alienated in his course: 'You're not into sport and you're not into the More Beer society ... SYN had a mix of really, really interesting and eclectic people that you couldn't find in other places. And SYN parties were excellent.'

When I meet him, Craig is working at 3MBS as the volunteer coordinator. 3MBS is one of the community broadcasting stations that received one of the first non-commercial licences in the 1970s. When Craig describes it as 'one of the oldest stations', he is talking about the age of the volunteers – a high proportion are retirees. At MBS, 'volunteer turnover' doesn't mean that people are going off to get jobs or move cities: 'In twenty years, 80 percent of their current volunteers will no longer be in this world.' Craig is used to being the young guy at MBS, he is only twenty-seven, old by SYN's standards.

The large folio he hands me is filled with newspaper articles, radio schedules, press passes, and SYN condoms and stickers. In amongst the paraphernalia is an A4 Melbourne University tutorial sheet. On one side it has a series of essay questions ('What do you understand by the transparency of monetary policy?'). On the other it has his notes for his radio show, *Melbourne's Bitter*. That week's work involved research for an interview with someone from the student union and compiling a list of album tracks he was planning on playing that week: Bob Dylan, Augie March and Art of Fighting. The essay on monetary policy obviously had to wait.

I also find an old envelope addressed to Craig. On the back, someone from SYN had scrawled: 'stop ripping off our humble radio station and renew your membership! You shame us all.' Craig renewed his membership. In fact, not long after our meeting, he left 3MBS and returned to SYN as the assistant station manager to help get the finances in order. One day he forwards me a bunch of files from the SYN newsletter archives from the time of the merger. An SRA newsletter shows an inflated, undergraduate identity – demonstrating that the transition from a university club to an open organisation was not entirely smooth. During the temporary broadcasts, the two groups initially decided to share the airtime – a fifty–fifty split – whilst maintaining distinct identities. Craig recalls that SRA was appalled by the content being produced by the 3TD kids. SRA might have been just a bunch of uni students compared with the bullies that dominated Australia's mainstream media, but they still protected their turf when the kids asked to join the club. The SRA newsletter consoled its membership about the drop in standards, assuring them the merger would greatly increase the station's chances of getting a full-time licence.

The Australian Broadcasting Authority, luckily, was not impressed by the line-in-the-sandpit approach to airtime and made it clear that the groups had to fully amalgamate if they wanted a shot at the licence. Turning SYN into a cohesive whole meant implementing training and coming up with a programming structure where all shows were subject to an evaluation process. The process was lax by SRA standards but a completely new concept for 3TD. Van Eedon and Thommo fought against demo tape applications and in favour of younger representation on the board, including a rotating president (one year tertiary, secondary the next). They didn't succeed.

The licence application process was arduous and competitive. Mary Delahunty, the Victorian Arts Minister at the time, helped out with funds for a business plan and the support of key politicians. Stations were permitted to comment on other applications. SYN pitted itself against two dance music stations, Hitz and Kiss, arguing that young people could not be represented with a single music genre. The dance stations were faddish and would cease to be relevant when the music was no longer new and interesting. SYN would offer diversity by nature of its accessible programming grid. Music tastes could come and go, and the station would always be relevant to what young people were listening to. That was the argument, anyhow.

The Sydney licence round came up first and when the 'cool' station there beat its dance music competitor, SYN saw the win as a good sign.

Paul Van Eedon describes the Melbourne ABA hearing as 'almost like a trial'. Wanting to fill the cavernous, grand auditorium of the Melbourne Town Hall with SYN supporters, the teachers decided to bus in school classes. The interrogation lasted for an hour and a half, and the school kids got 'bored silly'. When the hearing was over and the ABA members stood up to leave, the girls and boys broke out into thunderous applause. Van Eedon remembers the mistaken response: 'We heard back that they were really impressed with our kids because they were passionate. But the kids all clapped and cheered because they could finally get out of the place.' Adults, he observes, have different ideas of youth empowerment from the youth they are claiming to empower.

There was genuine surprise and relief when SYN won one of the Melbourne licences, despite less publicity than the dance stations and only being on the scene for a short time. The broadcasting authority then issued a further five youth radio licences around the country, including Edge Radio in Hobart and Groove FM in Perth. Now the difficult business of establishing a radio station commenced. The SRA newsletter put it out there: 'Anyone got a rich uncle?'

The rich uncle turned out to be RMIT University, which paid for the transmitter. But as SYN evolved, the tertiary identity grew weaker as voluntary student unionism began killing campus life. And despite SRA's fears, the school kids were often better in front of the mike. The challenge was to keep the station young, accessible and fiercely independent.

Today, the SYNners regard Van Eedon and Thommo as two old guys who were instrumental in setting up the station, but who ultimately had to go. From my observation, everyone seemed to get on with the teachers whenever they were in the room. Private interviews suggest that the relationship between the teachers and SYN was more complex, with disparate interests and cultures. SYN could not have teachers involved and remain independent. The teachers felt that they were the protectors of the high school-age kids, who would be subsumed in university business without them.

Van Eedon and Thompson voluntarily left the SYN board. Under the current model, schools are treated as clients rather than having real ownership over the station and Thommo thinks 'we got shafted'. Van Eeden and Thompson's innovation was to bring a new kind of literacy into the school. Once it was established, SYN needed to become part of the media system. That demonstrated the importance of digital literacy to the education system and SYN was able to teach the teachers.

Most of the organisation's income comes from training programs, which were carefully redeveloped by Georgia Webster in 2007. She has since worked her way up through SYN's volunteer and staff ranks to become station manager. In her opinion, high school media studies rarely include production and focuses on a critical understanding designed to discourage media participation. When teachers come into SYN they are amazed at the way their students take to radio – not just as DJs, but in technical and production roles and researching issues to discuss on air. SYN offers a different way of learning which is in many respects the opposite of school. The founder of the Educational Video Centre in New York City, Steve Goodman, observes a similar pattern: 'The failure of schools and after-school programs to address the media as the predominant language of youth today, or to recognise the social and cultural contexts in which students live, has resulted in a profound disconnect.' I asked the SYNners if they agreed: 'What was it like being trained at SYN?'

'It's a bit of a sink or swim kind of thing so it was very practical, very hands on,' one replied. 'You sort of see immediate results from what you're learning. Not that you're learning an idea and then years later you get to put it into practice. It's very much "here's the button you need to press, you go and press it".'

Schools have historically taken an antagonistic approach, to the media in their studies of it. Critical media literacy has been the standard approach with students learning about stereotypes or news values, usually in an English class. This strand of media studies emerged with the study of radio propaganda in the 1930s. By the late 1960s, it had begun to focus on television and commercialised culture. Students learnt how to translate the semiotic meanings within images, press biases and the illusion of objectivity. However, by teaching students to 'read' the media, but not to 'write' it, schools distanced students from the media. Critical consumers are powerless, however wise they may be to the inevitable tricks of an unrelenting force. Elizabeth Daley, Dean of the School of Cinematic Arts at the University of Southern California, writes, 'These courses... enforce the belief that real education remains in books and that real knowledge is rational and linear. Students are taught to read visual texts in order to defend themselves against the onslaught of visual culture. Second, these courses have been extremely one-sided in the definition of literacy, focusing on a "read only" approach.'

Young people learn how to make media by figuring it out for themselves, especially through social networking sites and content-sharing networks such as Flickr. As media studies professor, John Hartley, has pointed out, digital literacy investment 'is almost all private, seeking to develop markets rather than citizens'.

By 2006, over five thousand young people had been members of SYN after only three years of full-time broadcasting. Many were active volunteers at some point, undergoing training and then working on a radio or television program. Others would have made it into executive volunteer roles, managing its operations, or working on the board, directing station policy. If you add the kids that come through in school groups, either as short half-day trainees or term-long radio announcers, the participation figure is much, much higher. Regular volunteer meetings are held to induct new SYNners into the organisation, often with fifty to a hundred people turning up on a school night. The vast majority of SYN members are under twenty-one.

Work experience is one of the primary reasons for getting involved in SYN and its alumni register – those who are known to have gone on to work in the media industries – is impressive. At the start of 2006 there were sixty people on the list; a year later there were around eighty. SYN's unconventional training system is successful because it encourages responsibility and initiative. Richard

Riley, US Secretary of Education in Bill Clinton's administration once said, 'We are preparing our students for jobs that don't exist, using technologies that have not been invented, to solve problems that we haven't even considered yet.' The technologies at SYN might be crude or out of date in comparison to what they will find in the workplace. But that doesn't matter so much when you are learning the vital skill of how to cope with change.

In contrast, doing work experience at commercial media companies was mundane. Statements like 'Well I had previously been working and volunteering at Austereo in more of a promotional capacity but they weren't giving me any training or on-air experience' were fairly common. A young woman, who is now a newsreader, pointed out that 'volunteering at a commercial station is a very strange concept. And at the time it was really overwhelming because you're like "Wow this is how a real radio station works and I'm actually in here getting paid in free movie tickets to sit and answer phones."' In her enthusiasm to be at a 'real' radio station she didn't consider that a commercial media company was avoiding paying for her menial labour. SYN is very bad at answering the phones – perhaps a good indication that people have more interesting things to learn.

At the end of 2007, I surveyed approximately three hundred and fifty media workers about their qualifications and transition into paid work. My intention was to find out how many had volunteered in a community media organisation. Over half had been involved in some form of community media – mostly radio, but also TV, print and web. That figure rose to two-thirds for those aged under thirty. Participation in community media was 'important' or 'vital' for getting paid work in the media industries.

Digital literacy is an ongoing and incomplete experiment. On discussion lists, in studios and at computer terminals, SYNners conduct a continuous conversation on the best way to create content. They soon realise that, to communicate effectively in the media environment, certain forms, standards and methods are useful. SYN gives them basic skills, but it also allows them to practise and enact a suite of audio, visual and textual content forms.

Obviously, the system of digital literacy in which SYN is engaged is unfinished business. Because of the nature of the digital revolution, students, trainees and amateurs are just as likely as professionals to influence the way that digital literacy evolves. The seemingly unstructured, casual environments that the youth media sector has developed are, in many ways, an entirely appropriate response to the growing demands of the creative economy. As it is youth run, the form of digital literacy that results will be what young people see as necessary, not something imposed on them through curricula and exams.

Schools still have an important role to play. It's fair to say that Paul Van Eeden and Colin Thompson have done more for media education and digital literacy than any other teachers in the country. The pair have stayed at Thornbury High and now dedicate their time to *Class TV*, broadcasting school-made video content on C31. They have also started a new project, ClassNet (www.classnet.com.au), and hope it will encourage more schools to engage in media production and distribution. In 2007, Paul Van Eeden was awarded Victorian Teacher of Year.

There is a poster at SYN headquarters, the House of SYN, dated 28.01.03. On the poster, in fine double-outlines of hot pink and black, abstract figures perform twenty-nine different coital positions. The poster is ridiculous, a little shocking and its reference to radio is obscure. The image makes you bend your neck to the side and squint. And there really is more than one way to look at it. The figures and the date signify SYN's moment of inception: the first day of full-time broadcasting. Then there is the naughty/smutty aspect, a teenage obsession with sex. The poster implies that here at SYN you won't be told off for acts of trivial expression, so long as it is done in a creative way. It made me think of *Oz*, the 1960s magazine which used sexually explicit cartoons to challenge the establishment (their 'Schoolkids' issue being the most controversial of all). Germaine Greer once wrote that *Oz* 'behaved as though the revolution had already happened'. The same can be said of SYN, although it's a different revolution this time.

The poster caused trouble – not everyone likes it – but it is still on display as school group tours traipse through The House. SYN has ended up with that bifocal role – a conservative black outline marking the bread and butter training programs, neat and polite for the public. The shadow is the real culture, cast in retro fluorescent pink, unpredictable, immature and ready to tell whomever to get f*cked.

There is another poster on the wall from the same time, which everyone still loves. Nestled inside an ear is a foetus, a life about to be born through the ear canal. SYN had just received its community radio licence and would bring new life to an old platform. Unlike a lot of other youth-directed media, SYN is never deliberately cool, but sometimes it gets it right. ■

Ellie Rennie is a Research Fellow at Swinburne University's Institute for Social Research. Her second book based on ARC-funded research, *Life of SYN: A Story of the Digital Generation*, is due for release this year.

Reportage:
Voice of the people

Reporter:
Brent Balinski

Image: Chris Madden / www.chrismadden.co.uk

Voice of the people

We love a good hoax. When it was revealed that Keith Windschuttle, editor of *Quadrant*, had accepted a bogus article on genetic engineering, the wide coverage provoked debate about Windschuttle's criticisms of historians for flawed footnotes. Comparisons to famous hoaxes were made, and Windschuttle's opponents relished his comeuppance. Earlier this decade, American news icon Dan Rather's use of hoax evidence regarding George W. Bush's National Guard record received worldwide coverage and led to the sooner than planned end of Rather's career as CBS's *60 Minutes* anchor. Closer to home – perhaps in one's car, or through headphones at the gym – smaller hoaxes can sometimes be heard, perpetrated on those whose job is ostensibly to inform others of the events of the day and be a voice for the everyman.

Talkback radio occupies a unique place in Australia's media landscape. Radio stations are given more time by political leaders during election campaigns than all the other media combined, and radio talkback is the preferred venue for selling policy and managing scandals. Its fans argue that it's where Joe Public can hold the Prime Minister to account, as well as listen in on an 'over the backyard fence' conversation between average Australians. But its critics argue that talkback's biggest stars are salesmen relying on flimsy research and stories already broken elsewhere.

'The reason is that radio has very limited resources, it usually works off what's on the front and the first five pages of the tabloid press and whips those up in stories over the morning,' says David Salter, author of *The Media We Deserve* (MUP, 2007) and editor of *The Week*. 'In other words, they get the early editions, at three o'clock in the morning, a little further they say, "Oh look, there's a fantastic story about no rubbish collection in Carlton or something," and they go for it … They are not at the start of the 24-hour news cycle.'

Talkback radio may not have the same resources or investigative muscle of other media, but it has a head-start in terms in breaking stories. It is always on and doesn't have to wait for a deadline to file final copy or submit footage. The print media can never give instant traffic updates.

'And just a traffic update … Wayne says to me, "I'm at work, I just saw the traffic mayhem on Enmore Road. You'd better tell Sallyanne to investigate because it's bad. What looks like a whole truckload of tennis balls has been unloaded on Enmore Road, Enmore. There are about ten thousand tennis balls blocking every lane, and one very embarrassed looking truck driver." Why would tennis balls be loose? Why wouldn't they be in tins?' This information and these questions were shared by 2UE's Steve Price – certainly no stranger to weird hoaxes. Though Price expressed scepticism at the 'tip', the station's traffic reporter Sallyanne Ryan was not so cautious, 'I can't find any confirmation that it's happened. But I'm sure it has … ' Despite the lack of confirmation, the station ran this as news in the next bulletin at 4 pm. As did 2CC Canberra at 4.30 pm, whose newsreader informed listeners that, in the Sydney suburb of Enmore, 'a truck has apparently dropped a thousand tennis balls'.

Neither ten thousand, nor even one thousand, tennis balls dropped on Enmore Road, Enmore that day. It was an just another day for most in the inner west suburb, including Lew Palaitis and Nick Fintan, who were going about their day-to-day running of the Hardware art gallery. Palaitis explains: 'I'd always been listening to talkback pretty earnestly,' while at work at the gallery and at his former picture framing business. He sent his first hoax email to Steve Price 'back in 2003 or 2004' and through 2007 and 2008 passed a lot of quiet time at work sending ridiculous email tips with Nick, under pseudonyms, to talkback stations. His goal was to goad and inflame the hosts at first, but then it became a contest to see how far the absurdness envelope could be pushed.

'Usually they don't check IPs … The scrutiny they put emails under is still not very thorough,' says Palaitis. 'We didn't use any IP disguising or any anonymiser programs at all. At first we were cautious, but after a while we'd just write anything – as their medium means they'll just get an email and not have time to check it.'

Palaitis and Fintan invented personae to write to talkback hosts. One of the most successful was 'Ravi Draptur from West Bengal', a caricature of an eccentric Indian who struggles with cultural differences. Draptur had a blog and there are still a few examples of his pranks on YouTube. 'There was a blog for a while that got taken down, with all the characters,' explains Palaitis. 'We had a friend at Media Monitors who used to send us all the audio, but then it got too much – that's why it stopped. There were five to ten a day.' Steve Price's then-producer Darren Flynn asked Ravi to report on Price's program from India, 'Can we call you in our first hour between 3 and 4 Sydney time? We don't have many listeners in India … so it would be great to talk to you. Let me know via return email.' Later the penny apparently dropped and they realised it was a joke.

Alan Jones, also on 2GB, also shared a stream of affectionate correspondence with 'Ravi', and even used some of Draptur's unusual stories to attack the NSW Government's progress on public transport: 'And Ravi continues to write to me from West Bengal in India,' Jones said before reading another of Ravi's emails to his listeners. 'When you mentioned the integrated transportation card, I was very shocked you didn't have one. We have one of sorts here in

Calcutta (sic.). And even back in my home village we've got something. In my home village everyone who gets on Vishnu's cart must pay with a small piece of silk, which he collects and sells back to the villagers in exchange for fish each day.' Jones concluded, 'So there you are. Ravi from West Bengal.'

Jones also wrote back to Ravi, again expressing amazement at Kolkata's public transport advancements: 'Thank you for your note. All the way from West Bengal. I can't believe it ... No, we don't have an integrated ticketing system. And you've got one in Calcutta. I can't believe, Ravi, you're writing to me again. Lovely to hear from you. Keep in touch.'

Did Jones ever consider that 'Ravi' was pulling his leg? Paul Christenson, a producer on the program, says no. 'We had no inkling the emails were dodgy. We work on the quaint old-fashioned theory that people write because they want to get in touch with Alan,' he wrote in an email interview. 'We use common sense when looking at emails and taking calls.' But 'common sense' is not always enough, and shortly after Ravi's letters petered out, Jones used a set of hoax statistics to highlight the plight of pensioners: 'I wonder who cares? Government doesn't seem to. A refugee gets $2,470 a month, the pensioner $1,012 and that's called just, just public administration.' The same hoax embarrassed Garth Russell on ABC Radio Newcastle later in the year.

Nick Marland, a former long-time employee of Media Monitors, who left earlier this year as broadcast operations supervisor in Sydney, concluded that hosts fall for these stunts because 'once you start engaging with the media in any kind of way, be it through work or study or whatever, it becomes painfully obvious that they keep beating the same drums. They have their pet topics, and they tend to be pretty ignorant.'

A kinder explanation – than sloppiness or ignorance – for why hosts fall for pranks could be that the time pressures of being live to air (give or take the seven-second delay) make it harder to discriminate between junk and useful listener contributions. Tim Webster, former Channel 10 anchor and now Steve Price's stablemate at 2UE, says 'it's something we battle with almost every day, and you get hoax calls almost every day – or somebody's just trying to stir you up ... And there is pressure, you're right, because if a caller rings and they've got a tip about something, it could be anything from a car accident to something they've heard or seen, I suppose your tendency will be to go "let's go with that," but you have to be careful. And nowadays my producers – I've got one on the phone and the other who produces the show – are very careful.'

Salter agrees that hosts are up against it when it comes to sorting quality contributions from the dross: 'Of course there are very few quality filters between an incoming call and being put to air. The first is the producer, who receives the call on the talkback number. And they have just a few seconds to ask the incoming caller "What do you want to talk about, and what do you want to say?" And they make a snap judgement as to whether they'll put them in a queue.'

But when there's nobody in the queue, and still a show to do, the problems get worse. Salter says 'the actual responsive listenership ... the proportion of the listening audience that actually pick up a phone and engage the talkback host is miniscule, absolutely miniscule. There are many times when even the most popular talkback hosts are reduced to scouting for calls on the air ... What that also means is that the talkback host and their producer have to grab at almost anything that comes along.'

And what about the fill-in jocks, who might generate an even smaller response than their full-time counterparts? Palaitis and Fintan found out about this last year 'on the Mike Carlton [2UE breakfast] program – when Steve Liebmann filled in – there was one show when every email read on the show was from us,' says Palaitis. Indeed, a comparison between Palaitis's 'pranks database' and Media Monitors' archives shows that every email read out, bar one, before lunchtime on 2UE was from Palaitis's and Fintan's characters, who informed the hosts about topics ranging from binge drinking to circus clowns stealing petrol.

Another avenue sometimes explored by the mischief-makers who participate in talkback is playing to a host's sense of outrage. This can be seen above with Jones' refugees vs pensioners episode. Another long-time Media Monitors employee, Patrick Kemp (not his real name), believes a hoax should ideally 'be something that the rational individual knows is a complete fabrication, but something that is scandalising to a shock jock: something that they're quite passionate about'. It's certainly true that talkback radio has been known to trade on conflict and anger. Those who are amused by media hoaxes often contend that the best ones involve embarrassment over a topic the host feels strongly about, or even campaigns over. A famous example of this is the Angry Dwarf hoax, perpetrated on Price, then at Melbourne's 3AW. Satirist John Safran became involved in a stoush with Price in 2001, after he mocked Price's stance on the drug ecstasy and its use at dance parties. Safran convinced Price that drug manufacturers had latched on to the latter's anti-drug campaign (in his *Herald Sun* newspaper column and on his drive-time talk program) and used it to market ecstasy pills bearing the 3AW logo, and referred to as 'Angry Dwarfs' – a reference to Price's short stature. Safran had a friend (dressed as a parody of a raver) deliver paracetamol tablets with the 3AW insignia stamped on them to Price at his workplace. Safran arranged for female callers to impersonate churlish old women (the kind who might make outraged calls to a talk radio station), and give irrational comments on the rumours that 3AW ecstasy pills existed and were being made by Price: 'Well if it has your logo on it, Steve, then I don't know how you can say that you're not doing it.'

The hoax managed to critique the worst of what talkback radio can offer: pointless moralising, uninformed outrage from both presenter and caller, and the dangers of accepting information from strangers. Neither Safran nor Price would agree to be interviewed for this article.

The possibility of on-air friction can often gain the attention of a shock jock, as conflict and lively arguments form a part of the spectacle of talkback radio. Ashley Blacker is a health services administrator and former media student. He fondly remembers his evenings listening to the late Stan Zemanek, and being moved to participate in Zemanek's conflict- and insult-heavy brand of talk radio. 'When I started university and I'd be up late doing homework in the living room I used to have him on in the background for a bit of laughter,' he says. 'I'd been considering making joke calls for a while, as that seemed to be the nature of the show … I'd say, "Aw Stan, I'm a bit stoned and I'm listening to Slipknot." Straight away he went for it. He didn't become too vicious – he wanted to prolong the conversation – and he said, "You're stoned, aren't you? You're a Labor supporter. You're …" and he gave me a few of his choice insults.'

Ashley called a couple more times, and found out that calling in character and pretending to be a stoned heavy metal fan got him on the air much quicker than being sensible would. He says while he's not much of a fan of shock jocks as sources of information, he can understand the appeal of their work: 'It's a bit like the *Jerry Springer* of radio. People think they're discussing serious issues, when really they're just trivial … If I was to ring up *Perspective* on Radio National of an afternoon and pretend to be stoned, I'd be hung up on.'

But what is achieved by all these ruses? There appear to be few safeguards on radio programs to rule them out. And they don't appear to be much of a concern to hosts or their producers: 'We assume … that people have better things to do with their time than fabricate things for their own childish amusement,' relates Christenson. Indeed, Jones' career in radio has flourished, despite far deeper embarrassments than being strung along by some ridiculous Mahatma Cote-type persona in a series of emails. And is the lack of intellectual rigour and discrimination displayed by a radio host in falling for a seemingly ridiculous prank anything worse than what's sometimes foisted on listeners by PR agents or political stooges pretending to be members of the public? Salter points out that 'it's the same slackness that can't winnow out someone who's pretending to have been savaged by a Rottweiler belonging to the Prime Minister; that same inability to sift out someone who's pretending to be a housewife in the western suburbs who is actually working for the Labor Party'.

Despite the ease with which someone can subvert a program that might seem to rely on a quick flick through the morning's tabloid and a few phone calls from bored housewives for its journalistic research, these pranks don't appear to have much more of an effect than hearty laughter and a bit of *schadenfreude* among those who are in on the joke. Webster affably sums up the attitude that a presenter might have towards hoaxes: 'I have to say, they can be funny, but when they come through and it happens and you're there three hours a day, five days a week, it ends up going through to the keeper and it's water off a duck's back. [You think] 'There you go, good on you,' then you move on ...' ■

References available at www.griffithreview.com

Brent Balinski is a freelance writer based in Sydney's inner west. His personal experiences with talkback radio are detailed in *Griffith REVIEW 23: Essentially Creative*.

Memoir:
Tribes of Berlin

Author:
Brigid Delaney

Image: Berlin Wall grafitti art / www.deviantart.com

Tribes of Berlin

The early days in a new city always feel similar to snorkeling, or taking hallucinogenics, or lucid dreaming – where nothing is fixed in place or context, where people and objects drift by as if disconnected from reality, where there are no memories.

And so it was for my first day in Berlin: men in *lederhosen* with fierce beards, bells as heavy as bricks hanging from their necks, were herding goats through the Brandenburg Gate. Ravers on a makeshift stage at Potsdamer Platz pumped out techno and smoke – protesting for the legalisation of marijuana. Those who weren't dancing rested like dogs in the afternoon sun – heavy-eyed, stoned.

That night, down the old swathe of socialism, Karl-Marx-Allee (formerly Stalinallee), on miles and miles of trestle tables steins of beer and bratwurst were sold. Hordes of double-demined, bleached blonde groups sung joyfully and drunk beer – men and women looking indistinguishable from '80s band Europe who provided the soundtrack from the last days of the Cold War: 'The Final Countdown'.

One day – one city. But there is nothing homogenous about these locals. Berlin is a city of tribes.

For a newcomer, you can find your tribe via the internet or in a club or through friends of friends, or connect through film nights, poetry readings, events advertised online on Toytown or in monthly expatriate magazine *Exberliner.* Pick your tribe: the artists, the American expats, the fashion people, the web-geeks, the burnt-out academics, the English teachers, the language students (who themselves are divided into castes and tribes depending on their school), the history buffoons who tour concentration camps, the nudists, the ravers, the people writing books (first novels about boy meets girl, set in Berlin), the DJs, the embassy crowd, the drag queens and the installation artists.

There are support groups in Berlin for mothers of neo-Nazis, and other groups for mothers of drug addicts. At night, they roam the gritty Kottbusser Tor, a U-Bahn station notorious for drug dealing, and menace the dealers in a way that only mothers can. Then there are the politicals: the anarchists, socialists, communists and collectivists. Each month posters go up around Berlin advertising the next protest. Sometimes anarchists came to Prenzlauerberg to protest against the yuppies. The lead singer from radio-friendly 'alternative' band Travis moved into the neighbourhood – seen as a sure symptom of decline. In black paint on the wall opposite my building: 'Fuck off yuppies.' This was the old East Berlin, where bits of the Wall, ugly and grey, still rise out of the earth like rotten teeth. In the old no-man's land, the death strip, still nothing grows, even twenty years later. Berlin is a city so hip that the locals wear mullets with an insouciance that says 'I look cool even with the White Snake hair' – yet still there is no denying Berlin is haunted.

On summer nights when I am not out on the street (at a beer garden in Mitte, dancing at Ankerklause, playing ping-pong in the park, on my bike, cruising, cruising) I am online: browsing, perusing, surfing. Craig's List is good – want a job, flat, new/old couch, lover, $5 haircut, German lessons, ride to Stuttgart – this is your site. I got all three of my Berlin sublets through Craig's List – and each owner seemed so idiosyncratic and distinct that only the most perverse ruler of the cosmos could engineer that I would live in their houses in my time in Berlin.

First is the Park Avenue princess who denuded her flat (nineteenth century in the old East) of furniture before I arrived, yet left her library of books which encompassed the works of Primo Levi and picture books of pornography, Hannah Arendt and the history of horse fisting. Pasted around the walls were magazine tear-outs of topless models, yet there were no plates in the kitchen. Did she eat? She told me that her tribe in Berlin 'was kinda Bloomsbury, you know, like the group' and I wondered if she said that because they were all fucking each other – or they fancied themselves as intellectuals. Maybe both.

Next sublet contact was a dead ringer for Keira Knightley: an artist and former girlfriend of a famous singer, whose light-filled, art-filled flat on a canal was the personification of the Berlin dream – cheap, gorgeous apartment opposite some hippie caravan collective where African drumming and chanting woke me in the late morning.

Lastly there was the spicy tea-drinking, punk rocking Romanian-born Egyptologist who answered the door with a swollen face (fall off a bike) and serious beard (solidarity with his Muslim brothers). He had soft porn taped to the back of his toilet door and the shower stall was in the tiny kitchen, so you could theoretically fry an egg on the stove whilst showering. 'It's old East,' he said, as if that explained its oddness. That I could afford to sublet these apartments while filing only the occasional travel story or op-ed back to Fairfax showed that in some parts of the world you can live by your pen.

As for work in Berlin, there are never any job ads on Craig's List that promise serious employment. 'Bloggers wanted' reads an ad up since last June. I browse the personals but I do not answer any ads. Too scared, I suppose.

One friend K put up an ad for a lover and met two different men through the site. I met her the day after she rendezvoused with a Serb who wore green Converse. She looks dizzy and is grinning: 'still fuck drunk,' she explains. Neither lover lasts long, but no matter – this is Berlin, a city of transients.

For friendship she also goes online – finding a mixer on a site called Toytown (for 'Germany's English-speaking crowd') that connects the native English speakers with the locals. She invites me along and we get quietly drunk on the couches while around us young Germans, Brits, Australians, Russians and Americans negotiate not the awkwardness of our different nationalities and languages, but the bumpier ride from virtual to real contact. You can flirt and be bold online in the banter and bounce of a real-time feed. In person you are just – well, you.

But a few more drinks and people loosen up. Could this be the birth of a new tribe we are witnessing? We wondered what it would be: a Russian/American/Australian tribe based on a love of Rilke perhaps?

Kreuzberg, and an English friend new to the city, and I are walking along a canal. We had been to a bar writers were said to frequent and had that lovely time where how you feel and where you are collide. Here we were drinking red wine and talking about books and writing – and all around us were people doing the same. The spine of a Goethe splayed on the table, someone talking about Kafka at the bar, while those at tables alone were not really alone: they had their pens and their notebooks and by candlelight, they appeared to be writing. So heightened was our mood that we carried on, certain Berlin and the night would provide.

Down a side street the bar has a glowing light above the door and a small sign. It looks cool, hidden; the secret 'insiders' Berlin of which we feel we are now part. We ring the buzzer and a woman opens the door in a gold dress slit to the navel. She looks at us blankly and leads us up the stairs, where sitting desolately around a horse-shoe shaped bar are dozens of men, alone, naked and drinking beer. Actually, they aren't all naked – some are wearing leather straps across their navels that join to a pouch over the groin and another strap that disappears between their buttock cheeks. Some look profoundly depressed, others simply melancholy. The woman moves towards us to relieve us of our coats and jackets while we, like actors in a David Lynch movie, go towards the bar, tittering nervously, 'I think I'd like a beer, wouldn't you? I wonder if they speak English.'

I wish I could say we stay, get to know this tribe a little better, but just before we place our order (in terrible, nervous German) we look at one another and wordlessly decide to leave. For all our libertine talk in the previous bar, we are bourgeois to the core. The woman in the slit dress gives us a look that Berliners do well – contempt. A look that says, 'pussies'.

There is a tribe for everyone in Berlin – and even if you don't really fit in, the door will open to you – and you can stay if you like, if you are game.

Suddenly it is winter: you can see your breath hanging out the front of your face like a speech bubble and the nights are longer. Luke and I are walking through the West Berlin suburb of Schöneberg past some lively bars. 'Skins' bars,' explained Luke. 'It's Skins Festival this weekend.'

While I try to digest all the possible things the festival could be celebrating (tattoo art, beauty products, a medical conference … ?), he explains it is for the sizeable German community of gay skinheads. Luke even knows one guy who is a member of all the minorities: 'he's a German-Turkish, gay, Jewish, skinhead Nazi.'

Wow, he's fucked up, we agree.

Later I met a German guy who is introduced to me as the country's most renowned fetish photographer. He is in Berlin for an exhibition of his work. I sit next to him at dinner: he is vegetarian and doesn't drink. He speaks openly and plainly about his profession: 'Sometimes we go to warehouse, empty of course and they, they bring their own things, and I just try to capture the moment.'

I have a terrible sensation during the dinner: one of acute melancholy – that we have only one life, and mine is not set on that course – that pleasure and pain in a chilly warehouse in Berlin will be someone else's experience, and I will hear about it second hand at a dinner party.

What brought me to Berlin? In truth I don't really know – I was drifting, unemployed, and supposed to be writing a book – dreaming of an England I could no longer afford – and Germany seemed as good a place as any to live. Not a Germanophile, I didn't speak the language and I did not worship its authors or its playwrights. I didn't even know any Germans. I was – as far as it is possible to be about a country – entirely neutral. But I was optimistic that I would find others in the city just like me and we could form our own tribe. What tribe was I hoping to join in Berlin? An expatriate creative underclass would be the answer.

Writer on the continent, not successful – yet in that golden haze before success. Poor and happy, with similarly positioned friends. Everyone poor and happy, no one so successful that there was alienation and envy, all of us on the edge of some spectacular future. It would be comradely. Canadian writer Margaret Atwood said of Paris in the 1950s: 'Paris was cheap, still intellectually alive, and thus still the place you felt you should go to write if you were young and romantic and broke, and dedicated to your art.'

American expat Henry Miller wrote in 1934 at the beginning of *Tropic of Cancer* of 'the fall of my second year in Paris ... I have no money, no resources, no hopes. I am the happiest man alive. A year ago, six months ago, I thought that I was an artist. I no longer think about it, I am.'

Today Paris and New York, those old hubs of bohemianism, require a corporate salary yet Berlin is El Dorado – a happening place in the centre of Europe where you can live on air and dreams, make a cool café your office, and return home to your wonderfully cheap, large apartment. At night if you want to go out, but are feeling poor you can drink at a bar right by the old church at Zionskirchplatz where you only pay what you can for wine, or brunch at the vegan socialist café costing between four and eight euros – 'whatever you can afford'. Berlin has, for a while now, been talked about as a destination *par excellence* for unknown writers: cheap, creative and with just the right level of melancholia to give it depth.

Of course the salad days are long gone, I am constantly told by jaded émigrés who squatted in the '80s and '90s and raved in abandoned buildings. It's now happening in Leipzig, or Sofia, Warsaw, or San Paulo they say. Yet I think Berlin's wonderful.

For a start there is an abundance of office space in the form of plenty of cool cafés with free wi-fi and comfortable, quirky, well-designed spaces. Secondly, rent is cheap and apartments are the sort that exist only in dreams: high ceilings – many rooms, moody half-light in the afternoons – buildings that have the melancholy feeling of ghosts in the stairwell, their outsides still pocked with bullet holes plus – a bonus for the itinerant subletting. And subletting is part of Berlin life, so it's easy to get a short-term rental in Berlin and you're sure to get a good apartment whether you want to stay a month or a year. And the third attraction to a stint in Berlin? Critical mass. Everyone, it seems, is broke and writing a book.

City mayor Klaus Wowereit expressly wants to attract creative types. Embedded in the city's strategy for post-reunification economic recovery is the call for artists, musicians and writers to call Berlin home. Berlin, he says, is 'poor but sexy', which is no doubt how many artists and writers see themselves. Wowereit told *Time* magazine: 'The most decisive aspect is to bring creative young people to Berlin. I like to compare Berlin to London in the swinging 1980s. London was in a bad economic situation, but had a great deal of creativity and a positive mood.'

While Berlin is not as good value as when David Bowie and Iggy Pop moved to the city in 1976 and flatted together in a giant ten-room apartment (which Bowie painted black) in a gorgeous old building, the still-low cost of renting and huge spaces attract the new nomads and the art crowd in their droves. By 2006, the census reported that over 13,000 Americans were living in Berlin. *The*

Guardian warned: 'Go drinking or record shopping in Kreuzberg, and it won't be long before you hear British voices'. Already, some warn of 'overkill'.

According to a recent report by AP, 'If you show up in Berlin strapped for cash, you're in good company. The German capital's sizable student population, high unemployment rate and swelling starving artist contingent make penny-pinching a citywide obsession.'

Now, looking back, it wasn't so much Berlin that I wanted to live in – but a sort of tribal land that existed in Berlin in my imagination. Let's call it Bohemia.

One day I ride my bike out to the atelier of one American expat who has a studio in Wedding – east of Mitte. I cycle past where the wall used to be, and up through streets and streets of brown-box apartment blocks until I come to a sprawl of rug shops and kebab houses.

Antony C., a former New York-based artist, has been in Berlin for five years. He is one of Berlin's growing breed – the non-integrated creative community whose members fly back and forth from New York several times a year, have art dealers and commercial interests in New York, but work in Berlin because of cheap studio rent.

He tells me, 'I've got my papers (visa) sorted, but a lot of American artists haven't. They are pretty relaxed about it – they don't really bother getting organised. But they don't get a lot of hassles.'

One thing Antony hasn't bothered to do is learn German. 'I can order in restaurants and bars and stuff – small talk but I can't hold a conversation. I'm hopeless.' He has a German girlfriend who speaks English and many of his friends are American artists who have also fled the high rents in New York.

'Studio space is insanely expensive in Manhattan. They are all coming here.'

But while they can make the art here, selling it is another story. Mary Hoeveler, the managing director of Citigroup's art advisory department, told the *New York Times*: 'The artists are there, but the market isn't, quite.'

Antony's studio is huge – and inexpensive. He shakes his head when he repeats the cost – it is so little money for so much space that he can scarcely believe it's his. 'I tried to get a long lease, because I know this is too good to be true and rents are going to go up,' he says. Along the floor there are bits of wire, lumps of clay, a match-stick model. He is already imagining working on massive sculpture projects – the sort that would be impossible in Manhattan with its tiny studio space and expensive materials.

Wedding is the next push for artists, in the process of gentrification – from grim Soviet style suburbs to hip haunts for expat artists. The main drag is a long, long row of mostly Turkish shops – kebabs, rugs, shops selling household goods such as kettles, toasters and tea sets. 'There's a Burger King, which is good,' says Antony. I find it later, just by the station and buy a junior whopper from a teen who repeats my order back to me in perfect English.

I meet another Australian, Laurel, at a gathering of expat freelance journalists, and she talks about coming to Berlin in 1990 just after the wall fell and squatting in one of the old buildings in the east. 'No one could believe we wanted to live in the east,' she says. The buildings had been abandoned after the wall had fallen, as some East Germans weren't sure if another wall would be erected in its place and they would be forced to return, so houses were effectively abandoned as they escaped. While the electricity had been turned off – and it was freezing in winter – it was perfectly legitimate to squat in one of the incredible old buildings and later – after years had passed – claim a sort of squatter's rights.

Laurel had just returned from an artist's colony. A disused abattoir in the Czech Republic, it was freezing cold 'but really interesting'. Her project involved going into the pens and photographing the shadows as they moved across and through the wooden slats and pens.

Quite quickly I found my tribe in Berlin, and we had a lot of fun. It was as I imagined it: a lot of us were writing books, or were journalists or photographers. Often we met in the afternoon and played ping-pong and drank beer, or had dinner parties, or met in the bars of Mitte. We were poor and happy. For a while. But September came and even in the Indian summer, lying in bed with a late summer flu and listening to BBC World Service, I felt a chill when I heard about the banks falling like dominos. I realised that it was one thing playing at being poor and bohemian for a while – but it only worked if you could opt out when you wanted: return to your job and stability, having visited Bohemia.

Now it seemed like an island where I was marooned. No money coming in, and as the media seemed to be falling apart, none would be for a while. It was time to pack away the ping-pong paddles before it stopped being fun. I'm back in Melbourne now and Berlin has receded like a dream. Did I really ride a bicycle along the line of the old wall one rainy Tuesday stopping for waffles on Oderberger Strasse? Did I really eat fried chicken at White Trash then dance to the Gossip, with drink in hand, sweat flicking off my hair? Did I really chain-smoke in a bar called Fire? The Berlin dream came true – truer probably than I wanted it to be.

Bad things sometimes happened in Bohemia – an obsession with money, or lack of it, a feeling of jeopardy when down to my last twenty euros, the pervasive sense of insecurity, of life being too light, of borrowed apartments and empty days.

That I once walked out of a Lidl with a packet of Arborio rice in the sleeve of my jacket because I was cooking for my tribe that night and I didn't have the money to pay for the ingredients seemed not an act of daring, but an indictment. It was time to leave before the police broke up the party. ■

Brigid Delaney is author of *This Restless Life: Churning Through Love, Work and Play*, to be published by MUP in August. She is currently writing a travel book based on living in fifty-five different houses and eight different countries in 2008. Her articles have appeared in the *Sydney Morning Herald, The Age, The Guardian* and on CNN.com. Her essay 'The vulnerability threshhold' appeared in *Griffith REVIEW 13: The Next Big Thing*.

Fax/Post Subscription Form on Page 264